WOMEN REVIEWING WOMEN IN NINETEENTH-CENTURY BRITAIN

To the Memory of Three Fine Scholars
W. Scott Allan (1958–2004)
David G. Wright (1952–2008)
Terry Sturm (1941–2009)

Women Reviewing Women in Nineteenth-Century Britain

The Critical Reception of Jane Austen, Charlotte Brontë and George Eliot

JOANNE WILKES

University of Auckland, New Zealand

ASHGATE

Published by
Ashgate Publishing Limited
Wey Court East
Union Road
Farnham
Surrey, GU9 7PT
England

Ashgate Publishing Company
Suite 420
101 Cherry Street
Burlington
VT 05401-4405
USA

www.ashgate.com

British Library Cataloguing in Publication Data
Wilkes, Joanne.
    Women reviewing women in nineteenth-century Britain: the critical reception of Jane Austen, Charlotte Brontë, and George Eliot. – (The nineteenth century series)
    1. Austen, Jane, 1775–1817 – Criticism and interpretation – History – 19th century. 2. Brontë, Charlotte, 1816–1855 – Criticism and interpretation – History – 19th century. 3. Eliot, George, 1819–1880 – Criticism and interpretation – History – 19th century. 4. Women and literature – Great Britain – History – 19th century. 5. Women critics – Great Britain – History – 19th century. 6. English literature – 19th century – History and criticism. 7. English literature – Women authors – History and criticism. 8. Book reviewing – Great Britain – History – 19th century.
    I. Title II. Series
    820.9'9287'09034–dc22

Library of Congress Cataloging-in-Publication Data
Wilkes, Joanne.
    Women reviewing women in nineteenth-century Britain: the critical reception of Jane Austen, Charlotte Brontë, and George Eliot / Joanne Wilkes.
        p. cm. – (The nineteenth century series)
    Includes bibliographical references and index.
    ISBN 978-0-7546-6336-2 (hardback : alk. paper) – ISBN 978-0-7546-9857-9 (ebook : alk. paper)
    1. Criticism – Great Britain – History – 19th century. 2. English prose literature – Women authors – History and criticism. 3. Women critics – Great Britain. 4. English literature – Women authors – Book reviews. 5. Women and literature – Great Britain – History – 19th century. 6. Austen, Jane, 1775–1817 – Criticism and interpretation – History. 7. Brontë, Charlotte, 1816–1855 – Criticism and interpretation – History. 8. Eliot, George, 1819–1880 – Criticism and interpretation – History. I. Title.
    PR75.W56 2010
    820.9'9287–dc22

                                                                                                2009023952

ISBN 9780754663362 (hbk)
ISBN 9780754698579 (ebk)

Printed and bound in Great Britain by
MPG Books Group, UK

Contents

The Nineteenth Century Series
General Editors' Preface

The aim of the series is to reflect, develop and extend the great burgeoning of interest in the nineteenth century that has been an inevitable feature of recent years, as that former epoch has come more sharply into focus as a locus for our understanding not only of the past but of the contours of our modernity. It centres primarily upon major authors and subjects within Romantic and Victorian literature. It also includes studies of other British writers and issues, where these are matters of current debate: for example, biography and autobiography, journalism, periodical literature, travel writing, book production, gender, non-canonical writing. We are dedicated principally to publishing original monographs and symposia; our policy is to embrace a broad scope in chronology, approach and range of concern, and both to recognize and cut innovatively across such parameters as those suggested by the designations 'Romantic' and 'Victorian'. We welcome new ideas and theories, while valuing traditional scholarship. It is hoped that the world which predates yet so forcibly predicts and engages our own will emerge in parts, in the wider sweep, and in the lively streams of disputation and change that are so manifest an aspect of its intellectual, artistic and social landscape.

Vincent Newey
Joanne Shattock
University of Leicester

Acknowledgements

This book is the result of several years' research into nineteenth-century literary criticism, research which has been aided by a number of people. I am especially grateful to Dr Ellen Jordan of the Centre for Literary and Linguistic Computing at the University of Newcastle (Australia) for sharing with me her and her colleagues' findings about Anne Mozley's likely contributions to the *Christian Remembrancer*, as well as her transcriptions of the correspondence between Mozley and members of the Blackwood publishing firm held at the National Library of Scotland. I would like to thank as well Professor John Morrow, of the Political Studies Department, University of Auckland, for guidance with sources on the 'Froude–Carlyle' controversy, Kristine Moruzi, of the School of Culture and Communication, University of Melbourne, for directing me to an article of Mary Ward's in *Atalanta*, and Dr Amanda J. Collins, formerly of Sydney University, for assistance with my work on Julia Kavanagh.

I am grateful also for the unfailing assistance from the staffs of the manuscript collections I have consulted – at the National Library of Scotland, the Wordsworth Trust collection at Dove Cottage, Cumbria, the John Rylands University Library of Manchester, and the Harry Ransom Center, University of Texas at Austin. I thank the National Library of Scotland for permission to quote from the correspondence in the Blackwood Papers between members of the Blackwood firm and Margaret Oliphant and Anne Mozley, and the Wordsworth Trust for permission to quote from their holdings of the letters of Maria Jane Jewsbury and Sara Coleridge. Gratitude is also due to Mrs Priscilla Cassam for permission to quote from letters and manuscripts of Sara Coleridge held in the Harry Ransom Center.

Some of the material here has been adapted from earlier publications of mine. I would like to thank the editors of *Women's Writing* for allowing me to reuse part of my article, '"Only the Broken Music"? The Critical Writings of Maria Jane Jewsbury' from *Women's Writing*, 7 (2000): 105–18, and the Editorial Board of Otago Studies in English for permission to reuse part of my chapter '"Clever Women": Anne Mozley, Jane Austen, and Charlotte Brontë', from Colin Gibson and Lisa Marr (eds), *New Windows on a Woman's World: Essays for Jocelyn Harris* (2 vols, Dunedin: Department of English, Otago University, 2005), vol. 2, pp. 297–308. I am grateful as well for having had the opportunity to present earlier versions of some of the material here at conferences: a paper on Jane Williams and Julia Kavanagh at the 2007 conference of the Australasian Victorian Studies Association at the University of Western Australia, and a paper on Anne Mozley at the 2008 conference of the Research Society for Victorian Periodicals at the University of Roehampton, London. Thanks are also due to the English

Department of the University of Auckland for funding my attendance at these conferences, plus some of my research travel to Edinburgh and Grasmere.

Aspects of my research into the reception history of Jane Austen, Charlotte Brontë and George Eliot have been aired in my graduate classes on nineteenth-century fiction. I would like to express thanks to the students in those classes, and particularly to my co-teachers, Aorewa McLeod and Dr Rose Lovell-Smith.

Three of my colleagues at the University of Auckland, Dr Scott Allan, Dr David Wright and Professor Terry Sturm, all fine scholars and good friends, have recently had their careers cut tragically short. This book is dedicated to their memory.

Chapter 1

Introduction

By the time George Eliot's second full-length novel, *The Mill on the Floss*, was being reviewed in 1860, the female identity behind the author's male pseudonym had become common knowledge. The reviewer for the *Saturday Review* in April of that year recalled that Eliot's previous novel, *Adam Bede*, had been 'thought to be too good for a woman's story', and welcomed the disclosure of the novelist's sex:

> We may think ourselves fortunate to have a third female novelist not inferior to Miss Austen and Miss Brontë; and it so happens that there is much in the works of this new writer which reminds us of those two well-known novelists without anything like copying. George Eliot has a minuteness of painting and a certain archness of style that are quite after the manner of Miss Austen, while the wide scope of her remarks, and her delight in depicting strong and wayward feelings, show that she belongs to the generation of Currer Bell, and not to that of the quiet authoress of *Emma*.[1]

This new novelist's work, then, evokes both the achievement of a predecessor, and that of a prominent (if now deceased) contemporary, and the reviewer goes on to explicate the resemblances. Eliot's fiction possesses Austen's 'neatness of finish, a comprehensiveness of detail, and a relish for subdued comedy'. This last trait, moreover, is one where '[w]e seem to share with the authoress the fun of the play she is showing us', without the story-line being broken, and the commentator declares that '[e]very one must remember the consummate skill with which Miss Austen manages this'.[2] On the other hand, George Eliot has a dimension to her mind 'entirely unlike that of Miss Austen, and which brings her much closer to Charlotte Brontë'. That is, '[s]he is full of meditation on some of the most difficult problems of life … the destinies, the possibilities, and the religious position' of her characters. In addition, the story of the protagonist of *The Mill on the Floss*, Maggie Tulliver, is 'entirely in the vein of Charlotte Brontë', showing that Eliot 'has thought as keenly and profoundly as the authoress of *Jane Eyre* on the peculiar difficulties and sorrows encountered by a girl of quick feeling and high aspirations under adverse outward circumstances'.[3]

---

[1] Review of *The Mill on the Floss*, *Saturday Review*, 14 April 1860, repr. in Stuart Hutchinson (ed.), *George Eliot: Critical Assessments* (4 vols, Mountfield: Helm Information, 1996), vol. 1, *Biography, Nineteenth-Century Reviews and Responses*, pp. 18–22, at p. 18.

[2] Ibid., p. 119.

[3] Ibid., p. 120.

This commentary on the fiction of Jane Austen and Charlotte Brontë is quite characteristic of the mid nineteenth century: it was typical to see Austen's work as notable for neatly constructed, well-observed 'subdued comedy', and Charlotte Brontë's for probing female emotional and spiritual experience. But what I would draw attention to is the incipient canon-formation here: the review sketches a history of nineteenth-century English women's fiction as early as 1860. Although there had been few published discussions focused specifically on Jane Austen's fiction since her death in 1817, literary historian Anne Katherine Elwood could note in 1843 'the popularity [her novels] have at last so generally attained'; the year after the 1860 Eliot review, too, Henry Fothergill Chorley commented in the *Athenaeum* that, despite the lack of impact made by Austen's novels on their first appearance, 'they have passed into the small library of English fiction, containing the tales which may endure so long as men and women read "story-books"'.[4] Meanwhile the first novels of both Charlotte Brontë and George Eliot, *Jane Eyre* and *Adam Bede* respectively, had been both commercial and critical successes. Then after Brontë's death in 1855, the 1857 *Life of Charlotte Brontë* by her friend and fellow-novelist Elizabeth Gaskell had further stimulated a fascination with the woman and her work which has really never abated. The critical and commercial history of George Eliot's fiction over the nineteenth century was more chequered, but as the part-publication of her penultimate novel *Middlemarch* approached its end in October 1872, critic Richard Holt Hutton claimed that it 'bid[ ] more than fair to be one of the great books of the world'.[5] Jane Austen, Charlotte Brontë and George Eliot, for all the vagaries of reputation among women novelists over the nineteenth century – including their own – remained central to the developing canon.

As the 1860 review suggests, the three novelists were not all valued for the same qualities. Jane Austen emerges from the cluster of late eighteenth- and early nineteenth-century women writers to be praised for her fiction's social observation, and also for its verbal economy in the age of prolix three-deckers. Charlotte Brontë's novels grab readers from the outset with their compelling narratives, expressed in *Jane Eyre* and *Villette* through passionate and independent female narrators, and probe their characters' inner lives. George Eliot's fiction, psychologically penetrating like Brontë's, renders in a vivid and detailed way British society past and present, infused with wisdom derived from wide reading and profound thinking.

None of the three novelists ventured into print initially under her own name. Jane Austen's first published novel, *Sense and Sensibility* (1811), appeared as 'by a Lady', and subsequent novels came out as 'by the author of' the previous novel(s). Her identity was only disclosed after her death, with the simultaneous

---

4   Elwood, *Memoirs of the Literary Ladies of England from the Commencement of the Last Century* (2 vols, London: Henry Colburn, 1843), vol. 2, p. 181; [H.F. Chorley], '*French Women of Letters*', *Athenaeum*, 30 November 1861: 717–18, at 717.

5   'George Eliot's Moral Anatomy', *Spectator*, 5 October 1872: 1262–4, repr. in Stuart Hutchinson, *George Eliot*, vol. 1, pp. 285–8, at p. 285.

release of *Northanger Abbey* and *Persuasion* at the end of 1817, accompanied by her brother Henry's 'Biographical Notice of the Author'. By contrast, Charlotte Brontë chose the implicitly male pseudonym of 'Currer Bell' for *Jane Eyre*, and Marian Evans, the definitely masculine sobriquet of 'George Eliot' for her first published fiction, her series of three novellas, *Scenes of Clerical Life* (1858). But the identity of each author was soon revealed: Charlotte Brontë's with the publication of her second novel, *Shirley* (1849), and Marian Evans's with the appearance of *The Mill on the Floss*.

This is all familiar information. Equally well-known is that, in the cases of Charlotte Brontë and George Eliot, the early fictions by the then-mysterious authors generated much speculation about the identities, including the sex, of the writers, and the disclosures of the female names behind the apparently male pseudonyms inflected the reception of the later works. Nevertheless, to the extent that the striking and innovative aspects of their novels were accepted, Charlotte Brontë and George Eliot extended the boundaries of what women were considered capable of in literature.

An aspect of nineteenth-century women's writing that has been much less studied than their fiction, however, is their practice of non-fictional writing for periodicals. With the extraordinary burgeoning of periodical writing over the century, women had the opportunity to publish on a very wide variety of subjects. An examination of the five-volume *Wellesley Index to Victorian Periodicals* discloses that, although women contributors were much outnumbered by men, especially in the politically and intellectually heavyweight periodicals, they did write on topics in history, biography, travel, science, theology, philosophy, art, and sometimes politics and economics; as far as fiction, poetry and drama were concerned, they published copiously in these areas, including sometimes on the Greek and Roman literature that was seldom included in a woman's education. Other studies have brought to light women's contributions – as both writers and editors – to a larger range of periodicals and newspapers than was covered by the *Wellesley Index*, including periodicals directed specifically at women and children: Margaret Beetham's *A Magazine of Her Own? Domesticity and Desire in the Woman's Magazine 1800–1914* (1996), Barbara Onslow's *Women of the Press in Nineteenth-Century Britain* (2000), and *Gender and the Victorian Periodical*, by Hilary Fraser, Stephanie Green and Judith Johnston (2003).

Looking at the *Wellesley Index* and at the studies just named puts one in awe of the extraordinary versatility and energy of so many women who wrote for periodicals. My focus here, however, is on several women who practised as literary critics, and on what they had to say about women writers – and especially about those increasingly prominent literary entities, Jane Austen, Charlotte Brontë and George Eliot. If these three novelists evidently found venturing into print as women problematic, then how far did women, working in the same environment but as literary critics, respond to these writers specifically as women novelists? Moreover, to what extent was their writing as critics affected by their own awareness of a literary context where women's writing was often seen as different from men's, and where a woman's intellectual capacities for making authoritative judgments were not universally assumed? Where a novel like *Adam Bede* might be considered 'too good for a woman's story'?

There is now extensive documentation accessible about the critical reception of all three novelists, from their initial publication up to the late twentieth century. Of recent note are the 'Critical Assessments' series from Helm Information.[6] Still very helpful, especially in their introductions, are the volumes in Routledge's Critical Heritage series: Brian Southam's two volumes on Jane Austen (1968, 1987), Miriam Allott's volume on the Brontës (1974), and David R. Carroll's volume on George Eliot (1971). There are also more analytical studies of the novelists' reception history, such as Kathryn Sutherland's magisterial *Jane Austen's Textual Lives: From Aeschylus to Bollywood* (2005), Patsy Stoneman's *Brontë Transformations: The Cultural Dissemination of 'Jane Eyre' and 'Wuthering Heights'* (1996) and, for George Eliot, J. Russell Perkin's *A Reception-History of George Eliot's Fiction* (1990). My study, however, focuses specifically on a number of women critics who were active from the 1820s through to the early years of the twentieth century, and who wrote about one or more of Jane Austen, Charlotte Brontë and George Eliot. There is one exception – Jane Williams – whose book *The Literary Women of England* (1861), a pioneering history of British women's writing focused mainly on poetry, can be related illuminatingly to the women's history produced by Hannah Lawrance, who published on Charlotte Brontë, and Julia Kavanagh, who wrote on Austen. The critics' writings on women novelists have either not been reprinted at all, or have been reprinted only in part. In one case, that of Sara Coleridge, almost none of her commentary on women writers was written for publication, and such as was published appeared mostly posthumously.[7]

The first two critics covered are near-contemporaries Maria Jane Jewsbury (1800–33) and Sara Coleridge (1802–52). Jewsbury's work has received welcome attention in recent years, notably from Monica Correa Fryckstedt, Norma Clarke, Dennis Low and Susan J. Wolfson. But Jewsbury's crucial contribution to Jane Austen's reception history, in producing the first article on the novelist known to be by a woman writer, has attracted little attention – not least because of its unlucky post-publication history, which is one dimension of my discussion of it here. Sara Coleridge, meanwhile, is of interest partly because she chose not to publish most of her literary criticism; much of it is scattered through her letters, only some of which were published in 1873, long after her death, by her daughter

[6]   *Jane Austen: Critical Assessments*, ed. Ian Littlewood (4 vols, 1998), *The Brontë Sisters: Critical Assessments*, ed. Eleanor McNees (4 vols, 1996); for the volumes on George Eliot, see n.1.

[7]   Solveig C. Robinson has edited a helpful sampling of literary criticism by Victorian women, *A Serious Occupation: Literary Criticism by Victorian Women Writers* (Peterborough, Ontario and Orchard Park, NY: Broadview, 2003), which includes items by Anne Mozley and Margaret Oliphant, plus the article on Jane Austen by Mary Ward that I discuss here, 'Style and Miss Austen'.

Edith Coleridge. As well as drawing on what has been published of her work, I will be dealing with some of Sara Coleridge's unpublished letters and manuscripts. She writes on both Jane Austen and Charlotte Brontë.

The next group of critics treated are those who wrote histories of women, and/or of women's writing. Hannah Lawrance (1795–1875) produced histories of Anglo-Saxon and medieval women, but also published a substantial review of Gaskell's *Life of Charlotte Brontë* in 1857 – one that is inflected by the ideas about women's capacities that are both evident in her histories, and expressed in an article on the most prominent woman poet of the mid nineteenth century, Elizabeth Barrett Browning. The venture of Jane Williams (1806–85) in producing in 1861 a copious history of women's writing from the Anglo-Saxon period onwards, focusing on poetry from the period after 1700, also involved her articulating ideas about women's literary capacities and the extent to which these differed from men's. In the following year, Julia Kavanagh brought out *English Women of Letters*, which covered women novelists from Aphra Behn onwards, and included substantial discussion of Jane Austen. Kavanagh had already published well-researched studies of women: *Woman in France during the Eighteenth Century* (1850), *Women of Christianity* (1852) and *French Women of Letters* (1861). Like Lawrance and Williams, she investigated how far women's writing differed from men's, and what its distinctive qualities might be. Although Kavanagh's work as a novelist has received some critical attention, little has been written about her literary criticism, or about that of Lawrance and Williams.

Anne Mozley (1809–91), the subject of the subsequent chapter, was the first to write on all three of Jane Austen, Charlotte Brontë and George Eliot, and two aspects of her work are particularly worth signalling. In reviewing the *Life of Charlotte Brontë*, she took up Brontë's own critical comments on Austen (as revealed by Gaskell), to try to define the strong differences between the two novelists in their lives and writing. Then in welcoming *Adam Bede* in 1859, in the review most appreciated by George Eliot herself, she identified the author as female on internal evidence alone. Since much of Mozley's writing, especially that for the *Christian Remembrancer*, is now difficult to identify in the absence of publishers' records, the computer analysis of the *Remembrancer* carried out by the staff at the Centre for Literary and Linguistic Computing at Australia's University of Newcastle has been invaluable in studying her work; so too has been the biographical research on Mozley by one of that team, Ellen Jordan.[8] But there exists as yet no study focused on the actual content of Mozley's literary criticism.

The literary criticism of the last two writers covered here, Margaret Oliphant (1828–97) and Mary Augusta (Mrs Humphry) Ward (1851–1920), is better known. They are of course noted novelists as well, a circumstance which influences their

---

[8]   Ellen Jordan, 'Sister as Journalist: The Almost Anonymous Career of Anne Mozley', *Victorian Periodicals Review*, 37/3 (2004): 315–41; Ellen Jordan, Hugh Craig and Alexis Antonia, 'The Brontë Sisters and the *Christian Remembrancer*', *Victorian Periodicals Review*, 39/1 (2006): 21–45.

practice as critics. Oliphant's prodigious output for periodicals has been looked at from various angles in recent years, with Joan Bellamy concentrating on her treatment of Charlotte Brontë.[9] Meanwhile Ward's writing on the Brontës has received valuable attention from Beth Sutton-Ramspeck.[10] Especially helpful is the coverage of both writers' responses to Austen, Charlotte Brontë and Eliot in Valerie Sanders's *Eve's Renegades: Victorian Anti-Feminist Women Novelists* (1996). But while I agree with the emphases of Sanders, Bellamy and Sutton-Ramspeck in their treatment of Oliphant and Ward's responses to Brontë, I think there is more to be said about their reactions to Austen and Eliot. In particular, both writers engaged with and appreciated Austen's writing more than Sanders allows for, while Oliphant's access, late in her career, to Eliot's correspondence with her publisher John Blackwood, complicated her reactions to the novelist.

If Jane Austen, Charlotte Brontë and George Eliot made publication choices that concealed their identities and/or their sex, then the same option was open to women critics. In fact, for much of the nineteenth century, choosing to publish in a periodical normally involved concealing one's identity, since the convention of anonymity prevailed up to the 1860s, and in some periodicals, for much longer. But as anonymity came under challenge, there was much debate over the implications of anonymity versus signature, some of which is relevant to the choices made by the critics studied here.

A significant new weekly review, the *Athenaeum*, started publication in 1828, and when it was bought by Charles Wentworth Dilke in 1830, he championed anonymity as an article of faith. Disgusted by the habit of some publishers of using reviews they owned to 'puff' their firms' own publications, Dilke believed that anonymous reviewing safeguarded critical independence, since in his view it protected reviewers from coming under pressure from authors and publishers.[11] When the issue re-emerged 30 years later, with some periodicals opting for signed articles, a writer in the *North British Review* argued that signature might make writers vulnerable to political pressure.[12] Meanwhile Eneas Sweetland Dallas claimed that anonymity made periodical writing less personal, and kept down

---

[9]   'Margaret Oliphant: "mightier than the mightiest of her sex"', in Joan Bellamy, Anne Laurence and Gill Perry (eds), *Women, Scholarship and Criticism: Gender and Knowledge c. 1790–1900* (Manchester: Manchester University Press, 2000), pp. 143–58, and 'A Lifetime of Reviewing: Margaret Oliphant on Charlotte Brontë', *Brontë Studies*, 29 (2004): 37–42.

[10]   'The Personal is Poetical: Feminist Criticism and Mary Ward's Reading of the Brontës', *Victorian Studies*, 34/1 (1990): 55–75; *Raising the Dust: The Literary Housekeeping of Mary Ward, Sarah Grand, and Charlotte Perkins Gilman* (Athens, OH: Ohio University Press, 2004).

[11]   Leslie A. Marchand, *The Athenaeum: A Mirror of Victorian Culture* (1941; repr. New York: Octagon Books, 1971), pp. 105–6.

[12]   'The British Press: Its Growth, Liberty and Power', *North British Review*, 30 (May 1859): 367–402, at 397–8; periodicals that adopted signature included *Macmillan's*

displays of egotism, such as trumpeting one's acquaintance with the famous, telling private anecdotes of others, and engaging in 'virulence' and 'bombast'. Another argument in its favour, according to W.R. Greg, was that articles were judged on their inherent merits, rather than on the reputation of the writers.[13]

Claims like Dallas and Greg's could, however, be turned on their heads. Writers such as Thomas Hughes, George Henry Lewes, John Morley, Anthony Trollope and J. Boyd Kinnear argued strongly in favour of signature. It was a more honest policy: writers could not hide behind anonymity to mount unjust attacks, or to produce lackadaisical writing. It encouraged writers to take more responsibility for their writing, from a sense of having no buffer between themselves and their readers, claimed Morley as editor of the *Fortnightly Review* in 1867.[14] Related to these points was an argument based on the 'market' model: anonymity concealed information vital to readers' judgment as to the value of the product they were buying.[15]

The assumption behind the convention of anonymity was that the voice of a periodical transcended those of its individual writers, was that of a collective entity which might claim to articulate widely held values. Greg described an anonymous article in a 'leading organ of opinion' as 'a mysterious, shadowy, unknown power, made impressive by secresy'.[16] The individual therefore should have a sense of responsibility to the wider 'we' of the journal.[17] This situation might well have a downside for the individual writer – Leslie Stephen, a prominent contributor to one of the *Athenaeum*'s mid-century rivals, the *Saturday Review*, once looked through the weekly's files and found he could hardly distinguish his own articles: 'I had unconsciously adopted the tone of my colleagues like some inferior organism, taken the colouring of my "environment".'[18] It could also mean that those who wrote for a variety of periodicals learnt to adapt their voice to suit the target: Eliza Lynn Linton once explained in a letter accompanying a paper she was sending to Richard Bentley, '[i]f you do not care for it, I will turn it into a different key for

---

Magazine (1859–), *Fortnightly Review* (1865–), *Contemporary Review* (1866–), *Nineteenth Century* (1877–), *Cornhill Magazine* (1878–).

[13]   [E.S. Dallas], 'Popular Literature: The Periodical Press', *Blackwood's Edinburgh Magazine*, 85 (February 1859): 180–95 at 185–7; [W.R. Greg], 'The Newspaper Press', *Edinburgh Review*, 102 (October 1855): 470–98, at 488–9.

[14]   John Morley, 'Anonymous Journalism', *Fortnightly Review*, ns 2 (September 1867): 287–92.

[15]   See Dallas Liddle, 'Salesmen, Sportsmen, Mentors: Anonymity in Mid-Victorian Theories of Journalism', *Victorian Studies*, 41/1 (1997): 31–58.

[16]   'The Newspaper Press', 489.

[17]   Dallas Liddle, 'Salesmen, Sportsmen, Mentors', 54–5.

[18]   Quoted in Merle Mowbray Bevington, *The Saturday Review 1855–1868: Representative Educated Opinion in Victorian England* (New York: Columbia University Press, 1941; repr. New York: AMS Press, 1966), p. 381.

another [periodical]'.[19] Or Mary Margaret Busk might review the same book for different periodicals, mimicking the style expected for each: lively and impertinent for *Bentley's Miscellany*, scholarly for the *Foreign Quarterly Review*, subdued and straightforward for the *Athenaeum*.[20]

Arguments for signature sometimes adduced the honest 'manliness' of the practice. But for women, it was anonymity which promoted manliness, in another sense. It offered them opportunities for adopting voices which, either implicitly or explicitly, might come across to readers as male. Periodicals directed at educated readers assumed a primarily male audience, so that readers would have assumed primarily male authorship. Alexis Easley, in her *First-Person Anonymous: Women Writers and Victorian Print Media, 1830–1870* (2004), has explored this issue in detail. She mentions *Fraser's Magazine* and its creation, in text and image, of a male editorial board and contributors affecting a male editorial 'we', whereas there were in reality women who wrote for it.[21] Periodicals in general took on women contributors, albeit the old political quarterlies established early in the century, the *Edinburgh Review* and the *Quarterly Review*, had few. Anonymous publication, Easley points out, 'provided women with effective cover for exploring a variety of conventionally "masculine" social issues', and 'allowed them to evade essentialized notions of "feminine" voice and identity'.[22] So when Harriet Martineau submitted her article on 'Female Industry' to Henry Reeve, editor of the *Edinburgh Review*, in 1859, she hoped that he agreed that she had 'succeeded in making it look like a man's writing'.[23] Easley also quotes the comment in 1865 of the proto-feminist activist Bessie Rayner Parkes, that 'if editors were ever known to disclose the dread secrets of their dens, they would only give the public an idea of the authoresses whose unsigned names are legion; of their rolls of manuscripts, which are as the sands of the sea'.[24]

Of the women critics covered here who chose to publish anonymously, Maria Jane Jewsbury evidently relished anonymity for the expressive freedom it gave her: taken on by Charles Wentworth Dilke when he bought the *Athenaeum* in 1830, she had already shown in some of her published work her strong awareness that the personae projected in writing were to a greater or lesser extent constructs,

----

[19]   Letter of 8 April 1894, Bentley MSS, quoted in Nancy Fix Anderson, *Woman Against Women in Victorian England: A Life of Eliza Lynn Linton* (Bloomington and Indianapolis: Indiana University Press, 1987), pp. 71–2.

[20]   Elaine Curran, '"Holding on by a Pen": The Story of a Lady Reviewer, Mary Margaret Busk (1779–1863)', *Victorian Periodicals Review*, 31/1 (1998): 9–30.

[21]   *First-Person Anonymous: Women Writers and Victorian Print Media, 1830–1870* (Aldershot and Burlington, VT: Ashgate, 2004), p. 27.

[22]   Ibid., p. 1.

[23]   Valerie Sanders, '"I'm your Man": Harriet Martineau and the *Edinburgh Review*', *Australasian Victorian Studies Journal*, 6 (2000): 36–47, at 44.

[24]   Bessie Rayner Parkes, *Essays on Women's Work* (London: Strahan, 1865), p. 121, quoted in *First-Person Anonymous*, p. 2.

often deliberate performances, and could be varied according to the intended audience. This awareness, however, also meant recognising that women writing overtly as women might feel obliged to perform in a constrained way. In reviewing *Woman, in her Social and Domestic Character* in 1832, she claims that when writing avowedly as females, women do so 'under a paralyzing fear of man', such that 'all they decry, and all that they inculcate is subservient to the opinions and tastes of man'.[25] Hence the author (who, incidentally, writes as 'Mrs John' rather than as 'Elizabeth' Sandford) recommends to women only those virtues and accomplishments which please men, rather than acknowledging that women possess 'a separate and responsible intelligence', and need a moral code that is 'based in broad general principles which appeal equally and indiscriminately to all human beings'. Glennis Stephenson has argued of Jewsbury's contemporary, the popular poet Letitia Elizabeth Landon ('L.E.L.'), that when publishing literary criticism as 'L.E.L.', she writes effusively, personally (using 'I' rather than 'we'), and with slapdash grammar, whereas her anonymous piece for the same periodical (the *New Monthly Magazine*), 'On the Ancient and Modern Influence of Poetry', deploys the authoritative 'we', and uses correct grammar and clear and precise diction.[26] That is, when writing overtly as a woman, Landon deliberately comes across as emotional and intellectually limited.

Anne Mozley too welcomed anonymous publication: although signature was adopted by some periodicals during her writing lifetime, she did not seek to publish in any of them, and her long and prolific career as a periodical contributor was only disclosed in 1892, shortly after her death. Anonymity gave her expressive freedom, including the capacity to cover topics not usually seen as women's province. Both she and Jewsbury, in addition, writing from strongly Christian positions, would have been affected by religious strictures against seeking worldly acclaim, reinforced by social strictures against such ambitions on the part of women. Margaret Oliphant, meanwhile, preferred anonymity: she occasionally published periodical criticism as herself, but was more often anonymous, and sometimes adopted an overtly masculine persona. Her attitude differed somewhat from those of Jewsbury and Mozley: known as a writer of novels and other books, she was not confident that she was respected either as a woman or as an individual.

Sara Coleridge is an interesting case, since her short venture into periodical criticism was ill-starred. One corollary of identity and character being invested in periodicals themselves rather than in the individuals who wrote for them was that editors sometimes altered the texts of contributions to fit in with their sense of the periodical's viewpoint. How common this was is now hard to gauge, but Sara Coleridge's review of Tennyson's *The Princess* for the *Quarterly Review* in 1848 was doctored by the editor, J.G. Lockhart, to excise any references to Keats:

---

[25] '*Woman, in Her Social and Domestic Character*', *Athenaeum*, 5 May 1832: 282–3, at 282.

[26] 'Letitia Landon and the Victorian Improvisatrice: the Construction of L.E.L.', *Victorian Poetry*, 30/1 (1992): 1–17.

Sara Coleridge treated Keats sympathetically as an influence on Tennyson, but Lockhart chose to protract into the 1840s the *Quarterly*'s hostility to the 'Cockney' poet expressed in John Wilson Croker's notorious article of 1818. And although Margaret Oliphant preferred anonymity, she suffered from a minor instance of interference from the very Henry Reeve for whom Harriet Martineau had been anxious to project a masculine voice. When she reviewed for the *Edinburgh* in 1878 the correspondence of French novelist Honoré de Balzac, Reeve added to the beginning of her article a reminiscence of his own about meeting Balzac – a move which invested the reviewer's voice with personal experience and possibly even venerability (since Balzac had died back in 1850).[27]

The foregoing, as it relates to both novelists and critics, suggests that in the nineteenth century the traits evident in women's writing were expected to be different from those in men's. The women critics' sense of both what was publicly acceptable in their own writing, and of the criteria they should use in assessing women novelists, is important to this study. Contemporary assumptions about women's writing, not surprisingly, derived from notions about the nature, capacities and social role of women themselves, and there was often a double standard. Elaine Showalter's identification in 1977 of the qualities attributed to the writing of the two sexes in the nineteenth century is justified by much evidence. Women, she says, were thought 'to possess sentiment, refinement, tact, observation, domestic expertise, high moral tone, and knowledge of female character', and correspondingly thought to lack the male traits of 'originality, intellectual training, abstract intelligence, humor, self-control, and knowledge of male character'.[28]

Moreover, the denial to women of creative and intellectual power could lead to patronising treatment, such as that in the *London Review* for 1860, which argued that women novelists had succeeded by dint of applying microscopic observation to what has lain closest to hand: they cannot generalise or reason, but offer 'abundance of quiet and vivid surface observation'.[29] On the other hand, if women demonstrated knowledge of life beyond the confines of the domestic sphere, then they risked being criticised as unfeminine. Another *London Review* commentary of 1864 argues that a 'great writer' must 'understand by long experience the meannesses of the world', including 'the various ways in which men undergo moral declension and decay', and yet must emerge to 'take a broad and comprehensive

---

[27] [Margaret Oliphant], 'The Correspondence of M. de Balzac', *Edinburgh Review*, 148 (October 1878): 528–58; Margaret Oliphant to John Blackwood, 9 October 1878, quoted in *Autobiography and Letters of Mrs Margaret Oliphant* (1899), ed. Mrs Harry Coghill, intro. Q.D. Leavis (Leicester: Leicester University Press, 1974), pp. 275–6.

[28] *A Literature of Their Own: British Women Novelists from Brontë to Lessing* (Princeton, NJ: Princeton University Press, 1977), p. 90.

[29] *London Review*, 1 (1860): 137, quoted in Elizabeth Helsinger, Robin Lauterbach Sheets and William Veeder (eds), *The Woman Question: Society and Literature in Britain and America, 1837–1883* (3 vols, Chicago and London: University of Chicago Press, 1983), vol. 3, *Literary Issues*, p. 53.

view of life after all the destruction of one's ideals and utopias'. But literary preparation of this kind subjects a woman to 'a defeminizing process', such that the 'strength and breadth of view' that she gains is not worth 'the sacrifice of that nameless beauty of innocence which is by nature the glory of the woman'.[30]

Comments like these suggest that a woman writer who demonstrated intellectual acumen and a wide experience of life was threatening to men, whereas women who remained within a limited literary sphere reinforced men's sense of superiority, and could therefore be safely patronised. This was certainly the conclusion implied by George Eliot's acute and now well-known comments in her 1856 essay, 'Silly Novels by Lady Novelists', about the critical reception of women writers:

> By a peculiar thermometric adjustment, when a woman's talent is at zero, journalistic approbation is at the boiling pitch; when she attains mediocrity, it is already at no more than summer heat; and if she ever reaches excellence, critical enthusiasm drops to the freezing point. Harriet Martineau, Currer Bell, and Mrs Gaskell have been treated as cavalierly as if they had been men.[31]

In the absence of evidence of authorship, however, it cannot be proven that the *London Review* articles were written by a man (or men) – or that the praise of *The Mill on the Floss* with which I began came from a female pen. In the nineteenth century, male critics had no monopoly on patronising or critical commentary on women authors, nor women any monopoly on sympathetic treatment of them. In this context, it is worth recalling the now notorious review of *Jane Eyre* published by Elizabeth Rigby, later Lady Eastlake, in the *Quarterly Review* for December 1848. This article argued, among other points, that the novel must be the work of a man, since it possesses 'great mental powers … a great coarseness of taste, and a heathenish doctrine of religion', none of which qualities was likely in a woman.[32] But what clinches the argument for male authorship is the novelist's apparent ignorance of things every woman should know. A woman writer, the review argues, would not have referred to a woman's trussing game and garnishing dessert dishes with the same hands, or given to a female character the costume worn by Blanche Ingram, or had Jane don a 'frock' when suddenly roused in the night. If by any chance the writer is a woman, then she can only be 'one who has, for some sufficient reason, long forfeited the society of her own sex'. What I would emphasise here, however, is that in making these pungent comments (and others), Rigby is taking on a male voice. As if aware that claiming knowledge of domestic matters might identify the reviewer themself as female, she accounts for it by referring, rather clumsily, to 'a lady friend, whom we are always happy to

[30] Ibid., pp. 20–21.

[31] *Westminster Review*, 66 (October 1856): 442–61, repr. in Solveig C. Robinson, *A Serious Occupation*, pp. 88–115, at p. 113.

[32] '*Vanity Fair* and *Jane Eyre*', *Quarterly Review*, 84 (December 1848): 153–85, repr. in Solveig C. Robinson, *A Serious Occupation*, pp. 46–73.

consult'. Whether 'Currer Bell' is male or female, Rigby does not feel she can get away with hard-hitting criticism of the novelist, especially in a very conservative organ like the *Quarterly*, unless she affects to be male herself. We will see Anne Mozley adopting the same move in reviewing Brontë's later novel *Villette* for the conservative *Christian Remembrancer*, with the difference that her rhetorical strategy is more complex and her response to the novel more nuanced.

This is not to say that all critics argued for strict demarcations between writing by men and writing by women. One recurrent practice is the attribution of 'masculine' qualities to some women and their writing, and this sometimes has positive connotations, as Susan J. Wolfson has observed.[33] So William Howitt says of *Shirley*, that although it is clearly by a woman, she possesses 'the intellectual power of a man'. For him, the combination of this 'intellectual power' and the 'tender sensibilities' of Brontë's femaleness enrich the novel.[34] In 1857, George Eliot would commend Elizabeth Barrett Browning's *Aurora Leigh* as androgynous, combining the qualities of the male poet and the poetess.[35] Similar kinds of praise are sometimes found in the writing of the women critics to be treated here.

But identifying a combination of 'masculine' and 'feminine' qualities in a woman writer was possibly less often a pitch for creative androgyny, than a means of averting gender-based strictures. Harriet Martineau, anxious to appear male in the pages of the *Edinburgh Review* in 1859, had been in her early career a victim of misogynist criticism. This was because, not only did she discuss politics and economics, but she was a single woman writing on population control, and one who came across as 'mannish'.[36] The prudence of identifying feminine traits in prominent women is especially clear in the works of women who memorialised groups of other women – texts where overarching notions of masculinity and femininity are perhaps more noticeable than in discussions of individuals. These histories sometimes sought to steer their subjects between the Charybdis of condescension and the Scylla of disparagement, by pointing out how the women reconciled 'masculine' qualities with 'feminine' conduct. In particular, those women who were held up for admiration were often learned, but they were not ambitious for literary fame. This will be a theme of my discussions of literary histories by women – but the critics I focus on were not alone.

For example, in Louisa Stuart Costello's *Memoirs of Eminent Englishwomen*, a long and polyglot account of a variety of women from the Elizabethan period to the

[33] Susan J. Wolfson, *Borderlines: The Shiftings of Gender in British Romanticism* (Stanford: Stanford University Press, 2006), p. 34.

[34] *Standard of Freedom*, 10 November 1849: 11, repr. in Miriam Allott (ed.), *The Brontës: The Critical Heritage* (London: Routledge & Kegan Paul; New York: Barnes & Noble, 1974), pp. 133–5, at p. 133.

[35] 'Belles Lettres', *Westminster Review*, 67 (January 1857): 306–10, at 306.

[36] Alexis Easley, *First-Person Anonymous*, p. 41; Hilary Fraser, Stephanie Green and Judith Johnston, *Gender and the Victorian Periodical* (Cambridge: Cambridge University Press, 2003), p. 36.

mid eighteenth century, the clever and ambitious estate-builder Bess of Hardwick is faulted for her lack of 'feminine qualities' – she was 'daring, masculine, forbidding and selfish'[37]– whereas Mary Evelyn (daughter of the diarist John Evelyn), although well-educated in the classical poets and in history, as well as talented in music and letter-writing, is praised for being 'modest' and for possessing 'unpretending piety'.[38] Lady Mary Wortley Montagu, meanwhile, was formidably learned, but her letters often shift from demonstrating erudition to 'some amusing image', and thus are 'so feminine and so agreeable'.[39] Concentrating specifically on writers, Anne Katherine Elwood's *Memoirs of the Literary Ladies of England from the Commencement of the Last Century* (1843) observes that Anna Letitia Barbauld's writings are notable for 'sound judgment', 'good sense' and 'a considerable degree of wit', but Elwood emphasises too that she was 'exemplary – as a wife, as a sister, a friend', and hence 'an ornament both to her sex and to her native land'.[40] Similarly, Fanny Burney was 'a dutiful daughter, an affectionate sister, a devoted wife, and a faithful friend', and concentrated on 'feminine avocations' before dinner. But Elwood praises her fiction, and notes that it was fortunate that in Burney's youth, dinner was eaten earlier than was usual in 1843 – otherwise posterity would have had only 'some old screen and chair-covers', instead of her fine novels.[41]

This approach to women writers had developed over the eighteenth century. Margaret J.M. Ezell and Norma Clarke have investigated the representation of them in biographical studies and editions of their works during this period, and have concluded that the women found worth publishing and memorialising were, increasingly, those who could be celebrated for being chaste, modest and retiring. They may have been erudite in many cases, but sometimes they did not write for publication, still less out of the need to make a living. So by the late eighteenth century, according to Clarke:

> To be hidden rather than seen, unknown rather than known, silent rather than speaking and self-deprecating rather than self-assertive became key attributes of the laudable woman writer at the very time women were using their speaking, writing and self assertion to enter the literary world in ever greater numbers.[42]

This kind of tension is evident as well in the work of some of the critics discussed here.

---

[37] Louisa Stuart Costello, *Memoirs of Eminent Englishwomen* (4 vols, London: R. Bentley, 1844), vol. 1, p. 10.

[38] Ibid., vol. 2, pp. 305–14.

[39] Ibid., vol. 4, p. 342.

[40] Vol. 1, pp. 239–40.

[41] Ibid., vol. 2, pp. 65, 36.

[42] Norma Clarke, *The Rise and Fall of the Woman of Letters* (London: Pimlico Random House, 2004), p. 308; Margaret J.M. Ezell, *Writing Women's Literary History* (Baltimore: Johns Hopkins University Press, 1993).

* * *

This study concentrates on how nineteenth-century women critics responded to women's fiction, so that poetry will not be covered in detail. There will be some attention given to prominent poets such as Felicia Hemans and Elizabeth Barrett Browning, as they were discussed by some of the critics treated here, and in ways which relate to concepts of masculinity and femininity in writing. But I focus on fiction, since not only did it become an increasingly prominent genre over the century, it was also one that was sometimes associated with women.

Indeed, a woman had been central to an early nineteenth-century attempt at canon-creation. This was the 50-volume *British Novelists* series, edited by Anna Letitia Barbauld, and produced by a consortium of 37 booksellers in 1810, just before Walter Scott and Jane Austen started publishing fiction. Not only was the series edited by a woman – eight of the 21 novelists featured were women: Clara Reeve, Charlotte Lennox, Frances Brooke, Elizabeth Inchbald, Charlotte Smith, Fanny Burney, Ann Radcliffe and Maria Edgeworth. In her introductory essay, 'On the Origin and Progress of Novel-Writing', Barbauld acknowledges the low literary status suffered by novels: she begins by saying that '[a] Collection of Novels has a better chance of giving pleasure than of commanding respect'. But she goes on to argue that novels both have a significant emotional impact on readers and can convey a 'grave impressive moral' – further, that all this requires considerable skill.[43]

Barbauld ends her essay by quoting the adage, 'Let me make the ballads of a nation, and I care not who makes the laws', and then asks: 'Might it not be said with as much propriety, Let me make the novels of a country, and let who will make the systems?'[44] By the middle of the nineteenth century, the dominance of the novel as a genre of creative literature was established. In introducing her review of *Adam Bede* in 1859, Anne Mozley briefly traces the form's development, plus the increasing respect it had garnered. She asserts that 'every man's favourite field of thought falls by turns under the illuminating ray' of the novelist, and that 'there are very few scenes in the world which skill cannot turn into a good picture'. Hence those who had resisted Scott, the most popular novelist of the early nineteenth century, had now succumbed to at least one of Dickens, Thackeray, Charlotte Brontë, Elizabeth Gaskell, Charlotte Yonge, Bulwer-Lytton, Charles Kingsley, or, finally, George Eliot.[45]

In October 1829, between the accounts of Barbauld and Mozley, prominent critic Francis Jeffrey discusses women's fiction in reviewing two collections of Felicia Hemans's poetry in the *Edinburgh Review*, and begins by giving a roll-call

---

[43]   *Anna Letitia Barbauld, Selected Poetry and Prose*, ed. William McCarthy and Elizabeth Kraft (Peterborough, Ontario and Orchard Park, NY: Broadview, 2002), pp. 377–8.

[44]   Ibid., pp. 417–18.

[45]   [Anne Mozley], '*Adam Bede* and Recent Novels', *Bentley's Quarterly Review*, no. 2 (July 1859): 433–72, at 433–4.

of the capacities he believes women writers lack. They cannot, he says, 'represent naturally the fierce and sullen passions of men – nor their coarser vices – nor even scenes of actual business or contention – and the mixed motives, and strong and faulty characters, by which affairs of moment are usually conducted on the great theatre of the world'. These comments foreshadow those of the *London Review* critic of a generation later, cited above, who identifies the areas of experience from which women are best protected, despite their ignorance of these areas making their fiction more limited. Jeffrey also speculates that women are 'incapable of long moral or political investigations, where many complex and indeterminate elements are to be taken into account, and a variety of opposite probabilities to be weighed before coming to a conclusion'. He is uncertain, nonetheless, about what in these circumstances derives from women's nature, and what from their upbringing and habitual way of life. For example, he refers to 'the delicacy of [women's] training and habits', but also to 'the still more disabling delicacy which pervades their conceptions and feelings'. He alludes to women's 'actual inexperience of the realities they might wish to describe' – yet in the next phrase, to 'their substantial and incurable ignorance of business', as if such 'ignorance' could not be overcome by efforts to inculcate knowledge.[46] The *London Review* critic, we recall, conceded that women could be exposed to certain kinds of experience, but in being so would lose an 'innocence' which this critic sees as part of their 'nature' – as if what is innate could also be radically changed.

The interplay of nature and nurture in women, and its implications for women's writing, are problematic for some of the women critics discussed here as well. But what I want to stress in Jeffrey's review is, firstly, what he goes on to say about women's writing in general, and secondly, the implications of his term 'delicacy'. He argues that women's 'proper and natural business is the practical regulation of private life, in all its bearings, affections, and concerns', where the questions they deal with are 'better described as delicate than intricate', and thus demand 'rather a quick tact and fine perception than a patient or laborious examination'. Women's lives develop in them 'the finest perception of character and manners', and 'train[ ] their whole faculties to a nicety and precision of operation' and a 'singular exactness of judgment' – skills which some then apply to writing. He gives as examples 'the Letters of Madame de Sevigné ... the Novels of Miss Austin [*sic*] ... the Hymns and Early Lessons of Mrs Barbauld ... the conversations of Mrs Marcet', plus some works by Maria Edgeworth, Mary Russell Mitford and Amelia Opie. These, moreover, are works that could not have been written as successfully by men: that they are 'essentially and intensely feminine' is the result of the female tendencies Jeffrey has mentioned, plus 'softness and delicacy of hand'. Their femininity is also evident in the fact that these texts 'accomplish more completely all the ends at which they aim, and are worked out with a gracefulness and felicity of execution

---

[46]   [Francis Jeffrey], 'Felicia Hemans', *Edinburgh Review*, 50 (October 1829): 32–47, at 32.

which excludes all idea of failure, and entirely satisfies the expectations they may have raised'.[47]

There is condescension in all this, of course. The implication is that women writers produce more perfect works than men, and writings which do possess distinctive female traits. But since women are unsuited for, or at least excluded from, very wide areas of experience, the perfection arises from the limitation of their aims. In this context, it is not surprising that 'delicacy' is both a limitation and a defining female trait. For Jeffrey, it seems to mean, variously, a fragility and a vulnerability in women which means that they should be protected from certain kinds of potentially coarsening experience; a kind of tact which enables women to deal with sensitive but not intellectually complex matters ('delicate' rather than 'intricate'); and a sort of gentle subtlety ('softness and delicacy of hand'). Margaret J.M. Ezell has observed that 'delicacy' is often attributed to women's writing in the nineteenth century.[48] What will emerge in Julia Kavanagh's histories of women's fiction in the 1860s is a deployment of this term as a trait specific to women's writing, but also a particularly insightful application of it to the works of Jane Austen, and in a wider sense than seems to have been in Jeffrey's thoughts when he referred to the same novelist.

In the early 1860s, Julia Kavanagh championed women's overall achievement in fiction. It is the genre where women have accomplished the most, she claims, and the dominant genre of the mid nineteenth century. She also argued that women, from early in the genre's development, were the innovators in making central to the novel, the inner experience of individuals. In 1857, Margaret Sweat, reviewing the *Life of Charlotte Brontë*, recalled *Jane Eyre*, published 10 years earlier, as adumbrating the now-common preference among readers for 'deeper insight into character, for the features of the mind and heart', over portrayals of the external aspects of either individuals or social life. Not long afterwards, in 1860, R.H. Hutton observed in the *National Review* that whereas in the past the inspiration of English fiction had largely been social, the impact of the Brontës, and even more of George Eliot, had meant greater profundity in the study of the individual, such that Eliot in particular could offer 'more insight into the deeper roots of character'; he compared the Brontës and Eliot favourably with male novelists like Thackeray and Trollope.[49]

This is not to say that psychological insight was generally thought to be the special preserve of the female novelist, albeit it was a talent with which they were increasingly credited. But in one arena of experience at least, women could be

---

[47]   Ibid., pp. 33–4.

[48]   *Writing Women's Literary History*, p. 121.

[49]   [Margaret Sweat], review of *Life of Charlotte Brontë* in *North American Review*, 85 (October 1857): 293–329, partly repr. in Miriam Allott, *The Brontës*, pp. 379–85, at p. 380; [R.H. Hutton], 'The Novels of George Eliot', *National Review*, 11 (July 1860): 191–219, at 191–4, quoted in Richard Stang, *The Theory of the Novel in England 1850–1870* (London: Routledge & Kegan Paul, 1959), p. 55.

argued to have greater insight than men – the arena of female feeling, and especially women's experience of love. Kavanagh in the early 1860s draws attention to women novelists' access to this sort of knowledge, which she considers denied to men. In writing about the Brontës at the turn of the century, Mary Ward still found distinctive of women's fiction an understanding of the depth of women's feelings, and argued that the probing of inner psychological life was something that might strike chords with male readers as well. That is, even where women's circumstances have cut them off from large areas of experience, their resulting focus on the inner life could afford insights of value to both sexes.

So during the nineteenth century – to take a positive view of developments for women writers – the novel becomes an increasingly prominent genre, while women come to attention as practitioners, valued for both their 'feminine' emotional insights and, in the case of George Eliot in particular, for their 'masculine' intellectual prowess and the comprehensive understanding resulting from it. But central too to the reception history of Austen, Charlotte Brontë and Eliot are the biographical accounts of them that followed their deaths. All three aroused fascination about their lives: Austen, because, with apparently feminine modesty, she had had no public profile in her lifetime; Brontë and Eliot, because, since they published initially under male pseudonyms and demonstrated 'masculine' traits in their fiction, readers were concerned to know how 'masculine' they had been as women. My investigation of women critics' responses to the biographical accounts of these novelists has been a particularly rewarding aspect of this project, because they sometimes commented sharply and critically on the biographical image-making in a way that male critics seldom did – especially on the versions of the writers offered by male relatives.

Henry Austen's 'Biographical Notice' of his sister Jane came out in 1817 with the posthumous publication of *Northanger Abbey* and *Persuasion*, and was expanded in 1832 to accompany the first volume (*Sense and Sensibility*, 1833) of Richard Bentley's new edition of the Austen novels. It stressed Jane Austen's lack of desire for public acclaim, and highlighted her tolerance of other people's 'frailties, foibles and follies', such that she was never publicly critical of these, according to her brother. It also quoted a letter Jane Austen had written jocularly to her young nephew James Edward Austen, with a description of her own art as 'a little bit of ivory, two inches wide, on which I work with a brush so fine as to produce little effect after much labour', a description which was to become celebrated.[50] Unfortunately, the comment was taken too literally by many commentators – Jane Austen is clearly being arch rather than seriously self-deprecating, as she compares her own writing to her teenage nephew's 'manly, vigorous sketches, so full of life and spirit'. The literal interpretation was fostered, however, by the wish to identify Austen as an 'essentially and intensely feminine' writer (to recall Jeffrey's terms).

---

[50] The 'Biographical Notice' is reprinted in B.C. Southam (ed.), *Jane Austen: The Critical Heritage* (London: Routledge & Kegan Paul; New York: Barnes & Noble, 1968), pp. 73–8.

Moreover, Jeffrey's comments suggest that this kind of writer was comfortably limited – she did what she aimed at perfectly, but she attempted nothing 'manly' or 'vigorous'.

There was no other first-hand published account of Jane Austen the woman until the addressee of the letter, now James Edward Austen-Leigh, brought out a *Memoir of Jane Austen* late in 1869. This was a much longer work, but its version of the writer was very similar to Henry Austen's. Neither the brother nor the nephew denied Jane Austen wit or intelligence, but they both stressed her self-effacing tendencies. Austen-Leigh claimed that she had been happy to pass her time 'in the performance of home-duties, and the cultivation of domestic affections',[51] and he made much of her feminine accomplishments, eliding any distinction between writing and the other arts he attributes to her. He therefore lauded, in succession, her throwing of spilikins, her adeptness at cup-and-ball, her handwriting, her folding and sealing of letters, and especially her needlework. Hence, he concluded, 'the same hand which painted so exquisitely with the pen could work as delicately with the needle'.[52] 'Delicacy', as in Jeffrey's account, is pressed into service as a distinctly female trait, and recalls also the gentle fingering of the miniaturist on ivory.

Between the 'Biographical Notice' by Henry Austen and the *Memoir* by Austen-Leigh came the *Life of Charlotte Brontë*, which, according to Kathryn Sutherland, had an influence on the latter version of Austen. Gaskell's text had set, she says, 'a high standard for the simultaneous memorializing and effacing of its difficult subject, the woman writer'.[53] Gaskell was concerned in her biography to counter some of the implications of critical responses to Brontë's novels, such as Elizabeth Rigby's, that the novelist had been unfemininely outspoken and overfamiliar with aspects of life of which it behoved women to be ignorant. Designed to 'exonerate and iconise' Charlotte and her sisters, the book emphasised Charlotte Brontë's isolation, her bleak social and natural environment, her relentless experience of bereavement, and her struggle to make a living, as well as her consistent and willing fulfilment of the duties of a Victorian daughter and sister. Charlotte Brontë was not worldly or sophisticated, and the wild, passionate and 'coarse' aspects of her fiction were explained by her unusual but restricted environment and range of experience, and the outré kinds of people she knew. As Lucasta Miller has emphasised in *The Brontë Myth* (2001), it created a widely influential image of the sisters 'playing out their tragic destiny on top of a windswept moor with a mad misanthrope father and doomed brother'.[54]

---

[51]   *A Memoir of Jane Austen and Other Family Recollections*, ed. Kathryn Sutherland (London and Oxford: Oxford University Press, 2002), pp. 147–54.

[52]   Ibid., pp. 77–9.

[53]   Kathryn Sutherland, *Jane Austen's Textual Lives: From Aeschylus to Bollywood* (Oxford: Clarendon Press, 2005), p. 85.

[54]   Lucasta Miller, *The Brontë Myth* (London: Jonathan Cape, 2001), p. 57.

Although much in Jane Austen's life was very different, Austen-Leigh picks up on the isolation and unworldly aspects of Gaskell's image of Charlotte Brontë, so as to emphasise his aunt's modesty. Charlotte Brontë may have had limited contact with public life, but Jane Austen's 'seclusion' was unrivalled among women writers since, unlike Charlotte Brontë, she never met any literary celebrities at all.[55]

The women critics treated here generally accept Elizabeth Gaskell's version of her friend as genuine, although their responses to Brontë herself as a person are varied. But there is some scepticism about the versions of Jane Austen offered by her male relatives. Maria Jane Jewsbury (who had access only to Henry Austen's 1817 account) could only think that the 'real' Jane Austen emerged in the fiction; Julia Kavanagh, having access to both of Henry Austen's accounts, did not query them, but offered an interpretation of the fiction which went beyond their implications; Margaret Oliphant, reviewing Austen-Leigh's book, concluded that the Austen family were obtuse about the clever female in their midst; Mary Ward attacked another effort by an Austen male, her great-nephew Lord Brabourne's inept edition of Jane Austen's letters. That is, these writers countered the image of the witty, but unthreatening, pleasant and gentle spinster introduced to the world by Henry Austen and given longer life by Austen-Leigh's account (it survived well into the twentieth century).

As far as George Eliot was concerned, her widower John Walter Cross brought out in 1885, five years after her death, a three-volume compilation of letters with connecting narrative, the *Life and Letters of George Eliot.* This put more emphasis on the woman novelist's writing life than had the *Life of Charlotte Brontë*, or, especially, the Austen men's versions of Jane. But Cross made Eliot's intellectual development seem the result of a series of male influences, and also edited out evidence of wit, gaiety and spontaneity from the letters. Moreover, he made little of two great crises of Eliot's life, her abandonment of religious faith and her choice to live extra-maritally with George Henry Lewes. Hence the novelist came across as an unoriginal thinker, as well as ponderous, humourless and dull.[56] But as with the Austen-Leigh biography, Margaret Oliphant was dubious about Cross's version of Eliot, recognising it as an exercise in image-making.

The treatment of Emily Brontë in this study requires some explanation, since *Wuthering Heights* made a considerable impact, and she was naturally often discussed in tandem with her more prolific older sister. She was also a writer who attracted increasing interest and respect over the second half of the nineteenth century. Of the critics studied here, Anne Mozley discussed Emily Brontë in her review of the *Life of Charlotte Brontë*, and Mary Ward of course included *Wuthering Heights* in her edition of the Brontë novels at the turn of the century: I will consider

---

[55]   *A Memoir of Jane Austen and Other Family Recollections*, pp. 90–91.

[56]   See Joanne Shattock, 'The Construction of the Woman Writer', in Joanne Shattock (ed.), *Women and Literature in Britain 1800–1900* (Cambridge: Cambridge University Press, 2001), pp. 8–34 at pp. 26–8, and Joanne Wilkes, 'Remaking the Canon', ibid., pp. 35–54, at p. 50.

their responses here. But the overall reception of Emily Brontë's writing in the period has already received detailed attention. The extent to which early reviews of *Wuthering Heights* were inflected by assumptions about gender has been covered by Nicola Diane Thompson in her *Reviewing Sex: Gender and the Reception of Victorian Novels* (1996), while the later dissemination of the novel is treated in Patsy Stoneman's *Brontë Transformations* and Lucasta Miller's *The Brontë Myth*. The reception history is complex, but I would also argue that Emily Brontë, via both her writings and what was published about her life, came across as too unusual a person to be easily discussed, either then or now, in terms of the nineteenth-century conceptions of gender that concern me here. She was too hard to categorise, and her writing bewildered as much as it intrigued – she was perhaps the exception that tested all the rules.

Chapter 2
Maria Jane Jewsbury and Sara Coleridge

Maria Jane Jewsbury

After Maria Jane Fletcher, née Jewsbury, died of cholera in India in October 1833, shortly before her thirty-third birthday, several people commented on how her literary talent had not been fully disclosed in her published works. For example, her closest friend, Felicia Hemans, lamented:

> How much deeper power seemed to lie coiled up, as it were, in the recesses of her mind, than was ever manifested to the world in her writings. Strange and sad does it seem, that only the broken music has been given to the earth – the full and finished harmony never drawn forth![1]

Hemans's sister Harriett Hughes agreed, claiming that Jewsbury was 'endowed with masculine energies, with a spirit that seemed born for ascendency, with strong powers of reasoning, fathomless profundity of thought', but that these qualities were never 'appreciated as they deserved' – not indeed 'fully manifested except to the few who knew her intimately'.[2] Some years later, Elizabeth Barrett, after reading the letters of Jewsbury's quoted in Henry Fothergill Chorley's *Memorials of Mrs Hemans* (1836), commented that she had been 'a woman of more comprehensiveness of mind & of a higher logical faculty than are commonly found among women', such that her letters demonstrated a '*working power*' – but Barrett too regretted that 'no worthy work was left behind'.[3]

This response reflects more than the fact that Maria Jane Jewsbury died in early adulthood. She had, after all, published four works in volume form by the age of 30: a miscellany of short stories, articles and poems called *Phantasmagoria* (2 vols, 1825), a collection in the genre of letters of advice to young women (*Letters to the Young*, 1828), a volume of poems (*Lays of Leisure Hours*, 1829), and three novellas, published as *The Three Histories* (1830). But there were other factors affecting Jewsbury's reception, factors relating to the choices she made

---

[1]   Quoted in C. Harriett Hughes, *Works of Mrs. Hemans, With a Memoir of Her Life* (2 vols, Edinburgh: William Blackwood and Sons, 1839), vol. 1, p. 226.

[2]   Ibid., vol. 1, pp. 141–2.

[3]   Letter to Mary Russell Mitford of 14 June 1845, in *The Letters of Elizabeth Barrett Browning to Mary Russell Mitford 1836–1854*, ed. and intro. Meredith B. Raymond and Mary Rose Sullivan (3 vols, Waco, TX: Wedgestone Press, 1983), vol. 3, pp. 118–19 (Barrett's emphasis).

in reconciling her literary career to the demands of domestic life, and also to her choice of anonymous reviewing as the vehicle for much of her later writing.

On the practical level, Jewsbury had found it difficult from her late teens to juggle domestic commitments with her literary endeavours. Born in 1800 as the eldest in a family of seven, daughter of a cotton manufacturer turned Manchester insurance agent, she had become responsible for her younger siblings when her mother died in 1819, soon after the birth of the last child. By 1821, nonetheless, Jewsbury was contributing to the *Manchester Gazette*, where her poetry attracted Alaric Watts, editor of the *Leeds Intelligencer* and later of the *Manchester Courier*. He and his wife Priscilla encouraged her writing, and in 1825 Alaric persuaded Hurst and Robinson to publish her miscellany *Phantasmagoria*.

But domestic duty always weighed on her: when Priscilla urged her to write a 'love-tale', Jewsbury could only explain:

> With one or two exceptions, I never have read a love-tale without seeing its ludicrous side … Three dear children are catechizing me at the rate of ten questions in every five minutes. I am within hearing of one servant stoning a kitchen floor; and of another practising a hymn; and of a very turbulent child and unsympathetic nurse next door. I think I could make a decent paper descriptive of the miseries of combining literary tastes with domestic duties.[4]

An admirer of Wordsworth, Jewsbury sent *Phantasmagoria* to him in 1825, a move that initiated a friendship with the Wordsworth family.[5] In a letter of 1826 to Catherine Clarkson, Dorothy Wordsworth noted sympathetically that most of Jewsbury's poems and prose pieces were written as she stayed up in a children's sick-room till the early hours of the morning.[6] Narrating her 'History of an Enthusiast' in 1830, Jewsbury would refer to her own 'spinster matronhood'.[7]

So Jewsbury's decision to marry the Rev. William Kew Fletcher in 1832 was not in itself a choice of domestic over literary life. She continued writing after her marriage: Fletcher's position as chaplain to the East India Company obliged the couple to travel to India, but Jewsbury sent back to the *Athenaeum* extracts from her travel journal, plus the best poetry of her career, and the magazine published

---

[4]   Quoted in Maria Jane Jewsbury, *Occasional Papers*, ed. Eric Gillett (London: Oxford University Press, 1932), pp. xvii–xviii.

[5]   Jewsbury's role as a protégée of Wordsworth is discussed by Dennis Low in *The Literary Protégées of the Lake Poets* (Aldershot and Burlington, VT: Ashgate, 2006).

[6]   Letter of 1 April 1826, in Alan G. Hill (ed.), *The Letters of William and Dorothy Wordsworth*, 2nd edn, III, *The Later Years, Pt 1, 1821–28* (Oxford: Clarendon Press, 1978), p. 435.

[7]   Maria Jane Jewsbury, *The Three Histories* (London: Frederick Westley and A.H. Davis, 1830), p. 5.

this material between December 1832 and December 1833.[8] Nor was her marriage necessarily responsible for Jewsbury's early death from cholera: there was after all a cholera epidemic in England in the early 1830s. But it seems that her widower did impede the posthumous dissemination of her works. According to her younger sister Geraldine, responding in 1836 to a Lancaster solicitor who had approached their father about a memorial volume to Maria Jane, she had taken out to India with her all her manuscripts, including some minor pieces she had intended to republish. But the material had disappeared, since Fletcher had remarried, and had not answered any letters from the Jewsbury family.[9]

The foregoing should suggest that in Maria Jane Jewsbury's case, the relationship between the domestic and the literary life was not straightforward. Moreover, the more complex issues of how far Jewsbury herself internalised early nineteenth-century ideas about what a woman's priorities should be, and how much this internalisation affected her writing, have attracted differing interpretations. Two early commentators included Sarah Stickney Ellis, to become famous as the nineteenth century's most popular champion of the domestic and maternal roles of women, and Jane Williams, who included Jewsbury in her *The Literary Women of England* in 1861. More recently, with the post-1980 revival of interest in Jewsbury, there have been insightful discussions of the issues by Norma Clarke, Dennis Low and Susan J. Wolfson.[10] The comments by Harriett Hughes and Elizabeth Barrett I have cited, moreover, are instances of the contemporary tendency to attribute to Jewsbury qualities then coded as 'masculine'. Jewsbury herself, in her literary criticism, discussed 'masculine' and 'feminine' qualities in writing, as will be illustrated below.

I shall return to the critical debate over Jewsbury's attitude to a literary career for a woman. What is undeniable, however, is that much of her literary energy from 1830 went into writing many anonymous reviews and articles for the weekly *Athenaeum* – covering a wide variety of texts, including poetry, fiction, memoirs and histories, conduct literature and writing for children. Many of her subjects were ephemeral, but they included Wordsworth, Ebenezer Elliott, P.B. Shelley

---

[8]   Jewsbury's poetry is featured and discussed in Isobel Armstrong, Joseph Bristow with Cath Sharrock (eds), *Nineteenth-Century Women Poets: An Oxford Anthology* (Oxford: Clarendon Press, 1996), pp. 215–33; extracts from her travel journal were reprinted in Jane Williams, *The Literary Women of England* (London: Saunders, Otley and Co., 1861), pp. 374–6 and Francis Espinasse, *Lancashire Worthies*, 2nd series (London: Simpkin, Marshall & Co., 1877), 330ff.

[9]   Maria Jane Jewsbury, *Occasional Papers*, pp. lxv–lxvi.

[10]   Norma Clarke, *Ambitious Heights: Writing, Friendship, Love – the Jewsbury Sisters, Felicia Hemans and Jane Carlyle* (London and New York: Routledge, 1990); Dennis Low, *The Literary Protégées of the Lake Poets*; Susan J. Wolfson, *Borderlines: The Shiftings of Gender in British Romanticism* (Stanford: Stanford University Press, 2006).

and – my focus here – a range of women writers of the past and present.[11] Among the latter was Jane Austen, and Jewsbury's 1831 article on her represents the first published critical commentary on Austen now identifiable as a woman's response. Jewsbury was part of the influx of new talent brought to this new weekly review by Charles Wentworth Dilke, when he took over the *Athenaeum* editorship in 1830 – one consequence of which was 'more liveliness and satiric punch in some of the reviews'.[12]

As Norma Clarke has highlighted, for Jewsbury, who seems to have been the *Athenaeum*'s only regular female reviewer during the years she wrote for it, critical anonymity also meant that she could conceal the fact that she was a woman. She could therefore more easily adopt a knowledgeable persona, assume an authoritative tone, and be at times witty and sardonic – contribute, that is, to the 'liveliness and satiric punch' of the periodical's reviews.[13]

I have mentioned Jewsbury's comments regarding Elizabeth Sandford's tome on women, on how publishing overtly as a woman may make a female writer feel constrained to accommodate male preconceptions. A corollary of the anxiety to please men evident in Sandford's book, she suggests, is the approach taken by Anna Jameson in her *Memoirs of Celebrated Female Sovereigns*. Jameson omits much political and historical material, and plays down the 'profligacy and cruelty' of many of her subjects, for fear of distressing or injuring women readers. Thus she both edits out information essential to a proper evaluation of her sovereigns and, it is implied, panders to limiting contemporary assumptions about women's intelligence and appropriate knowledge.[14]

Before turning to Jewsbury's *Athenaeum* reviews of works by female creative writers, it is worth considering some of her writing for her first book, *Phantasmagoria*. This collection was published simply as by 'M.J.J.', and therefore, like the *Athenaeum* reviews, did not appear overtly as the work of a woman; it shows too that Jewsbury was fully aware, like Landon, that the literary personae of authors – including literary critics – were not simply reflections of the authors' personalities, but involved a greater or lesser degree of deliberate construction. These personae, moreover, might also be influenced by an author's sense of what kind of style and viewpoint particular periodicals demanded.

---

[11]   For a full list of Jewsbury's *Athenaeum* contributions that can be identified, see Monica Correa Fryckstedt, 'The Hidden Rill: The Life and Career of Maria Jane Jewsbury', *Bulletin of the John Rylands University Library of Manchester*, Pt 2, 67/1 (1984–5): 450–473.

[12]   Leslie A. Marchand, *The Athenaeum: A Mirror of Victorian Culture* (1941; repr. New York: Octagon Books, 1971), p. 24.

[13]   Norma Clarke, *Ambitious Heights*, pp. 37–8, 88ff. In 1833, Dilke would take on Lady Morgan, and in 1834, Mary Howitt.

[14]   '*Memoirs of Celebrated Female Sovereigns*', *Athenaeum*, 12 November 1831: 730–731, at 730.

A full illustration of this point would involve an analysis of the myriad personae inhabited by Jewsbury throughout the numerous poems and prose pieces which make up the collection. More briefly, it can be shown in three articles where the 'constructedness' of an author's persona is foregrounded. 'The Young Author' is in fact presented as the story of a 'young gentleman' who 'had the misfortune, in very early life, to discover that he was a genius', and thus 'very soon began to *train* as a literary character'.[15] So he reads all the new novels, circulates commonplace critical cant, writes album verse on 'Forget me not' and 'Remember me', quotes Byron and Thomas Moore during ball suppers, and writes a volume of love poems, full of eccentricities and affectations. He pretends to nerves and sensibility, plus 'thoughts too deep for tears', becomes ostentatiously abstemious, cultivates pale, languid and melancholy looks, and even adopts a dry delicate cough to suggest his consumptive tendencies. If he finds his works neglected, he will pin his hopes on posterity, and commit suicide like Chatterton. That it is specifically the male aspirant after literary fame who is targeted here is brought out by another of the 'Young Author's' literary schemes – despite the dubiousness of his own claims to literary respect, he plans to cut up Landon's 'Improvisatrice' in a critique: '"perfectly infamous for a woman to write, and write well"', he says; '"ought to be satisfied with reading what men write"'. This passage also perhaps suggests Jewsbury's awareness that, however much a writer cultivates a 'feminine' image like Landon's, she is always vulnerable to criticism if known to be a woman.

Meanwhile another article, 'First Efforts in Criticism', which purports to be samples of literary criticism sent to a periodical editor by a writer hoping for employment, highlights the potentially arbitrary nature of the critic's judgments and critical voice.[16] Here the 'critic' offers two possible reviews of an (apocryphal!) publication called *Love and Idleness, with other Poems*, by Edgar Percival Clerimont. The first version lambasts the author for the 'affectation' of his name (assumed to be a pseudonym), and castigates him for pandering to the tastes of sentimental women rather than writing for men. The second version, however, is enthusiastic and even rhapsodic: it indulges in gushing reminiscences of the critic's own past experience as a poet, and goes on to laud Clerimont for possessing 'a deep feeling of the beautiful … a fervent aspiring after the unattained and incomprehensible; – after those beauties which mock mortal eyesight, and come to the longing spirit, in midnight dream and vision', and for celebrating 'Love' as his 'being's law, – his purpose and his duty'.

This 'critic', then, will adopt whichever voice most suits the editor of the periodical. Furthermore, if the editor is after a review which functions simply as an excuse to dilate on the critic's (or periodical's) social and political views, then

---

[15] *Phantasmagoria; or, Sketches of Life and Literature* (2 vols, London: Hurst, Robinson and Co., 1825), vol. 1, pp. 189–98, repr. in Maria Jane Jewsbury, *Occasional Papers*, pp. 53–9 (Jewsbury's emphasis).

[16] Ibid., vol. 1, pp. 233–47, repr. in Maria Jane Jewsbury, *Occasional Papers*, pp. 8–18.

'First Efforts in Criticism' offers a sample of this as well. This 'review' groups six books on mathematics, but, rather than discuss them in any detail, it declares that better teaching of arithmetic will be socially beneficial because it will lead to 'a diminution of extravagance and crime' and 'the general establishment of a sounder feeling in religion, literature, and politics'. That is, it goes on, as long as new discoveries and systems are not accepted, since these, 'in this day of mad restlessness and innovation, are destroying that national energy, and national identity, which we possessed while adhering more scrupulously to the precedents of antiquity, and the wisdom of our ancestors'. The 'review' then heads off into an excursus on the virtues of the past and the dangers of change. It ends in a summary from the aspiring critic: 'Here follows a disquisition of twenty pages on things in general, with particular mention of the Brazils, the Peninsular War, and Church History'.[17]

The last item from *Phantasmagoria* to be considered here again takes up the pretensions of authors in a comic way, but in so doing raises some serious concerns which have implications for Jewsbury's later career. This article, 'Religious Novels',[18] in which Jewsbury does not for once project an evidently fictional persona, takes issue with the then-current popularity of this genre. Most religious novels, the review declares, are 'miserably defective in the power of developing the passions and principles of human nature'; they 'exhibit little of natural circumstance, less of natural character, and almost nothing of knowledge of the world'. Indeed they are 'weak in talent whether inventive or descriptive – and lamentably deficient in vigour of thought, and strength of feeling'. A few pages on, the article extends these points by ridiculing the implausibility, sentimentality, and sheer bad writing characteristic of this fiction. The heroine is generally a 'beautiful doll' and the hero a 'handsome simpleton', and the novelists generally 'kill either the one or the other, by the help of consumption or love'. The critic, however, would 'recommend the latter disease as being the more *lingering* of the two, and therefore more profitable both for the author and the apothecary'. In descriptive passages, she points out, '[t]he sun and moon must, of course, be complimented with a separate description; but in general, it will be safer for the writers to describe something which the readers, not having had an opportunity of seeing, will have no alternative but to pronounce – "very fine"'. Some kinds of implausibility do nevertheless go too far: heroes and heroines on their deathbeds 'must not compose as much poetry, and talk as much prose on the day of their death, as would serve a man or woman in full health for a month'.

For all its wit, there is a more serious aspect to Jewsbury's attack here, which results from disquiet over authors seeking money and popularity while affecting to be motivated by religious and moral fervour. The article both expresses reservations about religious fiction being written for financial gain, and identifies

---

[17]   Both the subjects mentioned, and the critical practice satirised, suggest that Robert Southey was Jewsbury's main target here.

[18]   *Phantasmagoria*, vol. 1, pp. 41–9.

a meretricious quality about these novels which is created by the authors' efforts to attract interest: thus their readers are taken 'by easy stages from the prayer-meeting to the ball-room – from the church or chapel, to the theatre – with its choice poetry, and affecting death-beds'. In fact there are so many disturbing aspects to both the fiction itself and the motivations underlying it, that the article ends by saying that the 'evil' these novels do in a religious sense 'is of too serious a nature to be treated lightly'. If writing to Jewsbury is a performance, it does nonetheless have an ethical dimension.

Early in 1826, a few months after the publication of *Phantasmagoria*, Maria Jane Jewsbury entered what was to become a protracted state of illness, exacerbated by a spiritual crisis in which she turned the questioning of authorial motive evident in the article on religious novels on herself. Norma Clarke has argued that this was largely a reaction to the transgression of the traditional female role that venturing into print in *Phantasmagoria*, and venturing so irreverently, had involved.[19] (Her identity as the author seems to have become rapidly known.) In particular, according to Clarke, she was afflicted by guilt over the ambition for fame which her literary activities expressed. Such ambition could be construed as sinful on religious grounds, in that it demonstrated a worldly concern for temporal rewards and a failure to give her eternal destiny the serious attention demanded of the devout Christian. But guilt of this kind was, for a woman of this period, aggravated by her awareness that writing for public recognition transgressed traditional notions of womanhood.

A key text here is a letter Jewsbury wrote on her birthday (24 October) to Dora Wordsworth in 1826, representing her career as that of someone who 'made herself idols after her own heart & when she had made them she worshipped them': a woman who sought and grasped 'gaiety', 'friendship', 'power' and 'ambition', but found herself 'most wretched' at the point of 'unalloy'd success'. And the reason for this? That 'this misguided being sought to satisfy the immortal spirit within her, with mortal & therefore perishing objects – she sought to fill an infinite gulf – with finite matter! – the eternal with the temporal!'.[20] Dennis Low, downplaying any psychosomatic dimension to Jewsbury's illness, argues however that she is here rejecting the literary market and the quest for celebrity, rather than writing itself.[21] This view is I believe borne out by the letter, in that its extended ruminations move towards the contention that the kind of Christian Jewsbury now aspires to be should not necessarily alter his or her activities, so much as the spirit in which they are undertaken. Such a Christian might 'follow a thousand occupations' and 'indulge a thousand tastes' which have no obvious religious dimension to them. But rather than having self at their centre, these occupations would have a 'new *motive*':

---

[19] *Ambitious Heights*, 69ff.
[20] Wordsworth Trust, Dove Cottage, Cumbria, WLMS A, Jewsbury, Maria Jane, no. 8.
[21] *The Literary Protégées of the Lake Poets*, p. 158.

> a hearty, honest, constant desire to glorify & serve *God* – & his fellow creatures
> for the sake of *God*; a constant deference to the declared will of *God* as a standard
> of duty, – & a constant eye to the approbation of *God*, in the place of his former
> seeking for the approbation of his own heart & of his fellow men. [Jewsbury's
> emphasis]

Jewsbury's struggle extended beyond the time of this letter to Dora, nonetheless. Her first book after *Phantasmagoria*, *Letters to the Young* (1828), bears witness to the continuing inner conflict which preceded her decision in 1830 to concentrate on anonymous publication. It is a collection of letters from an older to a younger woman, where the writer expatiates at length about the importance of eschewing the pursuit of public success and fame for domestic life, and where piety, self-control and meekness are enjoined on readers, stridently and repetitively. Happiness for women is to be found in 'graceful and good-humoured attention to inferior employments, homely duties and ordinary associations'.[22] The real letters on which this collection was based survive, nevertheless, and they have a more contradictory message. Written to Maria Jane's adolescent sister Geraldine at school, they are somewhat in the same vein. Yet they convey the impression too that the writer is partly playing a role – the role of moral guide, possibly as expected of Maria Jane by the sisters' father. Moreover, the injunctions to piety and humility are interspersed with news about Maria Jane's publications and the notice they have received!

Maria Jane Jewsbury evidently edited out any disjunctive elements in projecting the persona she sought in *Letters to the Young*. They re-emerge, however, in her novellas in *The Three Histories* (1830), in the arenas of both religious belief and gender roles. So 'The History of a Nonchalant' begins with a powerful evocation of the hero's arid spiritual state, as he struggles to find something worthwhile to believe in, and confesses his anguish to his best friend. But the friend soon takes on a satanic aura, and turns out simply to be striving to usurp the young man's place in his father's affections: he succeeds in having the son disinherited in his own favour, and the rest of the story evades further treatment of religious issues. In the longest story, 'The History of an Enthusiast', the writer heroine Julia Osborne achieves literary success, only to find herself feeling corrupted by her desire for constant adulation, not to mention distraught and lonely because her fame has repulsed the only man she has ever loved. Hence her success seems worthless to her, and much of the narrator's commentary endorses such a view. Yet earlier in the story, Julia's efforts to cultivate her talents in the face of opposition based on gender stereotypes are portrayed with much sympathy. In addition, the tone of the narrative towards the love-object, Cecil Percy, verges on cynicism: his rejection of Julia as a wife is said to typify the common male tendency to back off from intellectual and talented women, since dealing with them 'interferes with his

---

[22]   *Letters to the Young* (London: J. Hatchard & Son, 1828), p. 113.

implanted and imbibed ideas of domestic life and womanly duty'.[23] At the end, too, Jewsbury departs from the text which would have been recognised as her model for the story of a woman torn between creative life and love: in Madame de Staël's *Corinne* (1807), the eponymous heroine dies from being rejected in love, whereas Jewsbury's denouement is both open and potentially positive, with Julia, chastened but very much alive, resolved to travel alone to Europe.

The mixed messages emerging from 'The History of an Enthusiast' have been ably discussed by Norma Clarke and Susan J. Wolfson, who observe the disjunctions between, on the one hand, Julia's and the narrator's moralising laments over the penalties of literary ambition for women, and, on the other, the text's ambivalent treatment of Julia's immense energy, plus the open ending that challenges the *Corinne* tradition.[24] Contemporary commentary tended to read the story as a cautionary moral tale, and the response in an 1838 obituary of Jewsbury by Sarah Stickney Ellis foreshadows the attitudes expressed in the series of conservative conduct books for women that she was about to launch (her first, *The Women of England*, appeared in 1839). For Ellis, the story shows 'the final wretchedness necessarily attendant upon the ungoverned ambition of superior intellect, when associated with the weakness, natural dependence, and susceptibility of woman'.[25] On the other hand, as Wolfson has noted, some reviewers refused to endorse the text's ostensible message: the *Edinburgh Journal* remonstrated at the story's apparent moral, 'that the higher the genius, the less likely it is that happiness will be within the reach of the possessor', while the *Literary Gazette* asserted that '[w]e neither can nor do believe that the possession of one of Heaven's noblest gifts is like that of the false fair – to be fatal'.[26]

When Jane Williams came to write on Maria Jane Jewsbury in her *Literary Women of England* in 1861, she seemed to endorse the moralistic interpretation of 'The History of an Enthusiast', declaring that Julia is 'a selfish woman of genius, full of worldly ambition, which predominates over her few and weak social affections', one who values her talents only as routes to 'fashionable distinction', and makes of her genius a mere 'ministering drudge to vanity and worldliness'.[27] But Williams had also been given access, by Maria Jane's siblings Geraldine and Frank, to some of Maria Jane's correspondence, including letters to Geraldine.[28] Of Maria Jane's writing in general, she says, I think tellingly, that 'her advice on theological and religious subjects tended rather towards dogmatism' – yet this

---

[23]   *The Three Histories*, p. 150.

[24]   Norma Clarke, *Ambitious Heights*, pp. 83–6, Susan J. Wolfson, *Borderlines*, 105ff.

[25]   'Mrs Fletcher, Late Miss Jewsbury', *Christian Keepsake, and Missionary Annual*, ed. William Ellis (London, Paris and New York: Fisher, 1838), pp. 30–42, at pp. 31–2, quoted in Monica Correa Fryckstedt, 'The Hidden Rill', Pt 2, p. 459 n.79.

[26]   *Edinburgh Journal*, 8 May 1830: 270, and *Literary Gazette*, 24 April 1830: 271, quoted in Susan J. Wolfson, *Borderlines*, pp. 126–7.

[27]   *The Literary Women of England*, p. 385.

[28]   Ibid., p. 372.

was because 'scepticism ... seems to have been through her life her besetting temptation', and she hence dreaded to communicate doubt.[29] What Maria Jane Jewsbury asserted in writing was not necessarily what she easily or consistently believed. As we shall see, Jane Williams was aware of nineteenth-century women writers' sometime tendency to project particular images of themselves to accommodate prevailing ideas about their sex.

Jewsbury was thus highly conscious of the potential constructedness of an authorial persona, and duly performed various personae in her writings; this fact is especially relevant to her two major articles on women writers in the *Athenaeum*, on Felicia Hemans and Jane Austen. She firstly colluded with Hemans's own self-presentation as the feminine 'poetess', while exploring the similarities and differences between men's and women's writing, and then in the Austen piece considered the different kinds of self-presentation that might be adopted by a woman writer in her daily life as compared with in her literary works.

Jewsbury's article on Hemans, published as 'Literary Sketches – No. 1', appeared in the *Athenaeum* on 12 February 1831.[30] She begins by drawing on the distinction between 'classical' and 'romantic' poetry promulgated by the Schlegel brothers and Madame de Staël, in order to characterise the development of Hemans's poetic career: her early poetry was 'correct, classical, and highly polished', but her later work possessed more 'warmth' and 'imagination', was more Romantic. Yet if Hemans now 'writes from and to the heart' (as a woman should), this is a sign that she has found her own voice. Further on, Jewsbury highlights the specifically feminine traits of this later poetry: Hemans's 'matronly delicacy of thought, her chastened style of expression, her hallowed ideas of happiness as connected with home, and home-enjoyments; – to condense all in one emphatic word, her *womanliness*'. She declares too that 'Mrs. Hemans throws herself into her poetry, and the said self is an English gentlewoman'. Like Landon, Hemans projected in her poetry a persona governed by the heart rather than the head, but, as befitted a mother rather than a single woman, with more emphasis on domestic life and family affections. As Jewsbury – but not the general public – knew, this image was particularly important to Hemans because she needed to conceal the fact that she was actually a deserted wife. (One opportunity afforded Jewsbury by anonymity in this case, was cloaking her close friendship with Hemans.)

To a modern reader, Jewsbury's characterisation of Hemans's poetry might seem sentimental and reductive, but Jewsbury by no means wishes to diminish the work of the 'poetess' vis-à-vis the efforts of male writers – rather the opposite, in fact. She argues that '[t]here will always be a difference between the poetry of men and women', but the upshot is that 'we have two kinds of excellence instead of one'. She goes on to identify the distinguishing characteristic of men's poetry as 'power', and that of women's as 'beauty'; she also associates 'power' with 'passion'. She is of course drawing on the famous discussion by Edmund Burke

---

[29] Ibid., pp. 373, 384.
[30] 104–5.

of the features of the 'sublime' and the 'beautiful', in which he had linked the former with the masculine and the latter with the feminine. But Jewsbury does not want to imply that the 'two kinds of excellence' in men's and women's poetry are mutually exclusive: 'occasionally', she explains, 'we reciprocate their respective influence, by discerning the beauty of power, and feeling the power of beauty', and she goes on to cite instances of 'the power of beauty' from Hemans herself. Hemans's 'womanliness', too, coexists with her intellectual capacity, acting as 'the morning mist to the landscape, or the evening dew to the flower – that which enhances loveliness without diminishing lustre'. Whereas Hemans's poetry was habitually seen as the quintessence of femininity – as it was in the review by Francis Jeffrey mentioned in the Introduction – Jewsbury wishes to valorise its 'feminine' elements while averting the patronising approach that writing coded 'feminine' tended to attract.

Moreover, the article further validates Hemans's poetry by arguing that the current popularity of the poetry of 'power' and 'passion' has gone too far, leading to outbreaks of overblown bad writing. 'PASSION', Jewsbury asserts, 'has become 'a species of literary Goule that preys upon good sense, good feeling, and good taste', such that '[n]othing now is considered to be said strongly that is said simply – every line must produce "effect" – every word must "tell"'. Similarly, 'POWERFUL' is used as an excuse for the 'monstrous and absurd'. Presumably she is thinking of writers in the Gothic mode, imitators of Byron, and figures like the pretentious Robert Montgomery, whose lurid and portentous verse on religious subjects was often ridiculed in the *Athenaeum* – including by Jewsbury herself.[31] In this context, the poetry of Felicia Hemans, graceful, tasteful, delicate and subdued, as Jewsbury presents it, could be advocated as a welcome antidote. 'Masculine' qualities in writing are not self-evidently desirable.

If Jewsbury is willing here to use her friend's preferred mode of self-representation to highlight the virtues of 'feminine' writing, the article itself, as Marlon B. Ross points out, exemplifies the kinds of qualities contemporary critics considered masculine, such as intricacy and analytical rigour.[32] The same might be said of the article on Jane Austen.

The Austen piece is 'No. 2' in a series now entitled 'Literary Women'.[33] Jane Austen, as Jewsbury presents her here, is a model for a woman writer, in that she achieved literary distinction without fame, and hence remained in the feminine private sphere:

> For those who may doubt the possibility of engrafting literary habits on those peculiarly set apart for the female sex, and may doubt how far literary

---

[31]   Marchand, *The Athenaeum*, pp. 139–45; Jewsbury ridiculed his poetry in the issue of 30 April 1831.

[32]   Marlon B. Ross, *The Contours of Masculine Desire*: *Romanticism and the Rise of Women's Poetry* (New York and Oxford: Oxford University Press, 1989), p. 249.

[33]   27 August 1831: 553–4.

reputation is attainable, without a greater sacrifice to notoriety than they may deem compatible with female happiness and delicacy, it is pleasant to have so triumphant a reference as Miss Austen.

Since she was 'endowed pre-eminently with good sense, and a placid, unobtrusive temperament', Austen was able to pass 'unscathed through the ordeal of authorship', while 'exciting enthusiastic affection in immediate friends' and never losing 'the general good-will of all who knew her'. It is notable here that Jewsbury does acknowledge doubts about women writers' capacity to reconcile a literary career with private life, but evades the question of whether or not she shares them: if writing overtly as a woman, as in 'The History of an Enthusiast', she might have found it difficult to avoid endorsing such provisos. She also defers to the assumption that it may not be decorous to bring women writers so much into the public gaze as to write about them in their lifetimes, assuring her readers of Austen that, '[b]eing dead, she may be quoted without impropriety' – albeit the starkly aphoristic quality of such a statement highlights the overstrained nature of the kind of 'delicacy' it seemingly approves. ('Delicacy' here seems to mean modesty or sensitivity.) It is also a statement of possibly Austen-like irony. Was Jewsbury perhaps recalling the narrator's comment in *Emma*, on Mrs Churchill's demise, that death is 'to be recommended as a clearer of ill-fame'?[34]

On the other hand, Jewsbury does emphasise that Austen did not actively seek literary fame:

> whilst literature was a delightful occupation, it was not a profession to Miss Austen; she was not irrational enough to despise reputation and profit when they sought her, but she became an authoress entirely from taste and inclination ... her unambitious temper was amply satisfied with the attention bestowed on [her works] by the public.

As far as Jewsbury's readers are concerned, she is reassuring them that Austen did not exemplify any unfeminine ambition; for herself, she is possibly registering a kind of satisfaction achievable via anonymous reviewing. Like Austen, who collected readers' comments on her novels, Jewsbury conceivably garnered praise for her reviews, even if readers were not aware of her authorship of them.

Jewsbury is reliant for her version of Austen's personality on the only published account then available, the 1817 'Biographical Notice of the Author' by Austen's brother Henry. This account highlights her lack of any desire for public recognition, claiming that '[n]either the hope of fame nor profit mixed with her early motives', and that although she was gratified by her novels' reception, 'no accumulation of fame would have induced her, had she lived, to affix her name to any productions of her pen'. It is also obviously the source of Jewsbury's comments about Jane

---

[34]   Jane Austen, *Emma* [1815], ed. James Kinsley (London and Oxford: World's Classics, 1990), p. 351.

Austen's attracting 'enthusiastic affection' from her intimates and 'general good-will' from others, since Henry says that no one could get to know his sister 'without feeling a strong desire of obtaining her friendship', and that she never suffered 'an abatement of goodwill from any who knew her'.[35] Henry's account makes clear too the reasons to which he wishes to attribute this 'goodwill':

> Though the frailties, foibles, and follies of others could not escape her immediate detection, yet even on their vices did she never trust herself to comment with unkindness … Faultless herself, as nearly as human nature can be, she always sought, in the faults of others, something to excuse, to forgive or forget. Where extenuation was impossible, she had a sure refuge in silence. She never uttered either a hasty, a silly, or a severe expression.

Jewsbury, however, while not directly challenging this account, does not accept it at face value, and her version of Jane Austen shows her awareness of one way a woman writer might choose to deal with the constraints on female self-expression. Austen, in Jewsbury's representation, chose to disclose more of her real personality in her novels than in her daily life. After commenting on the personal warmth and goodwill Austen the woman attracted, Jewsbury continues:

> This alone is a high tribute to the benevolence of her temper, and the polish of her manners in daily life; for in print, her peculiar forte is delineating folly, selfishness, and absurdity – especially in her own sex. In society, she had too much wit to lay herself open to the charge of being too witty; and discriminated too well to attract notice to her discrimination.

It is as if Austen, aware that people in her social circle might be repulsed by her if they thought her to resemble the delineator of 'folly, selfishness, and absurdity' in her novels, restrained her wit and her caustic judgments in social gatherings, and thereby conveyed a conventionally feminine demeanour. Jewsbury goes on to say that Austen in real life followed the advice that she had expressed through the narrator of *Northanger Abbey*, that 'if a woman have the misfortune of knowing anything, she should conceal it as well as she can'.[36] That is, Jane Austen might well have behaved the way her brother says she did, but this was partly so as to conceal aspects of herself which she was able to express more openly in her fiction. In her review of Elizabeth Sandford's conduct book in 1832, Jewsbury would point out that, whereas a woman's writing in her own voice was usually constrained by fear of male response, when writing fiction 'she then fancies herself veiled, and often

---

[35]   Repr. in B.C. Southam (ed.), *Jane Austen: The Critical Heritage* (London: Routledge & Kegan Paul; New York: Barnes & Noble, 1968), pp. 73–8.

[36]   'A woman especially, if she have the misfortune of knowing any thing, should conceal it as well as she can.' *Northanger Abbey* [1817], ed. Claire Grogan (Peterborough, Ontario and Orchard Park, NY: Broadview, 1996), p. 124 (Chapter 14).

enunciates important truths; the fear of man somewhat departs from her mind, and she becomes (by comparison), free, natural, and unconventional'.[37]

The latter part of Jewsbury's Austen article turns to the work itself, and, as we might expect from her article on 'Religious Novels', she praises the verisimilitude, or what might later be called the realism, of Austen's fiction. She draws attention to the lack of 'catastrophes, or discoveries, or surprises of a grand nature' in the plots, and the way 'the reader breakfasts, dines, walks, and gossips with the various worthies, till a process of transmutation takes place in him, and he absolutely fancies himself one of the company'. The reason for this effect, she goes on, is that 'Miss Austen was a thorough mistress in the knowledge of human character; how it is acted upon by education and circumstance, and how, when once formed, it shows itself through every hour of every day, and in every speech of every person'. In her view, too, Austen's capacity to draw readers into close relationship with the lives and personalities of her characters has a moral effect, and one which is more genuinely beneficial than that ostensibly aspired to by the authors she had castigated in 'Religious Novels':

> in Miss Austen's hands we see into [her characters'] hearts and hopes, their
> motives, their struggles within themselves, and a sympathy is induced which,
> if extended to daily life and the world at large, would make the reader a more
> amiable person.

Austen is therefore more than simply a delineator of 'folly, selfishness, and absurdity'.

Jewsbury's religious faith may be to the fore here, inducing her to point out how fiction may have a salutary moral influence via its verisimilitude, rather than through direct exhortation or through creating implausibly virtuous and high-minded characters. But she does express a proviso in this regard: Austen's novels, she claims, 'deal rather too largely with the commonplace, petty, and disagreeable side of human nature', giving insufficient attention to the 'wise and high-hearted'.

Jewsbury's article on Jane Austen was inscribed into the history of nineteenth-century Austen criticism, but without being attributed to her, and in a way which failed to represent all her perceptions. This was because of Henry Austen's continuing wish to offer the public a particular view of his sister. For when the publisher Richard Bentley began his new editions of Austen's novels with the republication of *Sense and Sensibility* in 1833, Henry Austen not only appended a slightly altered version of his 1817 'Biographical Notice', he added to it what he termed 'extracts from a critical journal of the highest reputation'.[38]

---

[37]   '*Woman, in her Social and Domestic Character*', *Athenaeum*, 5 May 1832: 282–3, at 282.

[38]   Quoted in David Gilson, 'Henry Austen's "Memoir of Jane Austen"', *Persuasions*, 19 (16 December 1997), 12–19, at 16.

The 'Biographical Notice', plus the 'extracts', were then reprinted in reissues of this volume in Bentley's Standard Novels until 1854, and in his collected editions of Austen until 1869; they gained further currency in editions brought out by the publishers to whom Bentley sold the plates, up till the 1880s.[39] Yet what Henry Austen presented as extracts from one critical journal were actually extracts from two. Most of what he quotes is from Jewsbury, but the last paragraph is from an earlier article, written by Richard Whately for the *Quarterly Review* in 1821 – one of the only two published commentaries of critical value on Austen which predate hers. (The other is Walter Scott's review of *Emma* in 1816, also in the *Quarterly*.) But Henry Austen's selection from critical commentaries is geared to amplify the impression of Jane Austen conveyed by the rest of his notice.

From Jewsbury's article, Henry Austen extracts the long passage from which I have quoted above, dealing with the realism of the novels' plots and characters and the moral value of this realism. He also quotes some of her comments which contrast the distinction of Austen's novels with the obscurity of her life – but he omits Jewsbury's notable perception that the personality which emerges from the fiction may be closer to the 'real' Jane Austen than the one which his 'Biographical Notice' offers as evident in her social dealings. The addition of the paragraph from Whately also serves to emphasise the piety which Henry had attributed to Jane in the 'Biographical Notice'. Henry Austen omits Jewsbury's stricture on the novelist for neglecting the 'wise and high-hearted'; he then adds a paragraph from Whately which begins, 'Miss Austen has the merit (in our judgment most essential) of being evidently a Christian writer', and which goes on to argue that her Christian convictions strongly underpin her novels.[40]

Henry Austen's doctoring of Maria Jane Jewsbury's article, plus the wide circulation of his extracts in over 50 years of editions of *Sense and Sensibility*, meant that her comments on the novels' realism and the moral dimension thereof were much read and were echoed in later critical commentaries with what became monotonous regularity. Together with the image conveyed by Henry Austen's own words, they contributed to the longstanding view of Austen as 'gentle aunt Jane', purveyor of amusing but morally sound stories of daily life, written with unrivalled verisimilitude. But in the only instance I know of where Jewsbury's words were both directly quoted and attributed, the attribution was not to her, but to Whately. This occurs in George Henry Lewes's article, 'The Novels of Jane Austen', which appeared in *Blackwood's Edinburgh Magazine* in July 1859. His misattribution, ironically, invests Jewsbury's words with an authority they could never have conveyed if known to have come from a woman. For after a quotation from Jewsbury on Austen's realism, Lewes declares: 'It is worth remembering that this is the deliberate judgment of the present Archbishop of Dublin, and not a careless

---

[39]   Ibid., p. 12.

[40]   Ibid., p. 18; Whately's article appeared in the *Quarterly Review*, 24 (January 1821): 352–76, and is reprinted in full in B.C. Southam, *Jane Austen*, pp. 87–105.

verdict dropping from the pen of a facile reviewer'.[41] Meanwhile Jewsbury's more original insight as a woman writer into the outlook, and possible literary strategies, adopted by another woman writer, had been edited out of critical history.

There was to be no 'No. 3' in Jewsbury's series on women writers called, firstly, 'Literary Sketches', and then, 'Literary Women'. But the shift in nomenclature may be significant, as is suggested by one of Jewsbury's reviews that was published between the articles on Hemans and Austen. This review of 28 May 1831 concerned a work by the veteran playwright and poet, Joanna Baillie. Baillie's *The Nature and Dignity of Christ*, by virtue of being theological, does challenge the boundaries of acceptable writing for women, despite her reputation as a playwright focusing on the powerful and the passionate. So, in deference to the likely assumptions of her readers, Jewsbury says nothing about the actual book except: 'It is controversial, and controversy is best left to learned divines – certainly better left alone by ladies.'[42]

But this tactic also enables Jewsbury to devote most of her space to praise for Baillie herself, and for other women writers of her period: like Jane Austen, Baillie was of a generation before Jewsbury's own (she was born in 1762, Austen in 1775), and Jewsbury also commends here Elizabeth Inchbald (1753–1821), Anne Radcliffe (1764–1823) and Mary Wollstonecraft (1759–97). She compares these writers with the women writers of her own generation, and seeks to foreground the strengths evident in the work of the earlier women – strengths which readers of her time would have construed as masculine. Being notable for 'power of mind', these earlier writers, she says, 'were, in the spirit of their intellect, more essentially masculine', while the younger, who 'abound in elegant accomplishments' are thereby 'integrally feminine'. Thus the work of the older generation is characterised by traits such as 'nerve, simplicity, vigour, continuity … and good English', while that of the current generation is more notable for 'grace', plus 'fascinating tenderness, brilliancy of fancy, and beauty of feeling'. Moreover, like Landon in her 'L.E.L.' mode, Jewsbury's contemporaries do not write with 'compact, artist-like diction'; while they possess 'fancy', they do not rise to 'sustained loftiness of imagination'. Most significantly, these younger women lack the intellectual rigour to sustain coherent works of fiction (like Austen's) – they are, rather, only 'sketchers'.[43] So perhaps in titling her article on Austen, 'Literary Women – No. 2', after giving the name 'Literary Sketches – No. 1' to that on Hemans, Jewsbury was implicitly identifying with the more 'masculine' women of Austen's generation, rather than with their 'feminine' successors of her own time, who demonstrated facility only as 'sketchers'?

Though she does not discuss Wollstonecraft in any detail here, Jewsbury brackets her with the other, more respectable, women writers of her generation, so

---

41   [G.H. Lewes], 'The Novels of Jane Austen', *Blackwood's Edinburgh Magazine*, 86 (July 1859): 99– 113, repr. in B.C. Southam, *Jane Austen*, pp. 148–66, at p. 155.

42   *Athenaeum*, 28 May 1831: 337.

43   The generational distinction Jewsbury is making is noted by Dennis Low, *The Literary Protégées of the Lake Poets*, pp. 29–30 and Susan J. Wolfson, *Borderlines*, pp. 96–7.

as to focus attention on her intellectual calibre rather than on her private life. Writing in 1843 in her *Memoirs of the Literary Ladies of England from the Commencement of the Last Century*, Anne Katharine Elwood cites an intriguing comment from an unnamed woman writer, that she had heard Maria Jane Jewsbury 'express an intention of remodelling [Wollstonecraft's] "Rights of Women" [*sic*], that it would not fail to become again attractive, and she thought useful'.[44] This intention was, unfortunately, never carried out, but it does suggest an awareness on Jewsbury's part that such a text, from what she evidently saw as a period less constraining for women writers, might need reshaping to suit contemporary expectations.

Finally Jewsbury, for all her ambivalence about women's writing and women's literary careers, remained highly conscious of the potentially damaging effects of assuming strong demarcations between the capacities of the sexes. In her 1832 review of Jameson's *Memoirs of Celebrated Female Sovereigns*, she not only pointed to the distortions to historical veracity resulting from Jameson's accommodating a belief that women readers should be spared certain kinds of information; she also denied Jameson's claim that her survey of women rulers demonstrated that 'the power which belongs to [women] as a sex, is not properly, or naturally, that of the sceptre or the sword'. According to Jewsbury, the historical evidence does not bear this out, and this is largely because men and women brought up with the expectation of exercising 'extreme power' are educated in similar ways and hence end up behaving similarly: 'sex is lost in circumstances: a female heir apparent is by recognition, duty, education, and temptation, a prince'.[45] But just as significantly, in contending that power is inappropriate for women, says Jewsbury, Jameson unwittingly argues also for their exclusion from a realm potentially much more open to women than royal power: the very realm in which Jameson – and her reviewer – are operating:

> Besides, if Mrs. Jameson proves that women have no business to succeed to the sceptre, how will she prove that they have any right to wield the pen? Power is power; and the power of disseminating opinions is not much less valuable than that of holding a levee or opening parliament.[46]

Nonetheless this 'power of disseminating opinions' was not easy to exercise overtly. As noted earlier, Norma Clarke and Margaret J.M. Ezell identify the pressure on women writers to be 'feminine', and especially self-effacing, as escalating over the eighteenth century. The early nineteenth-century reception of Landon and Hemans, including Jewsbury's writing on the latter, bears out this conclusion. Jewsbury's own career, moreover, suggests that it was the power behind the throne, as it were, that she eventually sought in her literary criticism.

---

[44]   (2 vols, London: Henry Colburn, 1843), vol. 2, p. 153.

[45]   '*Memoirs of Celebrated Female Sovereigns*', *Athenaeum*, 12 November 1831: 730–31, at 730.

[46]   Ibid., 731.

Sara Coleridge

Maria Jane Jewsbury, with her family background in business, had from her own account a scanty literary education: she recalled to Felicia Hemans that when she took over running the household in 1819, she knew not 'a single person of superior mind', let alone any authors. Unaware of 'how wretchedly deficient' her education was, she wrote and wrote, only recognising her need for knowledge when she was 21.[47] Sara Coleridge, on the other hand, grew up in a very literary ambience: she lived mostly with her uncle Robert Southey, had the run of his extensive library, knew the Wordsworth family well, and, from her early years, encountered many people with literary interests. She had the opportunity to learn several languages, including the classical Greek and Latin not usually taught to girls, and was doing translation work by her early twenties. But this upbringing, and particularly the ambivalent influence of her father, Samuel Taylor Coleridge, did impose constraints on her literary endeavours of a kind rather different from those affecting Maria Jane Jewsbury.

Sara Coleridge was a very learned woman, especially in disciplines where women of her period seldom had the chance to become erudite: as well as being very familiar with Greek and Latin texts in the original, she was extremely well-read in theology, which was one of her major intellectual interests. In 1844, Elizabeth Barrett – very learned herself, needless to say – observed that Sara Coleridge 'possesses perhaps more learning, in the strict sense, than any female writer of the day'.[48] The youngest of the three surviving children from the ill-starred union of Sarah Fricker and S.T. Coleridge, and the only female, she was clearly more intellectually gifted than her next brother Derwent, and more self-disciplined than her talented but wayward eldest brother Hartley. Hartley indeed acknowledged her, rather than either himself or Derwent, as the one who had inherited their father's 'mind' and 'genius', and said of her 1843 'Essay on Rationalism', that no one in the country other than she could have written it, since their father died.[49]

But as her biographer Bradford Keyes Mudge has emphasised, Sara Coleridge devoted most of her literary/scholarly endeavours to editing her father's works,

---

[47]   Henry Fothergill Chorley, *Memorials of Mrs. Hemans* (2 vols, London: Saunders & Otley, 1836), vol. 1, pp. 165–6, quoted in Maria Jane Jewsbury, *Occasional Papers*, p. xviii.

[48]   Letter to R.H. Horne, 6 March 1844, in *The Brownings' Correspondence*, vol. 8, ed. Philip Kelley and Ronald Hudson (Winfield, KS: Wedgestone Press, 1990), p. 247.

[49]   Letters of 1844 and 1845, in *The Letters of Hartley Coleridge*, ed. Grace Evelyn Griggs and Earl Leslie Griggs (London: Oxford University Press, 1936), p. 275, and in Earl Leslie Griggs, *Coleridge Fille* (London, New York, Toronto: Oxford University Press, 1940), p. 131, quoted in Alison Hickey, '"The Body of My Father's Writings": Sara Coleridge's Genial Labor', in Marjorie Stone and Judith Thompson (eds), *Literary Couplings: Writing Couples, Collaborators, and the Construction of Authorship* (Madison, WI: University of Wisconsin Press, 2006), pp. 124–47, at pp. 139, 147.

in tandem with her husband, Henry Nelson Coleridge, and then independently following his death in 1843. She had published in her twenties two translations requiring considerable erudition: one from the Latin of Martin Dobrizhoffer's work of 1784, published in 1822 as *An Account of the Abipones, an Equestrian People of Paraguay*, and, in 1825, *The Right Joyous and Pleasant History of the Feats, Gests, and Prowesses of the Chevalier Bayard*, translated from fifteenth-century French. But, following S.T. Coleridge's death in 1834, she concentrated on her father's oeuvre. Her work here was extensive, with long introductions and appendices – an introduction of 180 pages to *Biographia Literaria*, for example, and the essay on rationalism praised by Hartley which accompanied *Aids to Reflection* and was almost as long as the text itself. Her efforts were nonetheless subordinate to and in the service of her father's output, and thus comprised an enterprise of proper female selflessness.

Sara Coleridge's quest to promote her father's genius and recuperate his personal and intellectual reputation gave her an outlet for her learning and her aspirations to write, without obliging her to put herself forward publicly in her own right. Like her father, she seems to have believed that women should be 'feminine': in an autobiography that she abandoned for the sake of yet more editing of her father's work, she recalled his preference for 'everything feminine and domestic, pretty and becoming'.[50] S.T. Coleridge's wedding present to his daughter in 1829 was thus characteristic. A copy of William Sotheby's 1827 edition of Virgil's *Georgics*, he said it was intended to show his 'sense of the talent and industry, that have made her the Mistress of the Six Languages comprized in the volume'. But Sara's 'unusual attainments in ancient and modern languages' are not as admirable for her father as 'their co-existence with piety, simplicity, and characteristic meekness – in short, with mind, manners and character so perfectly feminine'.[51]

Nevertheless, Sara Coleridge had written to her brother Derwent in early womanhood (the letter dates from 1825 or 1826):

> I should have been happier, with my taste, temper, and habits, had I been of your sex instead of the helpless, dependent being I am. The thing that would suit me the best of anything in the world would be the life of a country clergyman. I should delight in the studies necessary to the profession.[52]

After her marriage in 1829, the duties of family life, including bringing up her two children Herbert and Edith, loomed large in Sara Coleridge's existence; as for Jewsbury, the demands of domestic life caused inner conflict, because of her wish to devote time to reading and writing. Sara Coleridge had protracted bouts of illness, which Mudge has interpreted as 'in part a violent protest against the selfless

---

[50]   Repr. in Bradford Keyes Mudge, *Sara Coleridge, A Victorian Daughter: Her Life and Essays* (New Haven: Yale University Press, 1989), p. 263.
[51]   Quoted in Earl Leslie Griggs, *Coleridge Fille*, pp. 66–7.
[52]   Ibid., p. 57.

matriarch who was expected to live in and through her husband and progeny'.[53] But illness also, by sometimes relieving Sara Coleridge from the care of her children and from other domestic duties, did clear time for her reading and writing. This was particularly the case in 1836, when she ensconced herself in an inn for several months, away from her husband and two young children, pleading illness, but also composing her long prose-poem for children, *Phantasmion*.[54] Later, she would articulate some of the frustration she felt at the competing demands on her time. When her widowhood made her solely responsible for her children, she lamented to her friend Edward Quillinan (Dora Wordsworth's widower) the hours she had to spend chaperoning them to balls and evening parties, and expressed relief that at one such event, she had encountered Barry Cornwall (the poet Bryan Waller Procter), since she thus managed 'a bit of poetical and literary talk'.[55]

When Sara Coleridge did engage in writing for publication, it was, as I have noted, usually in the service of promulgating her father's works. That she sometimes found this editorial endeavour unrewarding, and wondered about alternatives, surfaces occasionally. So after completing her edition of *Biographia Literaria*, she regrets the invisibility of much of the effort editing entailed, plus the sometime coldness of her work's reception, and asks, 'What *might* I have been?'.[56] And in the letter to Quillinan just quoted she says that, of her work on editions of her father's texts, 'the unseen part, which does not appear, is more than that which does appear', such that she 'might have written many volumes in the time – & of a serious sort, with far less trouble'.[57]

Sara Coleridge was also a very physically attractive woman – she was painted at the age of 15 by William Collins (father of Wilkie), as Wordsworth's 'Highland Girl', and when the painting was exhibited in 1819 at the Royal Academy, she became known as the 'Flower of the Lakes' and the 'Sylph of Ullswater'.[58] Having a reputation mainly for beauty is something she seems to have found troubling, however, to judge from her unpublished essay of 1826, 'On the Disadvantages Resulting from the Possession of Beauty'. Being remarkably beautiful, she argues, encourages a woman to value herself primarily for this, and therefore to agonise over the potential loss of any charm – whereas a woman not accustomed to being noted for beauty will be pleased at any compliment on her physical appearance. To illustrate this last point, Sara Coleridge quotes the narrator's comment near the beginning of Jane Austen's *Northanger Abbey*, on the heroine Catherine Morland's

[53]   *Sara Coleridge*, p. 88.
[54]   See Kathleen Jones, *Passionate Sisterhood: The Sisters, Wives and Daughters of the Lake Poets* (London: Constable, 1997), pp. 215–17.
[55]   Letter of 9 February 1850, in Edith Coleridge (ed.), *Memoir and Letters of Sara Coleridge* (2 vols, London: Henry S. King, 1873), vol. 2, pp. 291–2.
[56]   Diary entries of 28 October and 28 September 1848, quoted in Mudge, *Sara Coleridge*, p. 44.
[57]   Wordsworth Trust, WLMS A, Coleridge, Sara, no. 49.
[58]   Low, *The Literary Protégées of the Lake Poets*, p. 105.

improved looks: 'To look almost pretty, is an acquisition of higher delight to a girl who has been looking plain for the first fifteen years of her life than a beauty from her cradle can ever receive'.[59]

It is apposite to recall at this point Maria Jane Jewsbury's citation from the same novel: the narrator's ironic comment that, 'If a woman have the misfortune of knowing anything, she should conceal it as well as she can'. Jewsbury had been suggesting that in her daily life, Jane Austen may have behaved this way tactically, but disclosed more of her real self in her fiction. Jewsbury's point is relevant to her own choice of anonymous reviewing as a way of being more outspoken than she could be in texts published under her own name. Sara Coleridge's choices of means for self-expression, outside what was enabled by editions of her father's works, were different from Maria Jane Jewsbury's, but were equally calculated to avoid public notoriety.

Sara Coleridge did actually write a great deal of literary criticism not directly connected with memorialising S.T. Coleridge. It encompassed a wide variety of texts from various periods, covered poetry, fiction and drama, and included classical and European as well as British literature – but most of it was not published by her. Some was in the form of essays, now held in the Harry Ransom Center at the University of Texas at Austin, and a selection of these was usefully included in Mudge's book on her. Much of Sara Coleridge's criticism was included in letters written to various relatives and friends: her husband and his brothers, her own brothers Hartley and Derwent, Derwent's wife Mary, cousin John Taylor Coleridge, Dora Wordsworth, Edward Quillinan, the poet Aubrey de Vere, American academic contacts Henry Reed and Ellis Yarnall, friends Elizabeth Crump (later Wardell), Emily Trevenen, Mary Stanger, Mrs Henry Jones, Mrs Plummer, Mrs Richard E. Townsend, John Kenyon and Isabella Fenwick. The originals of these are in the Harry Ransom Center and in the Jerwood Centre at Dove Cottage, but many were published posthumously in 1873, in a two-volume collection edited by Sara Coleridge's daughter Edith.

For Sara Coleridge, letter-writing was a stimulus to organising one's thoughts: it was a way of 'visiting our friends in their absence', and one in which 'persons who have any seriousness of character at all' would take the opportunity to 'put the better part of their mind upon paper'.[60] This was far preferable to what she implied was the more usual style of letter-writing, consisting of 'a long history of comings and goings, visitings and being visited, allusions to Mrs A.B. and Lady C.B., and other folks whom I never saw, and do not care tuppence about'.[61] Letter-writing is ideally a means of exchanging ideas, rather than of showing off one's social activities and social connections – entering into a world where contact is personal, but where intellectual discussion is largely gender-neutral.

[59] Repr. in Mudge, *Sara Coleridge*, pp. 187–200, at p. 190. The sentence occurs in the first chapter of *Northanger Abbey*.

[60] Letter to Mrs Plummer, 30 August 1838, in *Memoir and Letters*, vol. 1, p. 211.

[61] Letter to Mrs Plummer, 21 October 1837, in *Memoir and Letters*, vol. 1, p. 193.

One of Sara Coleridge's correspondents was Maria Jane Jewsbury, whom she no doubt met after the latter became friendly with the Wordsworth family in the mid 1820s. The two women were near-contemporaries, with Jewsbury born in 1800 and Sara Coleridge in 1802. That they corresponded is clear from Jewsbury's letters to their mutual friend Dora Wordsworth, but the letters themselves have not survived. When Sara settled in London after her marriage, Jewsbury visited her.[62] In April 1832, Jewsbury mentions to Dora Wordsworth a long letter she has received from Sara Coleridge: 'She tells of her domestic state, & writes in a very happy strain'. On 17 September, in her last letter to Dora before her own departure for India, Jewsbury recalls with pleasure dining with Sara and Henry Coleridge, saying that 'they are quietly happy'.[63]

What can be construed of the two women's views of each other is interesting. As the letters just cited suggest, Jewsbury saw Sara's marriage as successful, which perhaps to her augured well for her own. Back when Sara had married in September 1829, Jewsbury had sent her via Dora a poem, 'The Bridal Band', which hints at how far Jewsbury registered the strong literary heritage that Sara possessed and she herself lacked. The poem is built on the conceit that although a floral 'band' may not be available for an early-autumn wedding, the presence of Sara's family and friends is the true 'bridal band'. It is a literary 'band' as well – Sara is 'A child of classic bowers' (l. 24). Jewsbury presumably did not know that Sara's father would be too ill to attend the wedding; in any case she does not evoke him directly, but rather, his most famous poem. Yet dragging in 'The Rime of the Ancient Mariner' is a rather awkward move, given that the poem's protagonist is notable for having delayed a guest on the way to a wedding! So the speaker of Jewsbury's poem has to hope for a rather different outcome for Sara's marriage:

> But no old man 'with skinny hand'
> Will mar I trow *thy* wedding band,
> Will utter words of moan, –
> And if perchance a 'glittering eye'
> Hold with its gaze the passer by,
> That eye will be thine own![64]

It is tempting to read the Ancient Mariner figure as S.T. Coleridge, who has to be sidelined as his daughter moves to centre-stage: Sara and Henry's marriage had after all been delayed partly by financial problems that might have been alleviated had her father been less feckless – the edition of Virgil was all she

---

[62]   Sara Coleridge mentions these visits in letters to her husband, 15 July 1830, and to Emily Trevenen, 9 September 1830, Harry Ransom Center, University of Texas at Austin.

[63]   Letter of 24 April 1832, Wordsworth Trust, WLMS A, Jewsbury, Maria Jane, no. 36; letter of 17 September 1832, Wordsworth Trust, WLMS A, Jewsbury, Maria Jane, no. 39.

[64]   Letter of 3 September 1829, Wordsworth Trust, WLMS A, Jewsbury, Maria Jane, no. 26.

received from him on the occasion. But in the absence of direct evidence about Maria Jane Jewsbury's views on the man, the poem at least highlights, if clumsily, Sara Coleridge's literary connections.

After Maria Jane Jewsbury's death, Sara Coleridge regretted her loss, and recalled her as apparently happy at the prospect of marriage in 1832. She also told Dora: 'there are few persons whom I have not seen more of that I remember so vividly … I fancy I see her walking on your terrace'.[65] But some of that vividness may have resulted from Jewsbury's inner conflicts: judging from what she had heard from Jewsbury in life, Sara told Emily Trevenen, she imagined her saying on her deathbed, 'few have my days been & evil I fear'. Jewsbury gave Sara Coleridge the impression of being 'like the nightingale "a creature with a fiery heart"', and she recalled Wordsworth's saying that she had been '*burning the taper at both ends*'.[66] In the years following these letters, Sara Coleridge herself would be 'burning the taper at both ends', as she tried to follow her intellectual interests, while also fulfilling domestic responsibilities, plus what she saw as duties to her father's memory.

One notable difference between the two women was their experience of periodical publication. I have argued that anonymous reviewing provided Maria Jane Jewsbury with the opportunity to reconcile her desire to publish with her reservations about seeking fame. Such experience as Sara Coleridge acquired of periodical publication, however, was quite discouraging. Anxious to increase her income following her husband's early death, she wrote two articles for the *Quarterly Review* in 1848, the periodical being edited at this time by John Gibson Lockhart, who had been a close friend of her husband's. But the experience brought home to her, not the opportunities for self-expression afforded by periodical publication, but the possible constraints therein.

Her first review, of Tennyson's *Princess*, was markedly distorted by Lockhart, as is disclosed by a comparison of the published version with the original MS held in the Harry Ransom Center. Sara Coleridge wanted to relate Tennyson's poetry to that of Keats, but Lockhart insisted on continuing the *Quarterly*'s hostility to Keats, evidenced in the notorious 1818 review of him as a 'Cockney' poet written by John Wilson Croker. In this case, Lockhart, rather than directly attacking Keats, simply omitted every reference to him in Sara Coleridge's review. He altered the review as well to make it more negative about Tennyson, whose early work Croker had also attacked in the *Quarterly*.[67] Moreover, he made tonal changes too, so that the anonymous reviewer of *The Princess* came across as a somewhat misogynist 'man of the world'. Where Sara Coleridge quotes the poem's descriptions of Lady Blanche and her daughter Melissa with almost no comment, Lockhart inserts, '[h]ow should this painted mummy contrive to be the mother of the budding

---

[65]   Letter of July 1834, Wordsworth Trust, WLMS A, Coleridge, Sara, no. 33(1).

[66]   Letter of 5 July 1834, Harry Ransom Center, University of Texas at Austin (Sara Coleridge's emphasis).

[67]   See *Quarterly Review*, 49 (April 1833): 81–96.

charmer just sketched'.[68] Lockhart also added an epithet to describe the poem's heroine Princess Ida in academic mode as 'a Buckland in petticoats': because of its implied slur on women of intellectual claims, Sara Coleridge found this addition particularly offensive.[69]

Sara Coleridge's second and final periodical review raised problems of a different kind, but problems which again made her see this mode of publication as constraining rather than enabling. Lockhart had asked her to review a new edition of the works of the Early Modern dramatists Beaumont and Fletcher, published by Edward Moxon, since Lockhart was 'wishing to give Moxon, the publisher, a lift'.[70] The difficulty here was that the subject was a large one, and that Sara Coleridge initially wrote what would have come to nearly a hundred printed pages. But she also considered herself prolix, and a comparison between the original and the published versions shows that she did tend to over-amplify biographical speculations and go off on tangents. She confessed to Mrs Richard E. Townsend that she was 'carried away' by her '*subject*', and so could not 'help going too deep into it and travelling too widely all about it – into all its inmost recesses and around all its extensive environs'. As a result, she could neither confine herself to the length of a literary review article, nor practise the required 'smart not-too-thought-exacting style as the general reader will like'.[71] That is, she could give free rein neither to her intellect nor to her expression, within the bounds of a periodical review.

For Maria Jane Jewsbury, hyper-aware as she seems to have been of the potential for adopting different literary personae, anonymous periodical reviewing gave her an outlet to adopt voices congenial to her. But Sara Coleridge's experience subjected her to the 'party line' of the periodical she wrote for, and prevented her from exercising what she saw as her natural tendencies. Letter-writing, especially to close friends and family, and articles that were never published, offered her on the other hand the chance of freer expression.

---

[68]   Published version, 'Tennyson's *Princess: A Medley*', *Quarterly Review*, 82 (March 1848): 427–53, at 442–3, contrasted with the second of two MS versions in the Harry Ransom Center, University of Texas at Austin. The changes have been explored in Bradford Keyes Mudge, 'On Tennyson's *The Princess*: Sara Coleridge in the *Quarterly Review*', *The Wordsworth Circle*, 15/1 (1984): 51–4, and my own 'Snuffing Out an Article: Sara Coleridge and the Early Victorian Reception of Keats', in Joel Faflak and Julia M. Wright (eds), *Nervous Reactions: Victorian Recollections of Romanticism* (New York: State University of New York Press, 2004), pp. 189–206.

[69]   Published version, 440; see her letter to Mary Coleridge, quoted in Mudge, *Sara Coleridge*, p. 140. William Buckland was a prominent geologist.

[70]   See her letter to John Taylor Coleridge of July ? 1848, Harry Ransom Center, University of Texas at Austin.

[71]   Letter of September ? 1848, Harry Ransom Center, University of Texas at Austin (Sara Coleridge's emphasis). Her review was published as 'Dyce's Edition of Beaumont and Fletcher', *Quarterly Review*, 83 (September 1848): 377–418.

One recurrent motif of this relatively unconstrained kind of writing on Sara Coleridge's part was, however, the need for women, and particularly literary women in the public eye, to behave in a 'feminine' way. In society, this appears to have meant, primarily, that they should not put themselves forward in company – should do nothing to remind those present of any claim they may have to admiration. To Aubrey de Vere, she lauded her friend Isabella Fenwick: 'her mind is such a noble compound of heart and intelligence, of spiritual feeling and moral strength, and the most perfect feminineness', and although Fenwick is 'intellectual', she 'never talks for effect, never *holds possession of the floor*, as clever women are so apt to do'.[72] To her friend Mary Stanger she declared: 'Certainly all the women of first-rate genius that I know have been, and are, diffident, feminine and submissive in habits and temper'.[73] Jane Austen, whom she never knew personally, commended herself to Sara Coleridge partly because of her personal obscurity: 'Miss Austen, the clever novelist', she wrote to Emily Trevenen in 1834, 'seems invested with a peculiar interest from her having glided through life so noiselessly'.[74]

When it comes to women writers' actual works, 'feminine' is also a term of praise for Sara Coleridge, and lack of femininity is grounds for criticism. She is more given than is Maria Jane Jewsbury to consider literary traits as proper to one sex or the other. So after reading Frances Trollope's *The Vicar of Wrexhill*, she returns it to her friend Mrs H.M. Jones with the comment that both this novelist and Harriet Martineau demonstrate 'an absence of feminine modesty'.[75] Back in 1835, she had already criticised the new female literary star Martineau for her 'unwomanliness', on the grounds that 'there is something in the not-marrying, all-destroying or (if that be begging the question) the assailing and church-finding-fault-with system which Miss Martineau has taken up that is very unmaidenly'.[76]

These comments on Frances Trollope and Harriet Martineau might come across as unthinking reiterations of contemporary cultural stereotypes about women who engage with political or religious issues. But Sara Coleridge could apply the standard of 'femininity' in more interesting ways, when trying to be more precise about particular writers and their works. So in the case of Martineau's book about North America, *Retrospect of Western Travel*, she succeeds in producing the most compelling account of Niagara Falls that Sara Coleridge has read, by dint of focusing the phenomenon itself and its surrounds, rather than drawing attention to herself or her writing:

---

[72] Letter of July ? 1846, in *Memoir and Letters*, vol. 2, p. 63 (Sara Coleridge's emphasis).

[73] Letter of 6 March 1849, in *Memoir and Letters*, vol. 2, p. 218.

[74] Letter of 5 July 1834, Harry Ransom Center, University of Texas at Austin.

[75] Letter of 1839 or 1840, Harry Ransom Center, University of Texas at Austin.

[76] To Hartley Coleridge, April ? 1835, Harry Ransom Center, University of Texas at Austin.

> It takes you through out-door scenes, and though the politics are overwhelming now and then, it freshens you up by wanderings amid woods and rivers, and over mountain brows, and among tumbling waterfalls. I think Miss Martineau made one more at home with Niagara than any other of the American travellers. She gives one a most lively *water-fallish* feeling, introduces one not only to the huge mass of rushing water, but to the details of the environs, the wood in which the stream runs away, &c. She takes you over it and under it, before it and behind it, and seems as if she were performing a duty she owed to the genius of the cataract, by making it thoroughly well-known to those at a distance, rather than desirous to display her own talent by writing a well-rounded period or a terse paragraph about it.[77]

It is as if Martineau is like a good social hostess, ensuring that all her reader-guests have the best possible opportunity to acquaint themselves with the guest of honour, the waterfall, rather than dominating the scene herself. Ironically, Martineau had herself been the victim of editorial interference in the *Quarterly*: the critical review of her *Illustrations of Political Economy* written by Poulett Scrope in 1833 had had 'ribaldry' added by Croker and Lockhart before being published.[78]

As might be expected from someone with such close connections among prominent poets, Sara Coleridge often commented on both contemporary poetry and that of earlier periods, including poetry by women. Before she became aware of Elizabeth Barrett in 1838, she did not think any nineteenth-century woman had produced the 'genuine article' in poetry, apart from Joanna Baillie, and, unlike Maria Jane Jewsbury, she was decidedly lukewarm about Felicia Hemans. For Sara Coleridge, Hemans's work lacked the quality so much celebrated by her literary mentors Wordsworth and S.T. Coleridge, 'poetical imagination' – it was proficient and demonstrated some feeling, but lacked variety: 'she keeps one so long in a sublime region of thin ether that one craves to come down and breathe the common air.'[79] A true poet's mind 'so acts on the things of the universe, material and immaterial, that each composition is in effect a new creation', she explained to her husband, but Hemans's practice was to take a theme from a source external to herself and to illustrate it 'in fifty different ways, the verses being like so many wafers, the same thing in blue, green, red, yellow' – and then to append 'a sentiment or a moral, like the large red bead of a rosary at the end of several white ones'.

---

[77] Letter to Emily Trevenen, October 1838, in *Memoir and Letters*, vol. 1, pp. 218–19 (Sara Coleridge's emphasis).

[78] *Quarterly Review*, 49 (April 1833): 136–52, discussed by Mary A. Waters, *British Women Writers and the Profession of Literary Criticism, 1789–1832* (Houndmills and New York: Palgrave Macmillan, 2004), pp. 162–4.

[79] Letters to Emily Trevenen, 12 July 1835, in *Memoir and Letters*, vol. 1, pp. 127–8, and to Mrs H.M. Jones, 1836, ibid., vol. 1, pp. 151–2.

Hemans's materials, according to Sara Coleridge, 'have undergone no fusion in the crucible of imagination'.[80]

Sara Coleridge seems to have been introduced to Elizabeth Barrett's work by the latter's cousin, John Kenyon, who sent her Barrett's 1838 volume, *The Seraphim, and Other Poems*, and her translation of Aeschylus' *Prometheus Bound* (1833). She wrote to Kenyon in response, and there are two MS versions of the letter extant in the Harry Ransom Center: since the second is more complimentary than the first, Sara Coleridge no doubt felt that the first was too harsh to send to someone likely to pass on its contents to the subject. Sensitivity to a recipient's feelings is, needless to say, one potentially constraining aspect of using personal correspondence as a means of self-expression. (That her comments were passed on to Barrett is evident in the latter's letter to Kenyon of 15 July 1838.)[81]

Sara Coleridge praises several of the poems in the 1838 volume: 'The Poet's Vow', 'A Romance of the Ganges', 'Isobel's Child', 'The Island', 'The Deserted Garden' and 'Cowper's Grave'. But she is critical of the title poem, 'The Seraphim', which deals with conversations among angels watching the Crucifixion, because she thinks such a subject, if treated at all, should be handled 'with a sober Miltonic majesty of style, rather than a fantastic modernism'. In the second version of the letter, she amplifies 'fantastic modernism' into 'wild modernism and fantastic rapture', but palliates the criticism by adding that 'perhaps no other single poem in the volume has impressed me so strongly with the writer's power'. As for the Aeschylus translation, that is 'very clever', but Barrett has 'slipped into some phrases which want the Homeric simplicity of Aeschylus', Sara Coleridge observes in both versions of the letter.

Sara Coleridge's most forcible criticisms, however, are directed at Barrett's commentary on the 'Homeric question' – the longstanding debate about whether the *Iliad* and the *Odyssey* were written by a single individual. Barrett argued that they were, and Sara Coleridge finds her tone and language arrogant, very disrespectful of the eminent scholars who take the opposing view: using epithets like 'wrinkled brow', 'thin dry lips' and 'cold eyes', to characterise them. So strident is Barrett, in Sara Coleridge's opinion, that in the first version of the letter to Kenyon, she implied that if Homer himself was by repute physically blind, then Barrett was metaphorically so – but she evidently thought better of the accusation.

In writing about Barrett to Emily Trevenen at around the same time, Sara Coleridge again offers a mixed response: she acknowledges that Barrett is 'the most learned of all the literary women of the age' that she is familiar with, and that the *Seraphim* volume possesses 'very considerable power' – but she also considers

---

[80] Letter to Henry Nelson Coleridge, 25 October 1836, in *Memoir and Letters*, vol. 1, pp. 161–2.

[81] *The Brownings' Correspondence*, vol. 4, ed. Philip Kelley and Ronald Hudson (Winfield, KS: Wedgestone Press, 1986), p. 63. The letters are dated Thursday and Friday, July ? 1838; the second version of the letter was published in *Memoir and Letters*, vol. 1, pp. 302–3, misdated 1844.

that Barrett's poetry betrays 'affectation and bombast'.[82] When Barrett's *Poems* of 1844 appeared, Sara Coleridge told her friend Mrs Richard E. Townsend that she expected to prefer this collection to the previous one, since the poems seemed to have 'a *quieter* strength about them', and to 'keep more within the range of human feeling and sympathies' than the divine subject of 'The Seraphim' had made possible.[83]

By 1851, Sara Coleridge was telling her sister-in-law Mary that the latest volume by the now Elizabeth Barrett Browning, *Casa Guidi Windows*, was 'full of genius': she praised the title poem, and declared 'one set of sonnets Shakesperian' – possibly the soon-to-be-celebrated *Sonnets from the Portuguese*.[84] But she still had criticisms to make of Barrett Browning's work: she wrote to the American Ellis Yarnall soon after the letter to Mary Coleridge, that although Barrett Browning 'has more poetic genius than any other woman living, – perhaps more than any woman ever showed before, except Sappho', she is guilty of 'forced and untrue' imagery, 'exaggerated' sentiments and 'unnatural and unpleasant' situations. Moreover, her versification, 'rugged' and 'harsh', with its imperfect rhymes, mars the clarity of her ideas, and makes her work less likely to gain a lasting reputation.[85]

To some extent, gender-based criteria underlie Sara Coleridge's ambivalence about Barrett Browning's writing. Attributing to the earlier work 'affectation and bombast' suggests a kind of public self-projection on the female poet's part that Sara Coleridge found unfeminine, while the epithet '*quieter* strength' applied to the 1844 collection is praise that implies in part a toning down of unfeminine self-display. Gender-orientated phraseology is more explicit too: in the letters to Kenyon of 1838, Sara Coleridge recommended to the poet greater 'feminine gentleness' – changed to 'feminine reserve' in the second version, perhaps to hint at the need for a dignified self-restraint? In commenting on the 1844 collection to Edward Quillinan, she observed that the volumes 'are much more agreeable … than her last collection – more human, natural, feminine and comfortable'.[86] The 1851 letter to Yarnall, meanwhile, implies that in essaying verse, Barrett Browning is possibly not making the best use of female talents – after her strictures on the poetry, Sara Coleridge goes on to observe: 'It has been ever a favourite saying with me, that there is one line of literature, and only one, in which women can do something that men cannot do, and do better; and that is a certain style of novel.' She goes on to cite the fiction of Elizabeth Inchbald, Fanny Burney, Maria Edgeworth, Susan Ferrier, Anne Marsh, Jane Austen and Charlotte Brontë.

---

[82]   Letter of 17 July 1838, Harry Ransom Center, University of Texas at Austin.

[83]   Letter of 12 February ? 1845, Harry Ransom Center, University of Texas at Austin (Sara Coleridge's emphasis).

[84]   Letter of 14 August 1851, Harry Ransom Center, University of Texas at Austin.

[85]   Letter of 28 August 1851, in *Memoir and Letters*, vol. 2, pp. 447–8.

[86]   Letter of 9 September 1846, Wordsworth Trust, WLMS A, Coleridge, Sara, no. 43(3).

Sara Coleridge's commentary on Jane Austen and Charlotte Brontë in particular, I would argue, illustrates some of the conundrums involved in linking literary qualities to the sex of the author. Unlike Maria Jane Jewsbury, for whom Jane Austen's generation was one of 'masculine' women writers, Sara Coleridge saw her and her writing as feminine, and although she lauded Austen's fiction for what she considered its distinctively feminine qualities, she was also concerned about the limitations possibly consequent on these. As for Charlotte Brontë – despite bracketing her with Austen in the letter to Yarnall – Sara Coleridge had initially found it very difficult to believe that the author of *Jane Eyre* was female.

Austen is one of the writers mentioned in an unpublished essay of Sara Coleridge's on Henry Fielding's novels, especially *Tom Jones*.[87] Here she grapples with the issue of the relationship between life as it is experienced by the reader, and the representation of it in fiction. She argues that a novel cannot be 'a mere copy of life', and a major reason for this is that '[t]he shades and interminglings of character, the ramifications and mixtures of event and circumstance in this actual world are too minute and complicated, the action of life's drama is too comprehensive', to be thoroughly represented in fiction. What a good novelist offers instead is 'the allegory of life epitomized … abstracts generalized from what he has seen and heard' which must 'play their part in a certain space of time'. Moreover, the novelist must bring to bear on their materials the power of their imagination – a novel is 'Life recast in the mould of Imagination', and Fielding's *Tom Jones* exemplifies this 'moulding, modifying combining energy'.

As a counter-example, Sara Coleridge seems to offer the novels of Jane Austen. Or at least, Austen's novels as they were claimed to be by one of her literary mentors, Wordsworth: 'It has been observed by Mr W[ordsworth] that the novels of Jane Austen are too much mere likenesses of every day life: – drawn with skill and evincing much fineness of observation, but with too small a portion of the shaping and glorifying power.' The relationship between this judgment of Wordsworth's and Austen's sex is more explicit in a discussion of women writers Sara Coleridge included in a letter of 1834. Here she recalls that 'Mr. Wordsworth used to say that though he admitted that [Austen's] novels were an admirable copy of life, he could not be interested in productions of that kind; unless the truth of Nature were presented to him clarified, as it were, by the pervading light of Imagination, it had scarce any attractions in his eyes'.[88] But she says as well that 'Miss Austen's works are essentially feminine', as if their purported lack of 'the pervading light of Imagination' was a corollary of this. The novels do have admirable qualities, and Sara Coleridge lists them as positives – but they are qualities linked to Austen's sex: 'delicate mirth', 'gently-hinted satire' and 'feminine decorous humour'. Austen is, she says, 'surely the most faultless of female writers' – but in a limited arena.

---

[87]   'Fielding', Harry Ransom Center, University of Texas at Austin.
[88]   Letter to Emily Trevenen, 1834, in *Memoir and Letters*, vol. 1, p. 75.

With the publication of Lockhart's biography of Sir Walter Scott in 1837, the high opinion of Austen held by her most popular contemporary among novelists became widely known. Scott wrote in his journal, in lines that were to become famous:

> The Big Bow-wow strain I can do myself like any now going, but the exquisite touch which renders ordinary commonplace things and characters interesting from the truth of the description and the sentiment is denied to me.[89]

Sara Coleridge welcomed this generous validation of Austen: S.T. Coleridge had praised her too, and here was another authoritative male literary voice which countered the judgment of Wordsworth. Here what is coded feminine ('the exquisite touch') is compared favourably to something like the 'bombast' Sara Coleridge attributed to Barrett, but here acknowledged by a man as a trait that he can perform so readily because it is so easy. Austen's capacity to make 'ordinary commonplace things and characters interesting', moreover, also implies that she did possess something of that 'pervading light of Imagination', rather than just the habit of microscopic observation often attributed to women writers.[90]

Along similar lines, too, Sara Coleridge incorporates a defence of Jane Austen into her article on Beaumont and Fletcher, where she is discussing the appeal of a dramatic character 'devoid of almost everything to esteem or to admire'. She goes on to say that, although many readers find that an Austen novel 'describes a set of persons so below the general standard in moral and intellectual characteristics, that one would be right sorry to have been confined to such a world of mediocrity and meanness', such a portrayal still generates readers' interest. This is because it is 'not a mere mechanical material copy of the outer surface of things', but a representation of 'their inner life and being' and a 'true report of the artist's individual mind'.[91] How Austen's 'individual mind' is manifested in her fiction, Sara Coleridge does not elaborate, but she implies here that the novels do convey a sense of depth in Austen's characters, a quality that results from her creative powers. It is notable too that, unlike Maria Jane Jewsbury, she does not fault Austen for what they both perceived as the predominance of commonplace, morally inferior characters in her novels.

Scott's comment perhaps elucidates what Sara Coleridge means by the 'certain style of novel' where 'women can do something that men cannot do'. Is there a kind of subtlety of representation at which women surpass men – so that Austen's 'delicacy', plus the kind of 'satire' which is only 'gently-hinted', are not only admirable literary qualities, but also beyond the capacity of men? In the letter

---

[89]   *Journal of Sir Walter Scott*, ed. J.G. Tait, entry of 14 March 1826, repr. in B.C. Southam, *Jane Austen*, p. 106.

[90]   Letter to Emily Trevenen, 24 January 1838, Harry Ransom Center, University of Texas at Austin.

[91]   [Sara Coleridge], 'Dyce's Edition of Beaumont and Fletcher', 412.

where Sara Coleridge enthusiastically cites Scott's praise of Austen, she claims that 'hers is almost the only literary line in which women are not only unsurpassed by men, but in which they have done that which women alone can do to perfection'.

Yet Austen's 'perfection' here comes at a cost. Her novels are 'agreeable wholes', 'entertaining' and 'pleasing', and in this respect, they are superior to the fiction of her contemporary Maria Edgeworth. But the latter's work, in Sara Coleridge's opinion, 'has deeper & stronger passages'. That Austen's oeuvre demonstrated perfection, but only because she was unambitious and limited in what she attempted, was to become a cliché of Austen criticism in the nineteenth century – fostered, as mentioned earlier, by her brother's citation of Jane Austen's comparison of her writing to miniature-work. Sara Coleridge's comments on Austen suggest that she would find such an image of the novelist convincing.

So, despite their lacking the formal unity of Austen's fiction, Sara Coleridge finds much to admire in Maria Edgeworth's novels. If Austen can convey her characters' inner life, Edgeworth likewise 'paints manners as they grow out of morals, and not merely as they are modified and tinctured by fashion'. Unlike Austen's, however, 'the best parts of [Edgeworth's novels] seem as if they have been written by a man', such that *Castle Rackrent* possesses 'genuine humour', something Sara Coleridge considers 'very rare in the writings of women'.[92]

In Edgeworth's case, the quality of humour is an asset to her fiction, according to Sara Coleridge, rather than being a sign of unwomanliness: Sara Coleridge was thus not automatically critical of 'masculine' aspects of women's fiction. Correspondingly, not all kinds of 'femininity' therein are admirable or desirable. Sara Coleridge was highly critical of what she saw as the idealisation of selfish, even immoral, conduct in two female-authored novels of the 1840s, Countess Ida von Hahn-Hahn's *Faustina*, and the debut novel of Maria Jane Jewsbury's sister Geraldine, *Zoe: a History of Two Lives* (1845). She declared to Aubrey de Vere that *Faustina* was 'entirely a woman's book, a continental woman's book'.[93] She attributes to it recognisably feminine strengths: 'in the style of execution very exquisite, full of grace, beauty, light rich fancy'. But its ethical underpinnings are dubious – the heroine is claimed to possess 'superlative *purity of heart*! the simplicity of genius, – an innocent desire to *mould her being*'. In Sara Coleridge's view, however, she is entirely self-centred: she acts like 'an unprincipled coquette, – a frail, fickle, faithless, self-indulgent, passionate creature; nay, more than that, heartless and cruel, in the extreme'. And although Faustina's successful life is claimed to be the result 'of genius', it is really due to the fact that she is 'exquisitely beautiful and graceful'. Sara Coleridge prefers *Zoe*, as possessing greater 'variety' and 'power', but it contains the same 'moral falsity … that of uniting noble qualities of head and heart with conduct the most unworthy and unvirtuous'. (Presumably she is referring primarily to the episode where the heroine, an unhappily married

---

[92]　Letter to Emily Trevenen, 3 August 1834, in *Memoir and Letters*, vol. 1, p. 75.

[93]　Letter of 1848, in *Memoir and Letters*, vol. 2, pp. 174–5; emphases are Sara Coleridge's.

woman with children, almost leaves her husband for Comte Mirabeau.) It is as if for Sara Coleridge, 'feminine' authorship risked an over-valuing of physical beauty, and having moral rigour neglected in favour of a sentimental special pleading for an attractive woman to be allowed to follow her heart.

The welcome alternative to this kind of practice among women writers, Sara Coleridge believed, was to be found in a novel which for her in 1848 was self-evidently 'that of an English *man*' – *Jane Eyre* – where the heroine is patently plain, and could be read as making a firm ethical stand against adultery. She asserted to Aubrey de Vere that this novel was 'vastly superior in truth and power' to *Faustina*, since Jane, 'without personal advantages, gains upon the mind of the reader by what she does, and we can well understand how she fascinates Rochester'. The novel is marred only by being 'coarse and hard in parts'.

As the foregoing suggests, Sara Coleridge was convinced that 'Currer Bell' was male. Edith Coleridge, in her note to this letter, recalls that her mother 'felt sure that the mysterious "Currer Bell" was a *man*', and declared that 'she could as soon believe the paintings of Rubens to have been by a woman as "Jane Eyre"'.[94] This novel, more than those of Maria Edgeworth, clearly disturbed Sara's ideas about the link between gender and literary identity. While still under the apprehension that Currer Bell was male, she also discusses *Jane Eyre* in relation to a male-authored novel that made a major impact in 1847–8, Thackeray's *Vanity Fair*. She told Isabella Fenwick that she considered them equal in 'knowledge of life & delineation of character', and wondered if Currer Bell's novel owed something to Thackeray's. (That it did, was later affirmed by Charlotte Brontë's dedicating the second edition of *Jane Eyre* to Thackeray.) The two novels have distinctive strengths, however: Thackeray's 'keen and subtle' characterisation is especially evident in his portrayal of Sir Pitt Crawley, while *Jane Eyre* is notable for its 'landscape painting'.[95]

By the time Sara Coleridge was writing in letters about Charlotte Brontë's next novel, *Shirley* (1849), the sex of the author was known. On 21 December 1849, she tells Edward Quillinan that she has just learned that 'Jane Eyre is by a lady, the daughter of a clergyman at York'.[96] To Emily Trevenen, she exclaimed in March of 1850 that she had been '*utterly mistaken* about the authorship of "Jane Eyre"', having felt 'so sure it was by a *man*'.[97] She still believed that this novel was 'wonderfully powerful', but observed that 'Shirley seems to have all its faults and less of the attractive'. (Since she died in 1852, Sara Coleridge did not live to read *Villette*.)

Sara Coleridge remained ambivalent about Charlotte Brontë's fiction. Although she expresses no enthusiasm for *Shirley* in the letter just cited, she did defend the

---

[94]   *Memoir and Letters*, vol. 2, p. 175n.

[95]   Letter of 3 November 1848, in *Memoir and Letters*, vol. 2, p. 187.

[96]   Wordsworth Trust, WLMS A, Coleridge, Sara, no. 48(2).

[97]   Letter of 20 March 1850, Harry Ransom Center, University of Texas at Austin (Sara Coleridge's emphasis).

novel when it incurred a critical reception in the *Edinburgh Review* in 1850. She wrote to Mrs H.M. Jones that 'we [her family?] are delighted with' the book, and believe that the review 'made far too much fuss about its little faults of style and breeding', since '[w]hen you read the sentences in question, *where they occur*, they do not appear very shocking'.[98] Possibly her comment on the novel to Emily Trevenen had been based on hearsay rather than personal knowledge? The review in the *Edinburgh*, by G.H. Lewes, is critical of many aspects of the novel: the section Sara Coleridge is referring to declares that Charlotte Brontë must 'sacrifice a little of her Yorkshire roughness to the demands of good taste: neither saturating her writings with such rudeness and offensive harshness, nor suffering her style to wander into such vulgarities as would be inexcusable – even in a man'. The review goes on to cite several instances from both narrative and dialogue, and then to castigate the 'impertinence' and the 'frequent harshness and rudeness' evident in the main characters' manners.[99] As the phrase, 'even in a man' suggests, the novel's various alleged faults are particularly reprehensible in a female-authored text, and the review quotes as apposite to Brontë's case, Goethe's misogynist comment on Madame de Staël's *Corinne*: '"This person wants everything that is graceful in a woman; and, nevertheless, the faults of her book are altogether womanly faults. She steps out of her sex – without elevating herself above it."'[100]

Paradoxically, like Harriet Martineau, Lewes here was apparently the victim of the sort of editorial doctoring similar to what Sara Coleridge herself had suffered in reviewing *The Princess*: when Elizabeth Gaskell in her *Life of Charlotte Brontë* cited the review and the target's aggrieved response, Lewes wrote to her explaining that Francis Jeffrey, as editor of the *Edinburgh*, had 'tampered with the article as usual, and inserted some to [Lewes] offensive sentences'.[101] If the misogynist parts of the review actually are Jeffrey's, then had his assumptions about women writers, evident in his 1829 discussion of Hemans, Austen and others, been seriously challenged by the advent of Charlotte Brontë nearly 20 years later?

Sara Coleridge does not comment specifically on the review's gender-based judgments, and her ambivalence about the 'unfeminine' capabilities disclosed in Brontë's fiction seems to have persisted. When writing to Ellis Yarnall a few months later, she reiterates the strictures on coarseness and hardness, saying that Charlotte Brontë's novels have 'a certain hardness of feeling and plebeian

---

[98] *Memoir and Letters*, vol. 2, p. 230 (Sara Coleridge's emphasis), misdated 1849.

[99] *Edinburgh Review*, 91 (January 1850): 153–73, partly repr. in Miriam Allott (ed.), *The Brontës: The Critical Heritage* (London: Routledge & Kegan Paul; New York: Barnes & Noble, 1974), pp. 160–70, at pp. 165–6.

[100] Ibid., p. 169.

[101] G.H. Lewes to Elizabeth Gaskell, 15 April 1857, in Gordon S. Haight (ed.), *The George Eliot Letters* (6 vols, New Haven and London: Yale University Press, 1954), vol. 2, p. 316, quoted in Laurel Brake, *Subjugated Knowledges: Journalism, Gender and Literature in the Nineteenth Century* (Houndmills: Macmillan, 1994), p. 15.

coarseness of taste'.[102] On the other hand, like Edgeworth's fiction, they have a 'masculine' quality she admires – a 'masculine energy of satire'. Ultimately, however, Sara Coleridge gives the impression of being more 'comfortable' (to recall a word she used of Barrett's 1844 collection) with fiction that confirms her assumptions about gender and writing – and so she ends her comments to Yarnall by declaring that all in all she prefers the novels of Mrs Anne Marsh, since they are 'thoroughly feminine'.

Yet Sara Coleridge found that Anne Marsh in social life was not so womanly. Marsh 'evidently desires to be considered and treated as a "lioness"', she tells Quillinan in the same letter in which she reveals her surprise as to the identity of the author of *Jane Eyre*. The contrast she makes here is with 'Jane Austen, & Miss Ferrier, who were most feminine & retiring'. It is as if, in the face of the strangely 'masculine' female who wrote *Jane Eyre*, and Mrs Marsh who is 'feminine' in fiction but not in life, Jane Austen functions as a kind of benchmark of femininity, in both life and works.

Elizabeth Rigby (later Lady Eastlake), whom Sara Coleridge knew socially, also differed in her personal and her textual self-representations, but in the opposite way. In 1846, Sara Coleridge had reported to her sister-in-law Mary that she liked Rigby 'better than any lady authoress that I have come in contact with for a long time'. This is because (unlike with Marsh) '[t]here is no *lionism* about her'.[103] Sara Coleridge was equally enthusiastic about her three years later – after the *Jane Eyre* review, whose authorship she evidently knew, and which she described as 'very clever'. Sara Coleridge wrote of Eastlake to Quillinan in 1849: 'She is perhaps the most brilliant woman of the day – the most accomplished and Chrichtonian … [T]he top of her perfections is, that she has well-bred, courteous, unassuming manners, does not take upon her and hold forth to the company … She is thoroughly feminine.'[104] In this respect, Sara Coleridge goes on, Eastlake resembles 'that princess of novelists, Jane Austen'.

It is striking that, when the question of women writers' femininity is at stake, Sara Coleridge repeatedly champions Jane Austen, whom she could not have met, in relation to women writers she knew personally. It is conceivable that she had some private knowledge of Austen via Quillinan – his first wife Jemima Brydges had been the niece of Jane Austen's close friend and mentor Ann Lefroy. But if Sara Coleridge lacked personal knowledge, it appears that, unlike Maria Jane Jewsbury, she simply accepted Henry Austen's version of his sister, and found that it dovetailed with her reading of the novels. One wonders, however, if Sara Coleridge's constant lauding of the 'feminine' in women's lives and writing is

---

[102]   Letter of 28 August 1851, in *Memoir and Letters*, vol. 2, p. 448.

[103]   Letter of 8 June 1846, Harry Ransom Center, University of Texas at Austin (Sara Coleridge's emphasis).

[104]   Letter of April ? 1849, in *Memoir and Letters*, vol. 2, pp. 224–5; see also letters to Mary Coleridge of 31 March 1849, in *Memoir and Letters*, vol. 2, pp. 223–4, and 26 January 1849, Harry Ransom Center, University of Texas at Austin.

in part a way of reassuring herself and others that – despite having sometimes moved beyond editing her father's works and promulgating his genius, despite sometimes having questioned the judgments of her male literary mentors, despite appreciating some of the 'masculine' traits in Charlotte Brontë's fiction – she was still herself 'thoroughly feminine'.

Chapter 3
Writing Women's Literary History: Hannah Lawrance, Jane Williams and Julia Kavanagh

The three critics who are the focus of this chapter differ from the other writers in this study in that, rather than concentrating on women's writing of the present and the recent past, they essayed historical accounts of women's achievements, including their literary achievements. Jane Williams and Julia Kavanagh produced histories of women's writing, Williams offering an overview of English women's literary output from the earliest times to 1700 and of their poetry up to 1850, and Kavanagh treating the tradition of fiction-writing established by women in both France and England, up to Jane Austen and beyond. Hannah Lawrance, in her histories of women from the medieval and earlier periods, was not concerned primarily with their literary achievements, but the ideas developed therein inform the two substantial articles she later wrote on Charlotte Brontë and Elizabeth Barrett Browning respectively.

Like more recent historians of women, Lawrance, Williams and Kavanagh saw themselves as rescuing notable women from oblivion, neglect or misrepresentation. Their enterprise of considering the achievements of numerous women over time also meant that they addressed, perhaps more explicitly than the other critics in this study, the question of whether women's writing as such possessed gender-specific qualities, or differed significantly from men's writing. As a corollary, they were particularly interested as well in women's intellectual capacities, and the extent to which the development of these over the centuries had been hampered by prejudice and lack of opportunity.

Although Lawrance and Kavanagh also reviewed for periodicals which practised the convention of anonymity, their book publications, together with those of Williams, appeared under their own names. No doubt partly because of this, each of the three implied only modest claims for her own works – while at the same time deploying strategies which would allow readers to register that the evidence for women's achievement and potential was significant and wide-ranging.

Hannah Lawrance

Hannah Lawrance (1795–1875) was a prolific and a learned critic whose output is little known, although her historical works have recently received attention in Rohan Amanda Maitzen's *Gender, Genre, and Victorian Historical Writing* (1998), a study to which I shall return. As well as possibly being the author of *London in Olden Time: Tales Intended to Illustrate the Manners and Superstitions of its Inhabitants, From the Twelfth to the Sixteenth Century* (1825, 1827), Lawrance produced two substantial works of women's history in her own name: *Historical Memoirs of the Queens of England from the Commencement of the Twelfth Century* (2 vols, 1838), and *The History of Woman in England and Her Influence on Society and Literature, From the Earliest Period* (1843). The first book covers the queens from the twelfth century to the end of the Wars of the Roses, while the second, dealing with the period up until 1200, was apparently intended to be the first of a number of volumes, but nothing further from Lawrance under this title was published. The reason for this is unclear, but in any case Lawrance was from the 1830s to the early 1850s a regular reviewer for the *Athenaeum*, where her specialty was works dealing with the literature and history of the British Isles from its earliest days up until the sixteenth century. For *Blackwood's Edinburgh Magazine* she wrote two articles on 'The Anglo-Norman Trouvères' (1836), and for *Fraser's Magazine*, two articles on medieval French literature (1844, 1847). She also contributed three pieces to the short-lived *Hood's Magazine* in 1844 – two short stories focusing on the mores of 'A Hundred Years Ago' signed 'H.L.', and an anonymous review of Hannah Mary Rathbone's *Diary of Lady Willoughby* (1844), a text which purported to be the journal of a woman's experiences during the English Civil War and its aftermath. In 1854–5, Lawrance published five articles in *Household Words* on the social and literary life of the seventeenth and eighteenth centuries, drawing on books, newspapers, pamphlets and MSS of the time.[1]

Lawrance was a lifelong Congregationalist, and her publishing activities in her later years were concentrated on articles for the serious Nonconformist quarterly, the *British Quarterly Review*, to which she made over 60 contributions from 1847 to 1870. Her subjects were very diverse in their range: as well as a substantial number about medieval, pre-medieval and Early Modern literature, there were also pieces on art, African explorations, and the education and employment of women. It was here as well that Lawrance published most extensively on contemporary literature, and her reviews included two dealing with important

---

[1]   See Anne Lohrli (ed.), *Household Words: A Weekly Journal Conducted by Charles Dickens: Table of Contents, List of Contributors and Their Contributions* (Toronto: University of Toronto Press, 1973), pp. 338–9, Rosemary Mitchell's article on Lawrance in the *Dictionary of National Biography*, and Frederick Korn, 'An Unpublished Letter by Thomas Hood: Hannah Lawrance and *Hood's Magazine*', *English Language Notes*, 18 (1981): 192–4.

women writers: one of Gaskell's *Life of Charlotte Brontë*, and one of Elizabeth Barrett Browning's oeuvre.[2]

Lawrance was evidently fascinated with the life and literature of earlier periods, and very well-informed about them. Much of her published writing was concerned in particular to make the medieval and earlier periods of British history and culture better known to her contemporaries. In ending her book on the medieval queens, she declares that a major aim of the work has been to offer the reader 'a picture of that important period of our history, so distinguished as the birth-time of our political institutions, our arts, our commerce, our language, our poetry'.[3] She later takes the opportunity afforded by a review of Tennyson's *Idylls of the King* in the *British Quarterly Review* to aver that the legends of King Arthur and the Round Table, 'these fables of the Celtic and Teutonic nations', have inspired British soldiers in the Crimea and in India, and that their influence is traceable in such modern fictional characters as Charles Kingsley's Tom Thurnall (in *Two Years Ago*, 1857), Thackeray's Captain Dobbin and Colonel Newcome (respectively in *Vanity Fair*, 1848, and *The Newcomes*, 1855), and Dickens's Arthur Clennam (in *Little Dorrit*, 1857).[4] In discussing the Anglo-Saxon period in *The History of Woman in England*, she argues that 'rude Saxons brought from their pine-forests principles, social and political, which have laid the foundation for our present greatness, the elements, and the essential elements of that tongue which will, ere long, be the birth-tongue of half the civilised world'.[5]

Another emphasis of Lawrance's writings on the past was the need to go to contemporary sources to gain a true understanding of a period: reliance on later material would only create erroneous beliefs. In her book on the queens, she draws attention to her own use of contemporary sources (I, iv), and points out that the thirteenth-century Rolls, then (1838) recently published, belie common negative assumptions about the Middle Ages concerning Norman/Saxon and aristocrat/serf relations, relative levels of wealth, and the treatment of the poor; in her *History of Woman*, she adduces as her sources monks' chronicles, legal records, household books, and the works of the Anglo-Norman poets (iv, vi).

To steep oneself in the writings of the medieval and earlier periods, needless to say, required considerable erudition and recourse to unpublished records. Lawrance

---

[2]   'The Life of Charlotte Brontë', *British Quarterly Review*, 26 (July 1857): 218–31; 'Mrs. Browning's Poetry', *British Quarterly Review*, 42 (October 1865): 359–84. Subsequent references to these articles will be included parenthetically in the text.

[3]   *Historical Memoirs of the Queens of England from the Commencement of the Twelfth Century* (2 vols, London: Edward Moxon, 1838), vol. 2, p. 450. Subsequent references to these volumes will be included parenthetically in the text.

[4]   'Tennyson's Idylls of the King', *British Quarterly Review*, 30 (October 1859): 481–501, at 482.

[5]   *The History of Woman in England and Her Influence on Society and Literature, From the Earliest Period*, vol. 1 *To the Year 1200* (London: Henry Colburn, 1843), p. 59. Subsequent references to this book will be included parenthetically in the text.

evidently read Middle English, Anglo-Saxon, Anglo-Norman, Old French and Latin. For example, she translates in her two books on medieval women sections of the Anglo-Norman 'Voyage of St Brandon', while an article on the Anglo-Norman trouvères talks of Philip de Thaun's *Bestiaire* as a text 'which we have frequently turned over with much interest … in the Cotton Library'.[6] Her treatment of Lady Charlotte Guest's translations of the Welsh 'Mabinogion' is interesting in this scholarly context. She reviewed this publication in the *Athenaeum* as it appeared in several parts during the late 1830s and 1840s, and found it valuable, both in showing that stories thought by many to originate from continental Europe had their basis in Celtic legend, and in illustrating the mores of early centuries, the 'rude, warlike and imaginative character of our Celtic aborigines'.[7] Lawrance also paid tribute to a fellow scholar of early literature, in commending Lady Charlotte Guest for the quality of her translation and her notes, and for funding the publication of a work of much interest to scholars but considered by publishers too risky a venture. But she also criticised Guest for her punctuation in her reproduction of the French versions of the tales.[8]

Lawrance's own erudition received admiring comments from well-informed women: Christian Johnstone, reviewing *Historical Memoirs of the Queens of England* in *Tait's Edinburgh Magazine*, claimed that Lawrance had 'dug deeper in the tumulus of antiquity, than many accredited excavators of the other sex', while in 1844 Elizabeth Barrett – unsuccessfully – encouraged her collaborator on *The New Spirit of the Age*, Richard Hengist Horne, to mention Lawrance in the work, since extracts Barrett had seen from the *Historical Memoirs* suggested that Lawrance was, compared to her fellow-biographer of the queens of England, Agnes Strickland, 'deeper-minded'.[9]

For Lawrance, one significant result of widespread ignorance of and misconceptions about Britain's past was that women's contribution to the nation's development, both individually and collectively, had not been recognised. Despite the proliferation of history-writing, she observes at the beginning of *Historical Memoirs of the Queens of England*, the queens 'have been passed over with scarcely the slightest notice' (I, iii), and at the end she claims that the queens she

---

    [6] 'The Anglo-Norman Poets of the Twelfth Century', *British Quarterly Review*, 5 (March 1847): 159–86, at 164.

    [7] Review of Pt IV, *Kilwch and Olwen*, *Athenaeum*, 30 April 1842: 378–9, at 378.

    [8] Review of Pt I, *The Lady of the Fountain*, *Athenaeum*, 24 November 1838: 833–5. The other Parts were reviewed in the *Athenaeum* as follows: Pt II, 14 September 1839: 694, Pt III, 23 April 1842: 360–61; Pt VI, 17 May 1845: 479–81, Pt VII, 17 November 1849: 1149–51.

    [9] Christian Johnstone in *Tait's Edinburgh Magazine*, ns 2 (1838): 257, quoted in Rosemary Mitchell, *Picturing the Past: English History in Text and Image. 1830–1870* (Oxford: Clarendon Press, 2000), p. 150; letters of 23 December and 29 December 1844, in *The Brownings' Correspondence*, vol. 8, ed. Philip Kelley and Ronald Hudson (Winfield, KS: Wedgestone Press, 1990), pp. 103–5, 116–20.

has covered 'have in some cases been misrepresented, but in many more dismissed with merely a slight passing notice' (II, 450). What emerges, moreover, in the cases of individual queens, insofar as they are known, is that they have been reduced to female stereotypes in a way that belies the more complex picture revealed by a proper study of the sources. Matilda or Empress Maude, the heir of Henry I and mother of Henry II (and England's only queen regnant, as distinct from queen consort, in the period Lawrance covers), may have treated her English subjects with pride and contempt, but as her son's regent in Normandy she was notable for works of religion and charity, and her attempts to reconcile him with his archbishop Thomas à Becket demonstrated 'the intellectual character of this gifted woman' and her 'clear-sighted policy' (I, 144ff.). As for her daughter-in-law Eleanor of Aquitaine, consort of Henry II, she is, according to Lawrance, now seen simply as a vindictive 'woman scorned', responsible for the death of her rival, Henry's mistress 'Fair Rosamond' Clifford. But Lawrance denies her guilt, and blames Henry for the neglect and infidelity with which he treated her. Henry's conduct, moreover, excuses Eleanor's support of their sons against him, and her devotion as a mother was shown in their son Richard I's reign, when she worked tirelessly for his release from foreign captivity. She had also, as regent during this reign, freed Henry's prisoners and rectified injustices he had perpetrated, while, as a woman of 'unquestioned talents', she played a notable political role, especially in important diplomatic missions (I, 200ff.). Meanwhile Henry VI's queen, Margaret of Anjou, active in the Wars of the Roses, was not the heartless and overweeningly ambitious woman she is generally assumed to have been: she did not in fact order either the beheading of her husband's rival the Duke of York nor the fitting on his head of a paper crown, and she was notable for more peaceable activities such as the founding of Queen's College, Cambridge. During the Wars, she showed 'steadfast courage' and 'heroic devotion', and when her husband was forced to disinherit their son, it was maternal feelings rather than political ambition that were to the fore: 'no *woman*,' writes Lawrance, 'will charge Margaret of Anjou with ambition' (II, 367ff., Lawrance's emphasis).

Hannah Lawrance's discussion of these three queens brings into focus an important aspect of her treatment of women. She attributes to the queens here qualities that in the nineteenth century were not commonly ascribed to women, which were seen as predominantly masculine: strong intellectual capacities, political acumen, and courage in time of war. When the queens were placed in situations that might call on these qualities, such as the role of regent or involvement in warfare, Lawrance implies, they could produce them. Lawrance also mentions that noblewomen were often empowered to handle and redress grievances on their husbands' estates (II, 30). But on the other hand, the queens engaged as well in behaviour that nineteenth-century readers would generally have construed as consistent with the female role of beneficent influence in a humanitarian cause, rather than the exercise of direct agency – such as Maude's efforts to reconcile Henry II with Becket, the celebrated intervention of Edward III's Queen, Philippa of Hainault, in the pardon of the burghers of Calais (II, 172–3), or Richard II's being persuaded by his Queen, Anne of Bohemia, to pardon those involved in Wat Tyler's rebellion (II, 222). The religious and charitable works ascribed to Empress Maude, as well as to other queens such as her mother Maude (Queen to Henry I), were also consistent with nineteenth-century assumptions about women's proper social role. Indeed in her *History of Woman*, Lawrance points to the overall 'softening and refining influence' of women in England after the Norman Conquest (216).

What Lawrance seems concerned to do, in her general histories and elsewhere, is to praise women's possession and practice of the virtues associated in her day with femininity, while at the same time suggesting that they can manifest intellectual and political capacities when these are required: her summing up of her enterprise at the end of the book on the queens includes the comment that she intended to illustrate their 'commanding talents' and their 'gentle virtues' (II, 450). Not that men and women are, in her view, innately the same. In her article on Elizabeth Barrett Browning, where she discusses the latter's 'Bertha in the Lane', Lawrance says the poem shows 'that secret, uncomplaining, almost Divine self-sacrifice which we recognise as especially characteristic of woman'. Although men are also capable of self-sacrifice, she goes on, 'the feminine nature is more forward to yield, to give way and adapt itself to circumstances, to work for those who … are unconscious of the love and care bestowed', whereas a man rather shows kindness 'when some outward recognition of it is possible'. Moreover, 'he is framed more to control and to command' (378). It is as if the two sexes possess the same basic capacities, but some are more predominant in men, others in women.

Women's capacities for long-suffering and self-sacrifice are also at stake in Lawrance's review of Elizabeth Gaskell's *Life of Charlotte Brontë*, a biography which stressed these aspects of its subject's life. Like most other readers until recently, Hannah Lawrance accepted Gaskell's version of Charlotte Brontë. She points to Brontë's 'stern sense of duty' and 'unselfish regard for others', and, after alluding to the dreadful family circumstances she endured in the late 1840s, declares: 'Little did those who censured so bitterly the passionate "unrest" of *Jane Eyre*, and the gloom so painful of some portions of *Shirley*, know amid what stern strife of conflicting feelings the one was written, amid what blank household desolation the other' (227, 229). Brontë's writing offered solace to herself, and pleasure to others, so how could 'wiseacres have found out that Charlotte Brontë's gifted mind was a fatal dowry?' (229). Brontë's suffering, her dutifulness, and the legacy of her writing to others, explain and excuse for Lawrance, as Gaskell hoped they would for readers in general, the traits for which Brontë's writing had been criticised.

But if Lawrance accepts that Brontë's feminine qualities manifested in life explain and justify her writing, there is also a sense in which she is using Brontë's life and works as ammunition to defend women's intellectual and literary aspirations in general. More characteristic of modern feminist critics than of her own contemporaries, for example, is her singling out Southey's now-notorious advice to Brontë of 1837, first disclosed in the Gaskell biography, as particularly reprehensible. Southey, she says, in his 'abundance of cold, formal advice', told Brontë that 'literature cannot be the business of a woman's life'. But in doing so, according to Lawrance, he was ignoring the achievement, already evident back in 1837, of women like Joanna Baillie, Harriet Martineau and Mary Russell Mitford. His real anxiety, she suspects, was a concern for female literary competition – and she goes on to align his motivation with that of the watchmakers and wood-engravers of the 1850s who were then trying to keep women out of their professions (225). Discussing the success of *Jane Eyre*, Lawrance expresses the wish, '[w]ould that Southey had been living to find out that literature could be a woman's business' (229), and he is presumably one of the 'wiseacres' mentioned a little further on who thought 'Charlotte Brontë's gifted mind was a fatal dowry'. Lawrance is also scathing about other significant men in Charlotte Brontë's life, such as her idle and dissipated brother Branwell, a cause of much tribulation to his sisters, and her father Patrick, whom she criticises at length for what she sees as his negligent, even cruel, upbringing of his children, and his indulgence of his only son: Lawrance uses Gaskell's revelations about both men to offer a more explicitly negative appraisal of them than does her source.

Although naturally not a focus of her discussion of Charlotte Brontë, salient in Lawrance's histories of women is their role as mothers, as her treatment of Empress Maude, Eleanor of Aquitaine and Margaret of Anjou might suggest: Maude and Eleanor were regents for their sons, Eleanor devoted herself to getting her son Richard released from prison, and Margaret's thoughts for the future during the Wars of the Roses were for her son. An explicit reason for writing both about medieval queens and about women of the twelfth century and earlier, is to highlight a neglected but crucial aspect of women's contribution to the nation's historical development: queens are important partly because their 'maternal counsels so frequently impressed a character of good, or ill, on the reign of the succeeding monarch' (*Queens*, I, iii), while the *History of Woman* aims to bring to light 'the women whose powerful influence moulded the characters of those, to whom we owe our national greatness' (iii–iv).

Motherhood in Victorian writing could of course be treated in a very sentimental way, and identified with womanhood to the extent that the role subsumed nearly all others, but in Lawrance's treatment of women, their role as mothers, while very important, is not all-consuming. The role also, in her view, demands attention partly because it has been neglected in history and literature. These points come together in the opening of Lawrance's survey article of 1865 on the works of Elizabeth Barrett Browning, a poet who for Lawrance, as for George Eliot, possessed the capacities usually associated with both men and women. Barrett Browning, she claims, had a 'far-seeing, masculine intellect' which 'fitted her for dealing ably with the great social questions of the day', plus a 'varied and extensive scholarship', and both a 'vigorous imagination' and 'eminent artistic power for the delineation of character'. The 'feminine' side was the emotional one: 'her ardent and impassioned temperament, her deeply Christian spirit, and overflowing sympathy and love' (359). This coexistence of 'masculine' and 'feminine' qualities in Barrett Browning evidently did not perturb Lawrance as they had done Sara Coleridge.

One of the main implications of Lawrance's account, moreover, is that all this power, masculine and feminine, could be harnessed to add a new dimension to literature: the revelation of the inner life of women. Men's poetry, argues Lawrance, focuses on the erotic effect of woman's beauty on men, on 'her tenderness or her fickleness', such that '[w]e see her now worshipped as an angel, and now cursed as if almost a fiend' (359–60). Woman is not portrayed from the inside, revealing 'feelings which lie concealed in the inmost depths of the heart', and one dimension of her experience particularly neglected in literature is her feelings as a mother. As we cannot remember 'the love which watched over us in our infancy, when consciousness was but just awakened', it is only a great poet that can evoke it, and that poet must be a woman (360). That is, a woman poet may possess the intellectual, conceptual and imaginative powers usually associated with male writers, while at the same time adding a dimension to literature that is beyond masculine ken.

Lawrance's account of Elizabeth Barrett Browning canvasses the question of why such a woman has only so recently emerged to give readers 'new ideas as to the capacities of her sex' (359), following the previous century and a half of women's poetry. Her answer is that women of the eighteenth and early nineteenth centuries were hampered by lack of education and encouragement, arising from assumptions about women's capacities and social role. She takes her cue from Barrett Browning's treatment of the issue in the account of her heroine's education in her epic about a woman poet, *Aurora Leigh* (1857), and then develops the subject (360–63). Women, Lawrance argues, had been 'taught to consider an intellectual career as a thing meant only for men', and that 'it was unwomanly and indelicate to speak out their healthy natural sentiments'; moreover, their only poetic models were 'artificial and insipid verse'. A girl of 'thoughtful and original intellect' would be considered 'masculine and unwomanly', almost a social outcast, while the 'geniuses … cast in a gentler mould' would 'give up thought, and write … sweet and graceful poems' of little real influence. The poetry of Felicia Hemans, according to Lawrance, bears witness to this latter trend. In addition, women were meant to be 'ignorant of the world of sin and shameful crime which lies but half concealed in our streets', and Barrett Browning is an innovator in this respect as well. She 'insists upon the independence of woman, and her ability to become, without loss of proper delicacy, an efficient worker in the world of mind', an insistence which Lawrance evidently endorses (363–4). Female 'delicacy' is at stake here, as so often in nineteenth-century discussions of women's writing, and Lawrance implies that there is no sacrifice of this quality entailed in a woman's having a strong awareness of the seamy side of life.

But the century and a half which incurs Lawrance's strictures here is for her a kind of nadir as far as the history of the education and opportunities open to women in Britain is concerned. One significant emphasis of her writing about earlier eras, especially the medieval and Anglo-Saxon periods, is that women's access to education, meaningful activity, lucrative employment and legal parity with men, was once much greater than it is in her own day. The situation as regards education is improving, as Barrett Browning's example suggests, but in other arenas there is a long way to go: one purpose of Lawrance's writings on women in earlier periods is not only to highlight the origins of multifarious aspects of modern life, but also to show implicitly how, as far as women were concerned, historical trends had actually been retrogressive.

Among the ancestors of the modern English, Lawrance argues, the northern races had a strong focus on individual rights, conceiving of the state as a collection of human beings rather than as an abstraction, and one consequence of this was to enhance the status of women. Moreover, on account of the influence of Christianity, there was a high value attached to the virtues which were in Lawrance's day conceived of as feminine, such as piety, devotion, caring, mercifulness and self-sacrifice (*Queens*, II, 3–4). Yet this valuing of feminine virtues went in tandem with the fostering of female education: money was actually set aside specifically for this purpose (II, 26). The early years of Christianity in Britain were notable for the spread of learning among women, including knowledge of Latin: for example, Alfred the Great founded three abbeys for women (Shaftesbury, Wilton and Winchester), which 'were established with a liberality to which later days can lay no claim as free schools for the instruction of his *female* subjects' (*Woman*, 100, 130–32, Lawrance's emphasis). Later, in the twelfth century, under Henry I, further abbeys and priories for women were founded, and women continued to have access to education in convent schools. Indeed for the Protestant Lawrance, the opportunities convents afforded for female education was their most significant feature (*Woman*, 263–5, 291).

Although the focus of Lawrance's histories of medieval and pre-medieval women is not specifically on women as authors, she does sometimes draw attention to their writings. These include 'The Lives of St Willibald and St Wunebald', written by a nun in the 780s, the learned correspondence of Henry I's consort Maude with Anselm (*Woman*, 101ff., 224f.), and the twelfth-century lais of Marie de France, which she declares to be superior to the works of the contemporary male Anglo-Norman trouvères 'both in grace and feeling' (*Queens*, I, 365n). In an article for the *British Quarterly* on 'George Herbert and Contemporary Religious Poets', Lawrance criticises publishers of series of British poets for some of their omissions, such as women poets Mary, Countess of Pembroke, and Joanna Baillie.[10] There is much emphasis too, in her histories of women, on their crucial roles as patrons of literature and the arts.

In describing convent education for women, Lawrance assures her nineteenth-century readers that, although the female students had the same literary instruction as the male, they also learned, and learned to respect, 'the duties and occupations of women' (*Woman*, 310–11). But these 'duties and occupations' might be, according to Lawrance, part of an important and responsible role in the convent or household.

---

[10] *British Quarterly Review*, 19 (April 1854): 377–407, at 377.

In convent life, women might take on positions of great responsibility, even being in charge of men (*Woman*, 69f., *Queens*, II, 27). In secular life, mistresses of households were the ones who got in the stores, and provided the clothing (*Queens*, II, 28ff.), as well as often being familiar with medicine and other sources of practical help (*Queens*, I, 25): they could be in sole charge, too, given the time men spent away at war. The comparison with the present is sometimes explicit: in the twelfth century, Lawrance declares, 'the mistress of an extensive household was not the mere creature of showy accomplishments' (*Queens*, I, 25).

Women of past centuries also had greater access to legal and property rights and to employment, according to Lawrance. In Saxon times, she explains in her *History of Woman*, women could possess, inherit or transmit property, could sue and be sued, and had rights to the clothes, jewels and plate they brought to a marriage – none of which rights were available to married women in Lawrance's society until near the end of her life, when the Married Women's Property Act of 1870 extended to them some property rights (44ff.). In the twelfth century, women were still 'in fuller possession of independent property, and, probably, more actively engaged in trade, than even in the present day' (357). In the book on the queens, Lawrance points out that the widows and daughters of guild members could practise their husbands' and fathers' trades, while women lower down in the social scale could earn a living from spinning and/or weaving. This is one reason why 'during these ages, miscalled dark and barbarous, every woman who sought to support herself by her industry, was secure, not merely of a livelihood, but of a comfortable and honourable independence', whereas the present affords 'so melancholy a contrast' (II, 155–6).

Embroidery and sewing, in Lawrance's account, function in the nineteenth century in very different ways than in past centuries: the 'melancholy' aspect of the present condition of women is that sewing for a living is the expedient of thousands of women with no education or access to skilled trades, a grinding task they practise for long hours and for starvation wages. On the other hand, impecunious middle and upper-class women, limited in their choice of employment, cannot have recourse to this means of livelihood without becoming declassed. By contrast, impoverished high-born women in the Middle Ages could take to embroidery to support themselves, without losing caste (*Woman*, 156). A further baneful aspect of sewing for nineteenth-century women emerges in Lawrance's article in *Household Words* on Hannah Woolley, author of the 1672 *Gentlewoman's Companion*. Woolley advocates teaching girls Latin, French and Italian, and criticises the contemporary parents who instead '"suffer their children to spin away their precious time, or pore over a sampler, untill they have pricked out the very date of their life"'.[11] Sewing, Lawrance suggests, is a desperate expedient for poverty-stricken lower-class women with no other options, but one closed to their middle and upper-class counterparts, while for those with no financial need to

---

[11]   *Household Words*, 4 August 1855: 18–22, at 19.

work, it can degenerate to a mindless way of occupying time better spent on more substantial pursuits.

Lawrance's writings on the history and achievements of women ascribe to women qualities considered in her day feminine, such as a penchant for self-sacrifice, charitableness, and beneficial moral influence; they highlight as well the historical and literary importance of women's roles as mothers. But they also draw attention to capacities in women generally seen as masculine, such as strong intellectual powers, managerial skills, and political acumen. Lawrance's approach to her own work as an historian, in terms of contemporary assumptions about female historians, replicates this double focus.

Rohan Maitzen has discussed Lawrance's historical volumes in the context of expectations of men's and women's historical writing in the nineteenth century. Women, she points out, were considered suited to writing memoirs rather than to writing history proper, as it was then conceived. The reason for this, expressed in the assertions of male historians such as John Mitchell Kemble and Thomas Babington Macaulay, was that women were thought to have narrative facility, and in particular a good eye for the details of individual facts, but, correspondingly, to lack an ability to grasp the big picture, to assimilate and analyse the facts they could accumulate, and to operate on an abstract level intellectually.[12] Such views are of course consistent with what was often said about women's aptitudes in writing fiction. Women's supposed eye for detail, however, especially as applied to private life, was apposite for composing social history, which focused partly on the everyday and on domestic life.[13] As my discussion here has already suggested, Lawrance's two works of women's history have a strong focus on cultural and social history: the one on the queens, for example, has a 30-page chapter on 'The Arts in the Thirteenth Century' (I, 381–412, covering architecture, decorative painting, stained glass, sepulchral effigies, glass-painting, sculpture, engraving, and illuminated manuscripts), extensive treatment of literature (I, 269–302, 437ff., II, 254–75), a detailed description of life in London in the early fourteenth century (II, 124ff.), and 36 pages on 'Society in England During the Middle Ages' (II, 1–36) encompassing the political, social and religious condition of the English, and especially, of course, the lives of women.

A related contemporary development in historiography was a greater emphasis on the impact of indirect agency, on how events might arise from diffuse causes, and large changes take effect as the result of multiple small changes. This focus was amenable to the kinds of agency women might possess: influence rather than direct action, and operating on a micro rather than a macro level.[14] Such a trend is also relevant to Lawrance's histories, with their concern with household-level activity, their exploration of indirect agency such as that of mothers, and their

---

[12] *Gender, Genre, and Victorian Historical Writing* (New York and London: Garland, 1998), 8ff.

[13] Ibid., p. 16.

[14] Ibid., p. 40.

identification of female influence. She engages with the arenas in which she sees women functioning in the past, and points to their importance.

But this does not mean that Lawrance eschews history proper (as her contemporaries saw it) – the worlds of politics, battles, diplomacy and ecclesiastical developments. She does say early in the book on the queens that she does not 'intend to encroach upon the province of general history' (I, 60), and later, in broaching the conflict between Henry II and Becket, she observes that since this belongs to 'the political history of the day', it is 'hence inadmissible here' (I, 210). But these are tactical disclaimers – Lawrance by no means ignores political, military, diplomatic and ecclesiastical history. This is partly because her queens sometimes participated in such matters, of course, but she also treats of events beyond their involvement. She takes the opportunity to write quite extensively, for example, about the Henry II–Becket struggle, partly to emphasise that she has consulted sources contemporary with the events being treated. Earlier accounts, Lawrance argues, have relied too much on biased, anti-Becket material deriving from Henry VIII's reign over three centuries later (I, 210ff.). Although the public dimension of history is not her overall focus, it does receive some detailed coverage in this book. That is, just as the women she writes about, in her view, manifest feminine and masculine qualities, Hannah Lawrance herself, as historian, displays her substantial erudition, and, despite her claims to the contrary, unites the fields of male history and female memoir.

Jane Williams

The literary output of Jane Williams (1806–85) was quite diverse. Much of it had a Welsh focus: although born in London, she spent much of her life in Nevadd Felen, near Talgarth in Brecon, where she had originally been sent for her health. Learning the Welsh language, she became part of Lady Llanover's circle, which was concerned with the language and the romantic Welsh tradition.[15] (This is an interest she shared with Hannah Lawrance, although there is no evidence that the two women knew each other.) Accordingly, in 1848, Williams defended the Welsh against the aspersions contained in the *Reports of the Commissioners of Enquiry into the State of Education in Wales* (*Artegall; or Remarks on the Reports of the Commissioners of Enquiry into the State of Education in Wales*), and several years later, published the *Literary Remains of the Reverend Thomas Price, Carnhuanawc* (2 vols, 1854–5); her religious interests had already been demonstrated in her *Twenty Essays on the Practical Improvement of God's Providential Dispensations as Means to the Moral Discipline to the Christian* (1838). In 1869 came the substantial *History of Wales Derived from Authentic Sources*.

[15]   *The Autobiography of Elizabeth Davis Betsy Cadwaladyr A Balaclava Nurse. Daughter of Dafydd Cadwaladyr*, ed. Jane Williams (1857), ed. with new intro. by Deirdre Beddoe (Cardiff: Honno, 1987), p. x.

Williams was also concerned with the history and achievements of women. Indeed, her interests in Welsh history and in the lives of women came together in her attempt to produce an autobiography of a Welsh working-class woman, Elizabeth Davis (or Betsy Cadwaladyr), in 1857. As her subject was illiterate, Williams transcribed Davis's words, adapting them somewhat for publication. This early attempt at oral history also had a topical resonance, since Davis had been a nurse in the Crimea, and was critical of Florence Nightingale. A few years later, Williams produced the work which I will concentrate on here, *The Literary Women of England*.[16] The book's scope is suggested by its protracted subtitle: *Including a Biographical Epitome of all the Most Eminent to the Year 1700; and Sketches of the Poetesses to the Year 1850; with Extracts from Their Works, and Critical Remarks.*

If Jane Williams was induced to focus on issues of gender as an adult, it seems that as a child she inhabited an almost genderless fantasy. She was the second of the seven children of a civil servant in the Navy Office, three boys and four girls. From her account of them, the children lived for many years among the 'paper people', a whole world in miniature which they created out of paper cut-out figures, and the models and texts they produced as a context for these figures' lives – just as the Brontë children (slightly younger than the Williamses), famously created the lands of Angria and Gondal from Branwell's toy soldiers. The Williams children's paper world was, according to Jane, their principal means of education, and was truly comprehensive, encompassing many countries. For Britain alone, they constructed the Tower, the Treasury, the Horse Guards, the Bank of England, Buckingham Palace, Westminster Abbey, the Houses of Parliament, the GPO, railways, fully equipped houses, stables, inns and hotels, with figures representing the Government and the Civil Service, the universities, the clergy, mayors, judges and the armed forces. The texts included parliamentary proceedings and bills, 'hundreds of tiny letters minutely written, upon all imaginable subjects', plus verses, prose histories, essays, lessons, trials by judge and jury, documents relating to civil contentions and overseas wars, 'with innumerable inflexions, unisons, and combinations of circumstances continually arising'.[17]

As this summary suggests, this was very much a public world, focused on what at the period were male activities, and generally activities concerned with public life. The implication of Williams's account is that this masculine realm was as open to the imaginations and the play of the girls as to those of the boys. In one respect, however, the children imbibed contemporary notions of gender roles. Usually the boys played with male figures and the girls with female, with each child having particular figures in his or her charge. Each figure was accessible as well to the siblings of the same sex as its owner, and it was also the case that the male figures

---

[16]   (London: Saunders, Otley and Co., 1861). Subsequent references to this book will be included parenthetically in the text.

[17]   *The Origin, Rise, and Progress of the Paper People, For My Little Friends* (London: Grant and Griffith, 1856), pp. 15, 21ff., 27–31.

were available to the girls, whereas the female ones were not available to the boys. This was apparently not out of a desire for fair division (since there must have been more male figures than female ones), but because they 'all felt an instinctive horror of masculine women' – presumably they thought the female figures would behave in a masculine way once the boys got hold of them!

When Jane Williams came to write *The Literary Women of England*, she concentrated, as her subtitle suggests, on women's practice of poetry. Poetry was still in the mid nineteenth century considered an elevated literary genre, requiring a technical knowledge ultimately deriving from the classical Greek and Latin poets. Williams's comments on women's overall achievement in poetry, compared to that of men, suggest that the imaginative realm she was willing to grant them was much more circumscribed than that she had herself inhabited in her childhood: she declares that '[t]he women of every age take its spirit from the men, and their share in the national poetry is like their part in a concert, to which men's voices give fullness and power, and of which men are the musical composers and directors' (142). She has already ascribed to women writers characteristics then seen as feminine – 'intuitive fineness of perception, rapidity of apprehension, tenderness, delicacy and a certain persuasive sweetness' (132) – what she calls women's 'own soft glory'. Williams seems, then, to deny to women both a strong poetic voice, and poetic originality, while her childhood 'horror of masculine women' has apparently revived to limit her view of her own sex's powers. At the end of her volume, after detailing the lives and literary works of multifarious women over the centuries, she seems to want to contain their literary endeavours further. She asserts forcibly:

> no talent with which a favoured individual may be gifted, no capacity for knowledge, no aptitude for artistic accomplishments; no taste, however discriminating; no genius however fine and powerful, can constitute an admissible plea for the neglect of even the smallest act of domestic duty: that the claims of a parent or a brother, of a husband, a child, or a household … must take habitual and unhesitating precedence of all intellectual pursuits. (558–9)

The starkness of Williams's claims in her general commentary, about the limited and subordinate role of women's poetry and the pre-eminence of their domestic duties, is nonetheless contradicted by the actual content of her book, her treatment of an array of individual women writers. In asserting the importance of domestic obligations, Williams does in fact acknowledge women's potential for more than the qualities usually associated with femininity – for 'capacity for knowledge', and for 'genius … fine and powerful'. The overall premise of her study is indeed that women's literary achievements have been neglected. She had originally undertaken to write a critical and biographical sketch of Felicia Hemans, but had come to feel the need for '*a compendious work exclusively appropriated to a summary view of our literary countrywomen*' (4, Williams's emphasis). The *Biographia Britannica*, Williams found, was slapdash and demeaning in its treatment of women writers (cf. Lawrance's comments on the historiography of women), 'with the most important notice of female writers lurking in all sorts of improbable corners, carelessly treated, and often shut out from the index' (5–6).

Like Lawrance, Williams champions women's intellectual capacities throughout her work. Women's education in the Anglo-Saxon period, she claims, was the same as men's (has she perhaps read Lawrance?), and she discusses several learned women of the period, such as Hilda, Abbess of Whitby, Abbess Eadburga, Ethelfleda the daughter of Alfred the Great, Editha wife of Edward the Confessor, plus, from the medieval period, Henry I's successive Queens Maude (or Matilda) and Adeliza, the playwright Hroswitha, Juliana Prioress of Sopewell, and Marie de France (16–23). Later centuries produced Lady Margaret Beaufort (31–3, mother of Henry VII), the fine Latin scholar Queen Catherine Parr (45), the daughters of Sir Thomas More, adept at both Greek and Latin, and 'esteemed the most learned and accomplished women of their time' (40–41), Mildred, Lady Burleigh, notable for her knowledge of Greek, her sister Anne (mother of Francis Bacon), who translated from Latin to English Bishop Jewell's *Apologie* (59ff.), Mary Countess of Pembroke (73ff.), the neglect of whom Lawrance had also noted, and the eighteenth-century Catherine Cockburn, of 'extraordinary mental powers' (187). Among more specifically creative writers, Susannah Centlivre in the eighteenth century wrote plays 'all more or less remarkable for ability, and the comedies especially for cleverness' (152), while of the novelist and poet Charlotte Smith, Williams writes that '[h]er mind had naturally great scope, comprising the high imaginative power of an inborn poet, with the accuracy of detail and sound commonsense which constitute the woman of business and worldly wisdom' (224).

If Charlotte Smith could combine masculine and feminine qualities, she was not alone. For example, Lucy Hutchinson, the seventeenth-century biographer of her husband in her *Memoir of the Life of Colonel Hutchinson*, is in Williams's view remarkable for 'a combination of mental power and domestic ability with affections at once so tender and true' (93). Williams also points out that many literary women of the seventeenth century and earlier had been married, and concludes that 'it would appear that their mental pursuits had not weakened their domestic affections' (130): intellectual and literary activity are not really incompatible with feminine feelings and household duty. She makes the same point, in fact, about Maria Jane Jewsbury: although she was not married for most of her literary life, Jewsbury had strong domestic ties and responsibilities, and in Williams's view, combined 'an extraordinary mind' with 'an enlarged and noble heart' (373). Having had access via Jewsbury's siblings to her unpublished letters and journal of her voyage to India, and being aware that Jewsbury had been an *Athenaeum* contributor, Williams praises the descriptive powers evident in the journal, and regrets that 'many of the best pieces which she ever composed still remain entombed, though embalmed, in the thick quartos' of the magazine (369). Not a writer who herself published anonymously, Williams implies that doing so for a woman impedes the proper recognition of her contribution to literature.

On the other hand, Williams does perceive that publishing overtly as female might induce a literary woman to project a particular image of femininity in order to accommodate readers' assumptions about women's writing. This point emerges in her treatment of the early nineteenth-century poets, Felicia Hemans and Letitia Elizabeth Landon ('L.E.L.'), who both wrote, often desperately, to support themselves and family members. Like Lawrance, Williams recognises that the nature of Hemans's output was influenced by a felt need to fit in with contemporary conceptions of women's capacities. She quotes a letter of Hemans's where she regrets that financial pressures had obliged her to write so many '"desultory effusions"', rather than '"some more noble and complete work which … might permanently take its place as the work of a British poetess"' (473). In addition, Hemans had confined to her unpublished poems and letters, her talents for 'raillery' and 'drollery', her 'powers of wit and satire' (432). A similar effort to live up to a particular image of the woman poet is evident for Williams in the work of Letitia Landon, whom she presents as projecting a soulfully tragic and lovelorn persona at odds with her actual life and temperament: she quotes the comment by Laman Blanchard in his biography of Landon, that she '"aimed at assuming a character for the sake of a certain kind of effect"', such that '"[s]orrow and suspicion, pining, regrets for the past, anguish for the present, and morbid predictions for the future, were, in L.E.L., not moral characteristics, but merely literary resources"'. Landon wrote, affirms Williams, 'in accordance with her own idea of a poetess' (502–3) – a perception which foreshadows Glennis Stephenson's comments on Landon's literary criticism, mentioned in my Introduction. Femininity is therefore for Williams to some extent a performance, rather than a manifestation of innate tendencies, and the need to perform it could oblige women writers to constrain the expression of their intellectual and creative talents.

Moreover, if a woman was to demonstrate capacities generally construed as masculine, it was helpful if her physical appearance and demeanour were particularly feminine, as Williams observes in discussing the polymath Anna Letitia Barbauld. Barbauld had learned Latin and Greek (282), had become conversant with the physical sciences through her friendship with scientist Joseph Priestley and his circle (284), and had attained a 'fertile and richly-cultivated mind' (289). Her writing was notable for 'extensive and exact knowledge … sagacious and acute powers of original thought, a lively and inventive fancy, a copious treasury of English diction, a correct application of words, and a polished brightness of style more generally attained by the masculine than feminine intellect' (294). Hence '[h]er Essay "On Monastic Institutions" would do credit … in comprehensive grasp and rhetorical power, to a University Professor of Modern History', while '"The Hill of Science" might have passed unquestioned by the keenest critics as an allegory worthy of Addison's elegant mind, and of winning even for him additional glory' (294). But crucially, Barbauld garnered admiration for her abilities, rather than criticism or jealousy, because her appearance and behaviour rendered her attainments unthreatening:

Her personal beauty, fine figure, exquisite complexion of red and white, delicately-chiselled features, dark-blue eyes radiant with intelligent vivacity, an air of perfect health and social enjoyment, sufficed to procure pardon from the most invidious scholars; while the absence of pride and pretension in every form, and the charm of invariable affability, secured her from the envy of her female acquaintance. (284)

Williams implies that Barbauld's conduct was unforced rather than consciously performed, but also that the prejudices against intellect and literary talent that her appearance and behaviour countered, were in themselves unwarranted.

So although Jane Williams ostensibly argued in *The Literary Women of England* that women's literary capacities were limited, and that they should always be sacrificed to domestic duty, these comments in themselves may be efforts on her part to accommodate contemporary notions of women, to make her own book seem unthreatening while advancing its claims for women's achievements. This perhaps recalls her childhood stance in relation to the 'paper people': the Williams girls' denying their brothers access to the female figures ostensibly reflected the siblings' 'horror of masculine women', but, since the girls could use the male figures, it was a strategy that gave the girls a full experience of their imaginary world.

Julia Kavanagh

As I have suggested, one reason that Williams is circumspect in her claims for women's writing is that she is concentrating on the elevated genre of poetry. Publishing in the wake of *The Literary Women of England*, the two literary histories by Julia Kavanagh (1824–77), *French Women of Letters* (1861) and *English Women of Letters* (1862) focus squarely on women's contribution to the novel. This genre, although gaining in respect, still carried less prestige than poetry, because it was newer, did not require erudition, and had no obvious rules to be mastered. But partly because of this, it was easier to claim that women had a significant role in establishing and developing the genre, and this is what Julia Kavanagh did. In the Preface to *French Women of Letters*, she declared that the novel was the 'only branch' of literature 'in which women have acquired undisputed eminence', but also 'the great feature of modern literature', and for many people, 'the teacher[-] of good or for evil'.[18] The great pioneers here were Mlle de Scudéry and Mme de la Fayette, in the seventeenth century; in England in the same century, meanwhile, Aphra Behn's *Oroonoko* inaugurated the 'great English school of passion and nature, of dramatic and pathetic incident', and in the last 70 years, '[t]he character

---

[18]   *French Women of Letters: Biographical Sketches* (2 vols, London: Hurst and Blackett, 1861), vol. 1, p. v. Subsequent references to these volumes will be included parenthetically in the text.

of the English novel has … been much modified by what threatens to become an overwhelming influence – that of women'.[19]

Like Lawrance and Williams, Kavanagh was versatile in her literary repertoire, although she apparently did not manage to publish on all the subjects that interested her. As a young woman she began to support herself and her invalid mother through her writing: she was the only child of Sophie (also known as Bridget) Fitzpatrick and Morgan Kavanagh, and the family spent most of Julia's childhood in France, making her conversant with French literature and culture. Morgan Kavanagh, who devoted much of his energy to publishing dubious theories of linguistics, seems to have deserted his wife and daughter some time in the late 1840s.[20] So Julia began to publish work in periodicals, including *The Athenaeum*, *Chambers' Journal*, *Chambers' Miscellany*, the *Popular Record*, the *People's Journal* and *Eliza Cook's Journal*. Her specialty was reviewing French works, such as Lamartine's *History of the Girondins* (*Athenaeum*, April–September 1847), and writing about French proletarian and peasant culture. There is evidence in her correspondence with the editors of the *Chambers'* publications that she would have liked to range more widely: she offered, unsuccessfully, to write on ancient Roman manners and customs, the life and manners of the inhabitants of the Polar regions, the indigenous inhabitants of Australia and Polynesia, and the history of Venice and its government.

Julia Kavanagh was also a prolific novelist, and, with the success of *Nathalie* in 1850, reached a financially firmer footing: the publisher Richard Bentley offered her £300 for the copyright of her next three-volume novel. A year later, her father was not above boasting about her achievements, as Sara Coleridge's correspondence reveals: Sara Coleridge was employing him as a mesmerist, and her letters to her brother Derwent and sister-in-law Mary late in 1851 show Morgan Kavanagh discussing his daughter's literary career, remarking on how she had apparently written for years in vain before her recent success.[21] In 1857, the rascally publisher T.C. Newby would take advantage of her fame to publish a poor novel of her father's, *The Hobbies*, under her name. (This was the publisher who had exploited the popularity of *Jane Eyre* by promoting *Wuthering Heights* and Anne Brontë's first novel, *Agnes Grey*, as also the works of 'Currer Bell'.)

In her Preface to *French Women of Letters*, Kavanagh said that she aimed as a woman at 'rescuing from forgetfulness the labours and the names once honoured and celebrated of other women' (I, vi). Before embarking on her two specifically

---

[19]   *English Women of Letters: Biographical Sketches* (2 vols, London: Hurst and Blackett, 1862), vol. 1, pp. 48, 4. Subsequent references to these volumes will be included parenthetically in the text.

[20]   For information on Kavanagh's life and publications, I am indebted to Amanda J. Collins, 'Grave Duties of the Caretaker in the Lives of Charlotte Brontë' (PhD thesis, Sydney: University of Sydney, 2004), 18ff.

[21]   Letters of 28 October 1851 to Mary Coleridge, and 7 November 1851 to Derwent Coleridge, Harry Ransom Center, University of Texas at Austin.

literary histories of women, however, Julia Kavanagh had published two other works of women's history: *Woman in France During the Eighteenth Century* (1850) and *Women of Christianity: Exemplary Acts of Piety and Charity* (1852), which shared something of the same purpose. In *Woman in France*, she wanted to draw attention to a circumstance not fully acknowledged by other historians – the unparalleled power that eighteenth-century French women exercised, a power more 'real' than had been evident in the 'idolatrous homage' which their beauty and defencelessness had attracted in the days of chivalry.[22] In *Women of Christianity*, she strove to draw attention to more traditionally feminine but also powerful forces that had acted on the world since the advent of Christianity – forces which had been neglected by male historians in favour of men's deeds in politics, in war and peace, and in intellectual developments.[23] History had barely registered 'woman in the peace and quiet beauty of her domestic life, in the gentleness of her love, in the courage of her charity, in the holiness of her piety' (1). Whereas men may gain renown because they 'liberate nations and win realms', what is forgotten is the multitudes 'redeemed from misery' or 'conquered to heaven' by women (466).

There are differences of emphasis between these two early works. The prominence of women in eighteenth-century France, Kavanagh argues, derived from the system of monarchical absolutism, where almost all men lacked political power, and there was no forum for the open debate of political issues: hence men had little more political agency than women. The book on Christian women, by contrast, presupposes a strong demarcation between the social roles of the sexes. But the two works share a focus on women in the female role of exercising influence rather than agency, while claiming for this influence great significance. In pre-Revolutionary France, Kavanagh claims, salons hosted by women were the key sites for bringing together those of both sexes interested in literary, scientific and political issues. Although the women were not always well-educated, this could also be an asset, in the sense that male intellectuals therefore needed to explain their ideas with great clarity (I, 162), and while salon women were not generally prominent as authors, they sometimes influenced notable male writers, such as Mme de Tencin's impact on Montesquieu's *De l'Esprit des lois* and on Helvétius's *De l'Esprit* (I, 98). The ideas and works fostered in the salons, Kavanagh contends, had tremendous influence on the intellectual and social trends which eventually helped to precipitate the Revolution. She even argues that, in the private salon world and in her letters, Mlle de l'Espinasse reveals herself to be a sort of female version of the outspoken Rousseau: she experienced the private

---

[22] *Woman in France During the Eighteenth Century* (2 vols, 1850, repr. London: G.P. Putnam's Sons, 1893), vol. 1, pp. 3–4. Subsequent references to these volumes will be included parenthetically in the text.

[23] *Women of Christianity, Exemplary for Acts of Piety and Charity* (London: Smith, Elder, 1852), p. 1. Subsequent references to this book will be included parenthetically in the text.

effects of the social inequality that Rousseau felt and wrote of so forcibly, since her love affairs were always hampered by her poverty and her illegitimacy (I, 191–2). Ironically, however, the Revolution itself curtailed women's power, by confining political rights to men and keeping women shut out from many means of livelihood (II, 251).

Women in eighteenth-century France demonstrated, for Kavanagh, considerable intellectual powers, even if these did not usually manifest themselves in publications. Like men, women were 'earnestly seeking, through all the mists and errors of human knowledge, to solve the great social and political problems which still agitate us in our day' (II, 259). Intellectual attainments are also prominent in some of the Christian exemplars Kavanagh discusses: the early Christian women of Rome and Greece could be 'learned as well as pious' (34), such as Eudocia, wife of Emperor Theodosius II (48ff.), while later the cloister attracted many women possessing 'a love of study and science' (71), including the playwright Hroswitha also mentioned by Williams; the sixteenth century, meanwhile, was 'eminently the age of learned women' (147). Some women even exercised political influence, such as Theodosius II's sister Pulcheria, the only member of the imperial family equal to state duties (45), and, much more recently, Hannah More's writings had had an impact that was 'political, moral, and religious' (319).

Women of Christianity thus recalls Lawrance's histories in its implication that intellectual and political abilities might coexist with more conventionally feminine qualities. It also resembles these earlier histories in seeking to complicate representations of women of the past. Just as Lawrance combated stereotypical views of some of her queens, Kavanagh strove to alter the reductive images of pious women contained in other biographical accounts. Whereas the accepted images of some of Lawrance's queens fitted very negative stereotypes, the images of pious women offered by biographers fitted positive ones – but stereotypes which for Kavanagh denied the possible complexity and individuality of women's spiritual lives. In a frustrated tone, Kavanagh in her Preface complains of the problems presented by her sources: the biographers' sympathies are limited, and they cater to 'fastidiousness' in their readers, so that the biographies possess a 'painful and wearisome similarity'. The good are not really alike, but the biographies 'praised when they should have painted, and suppressed characteristic touches as undignified' (iv–v). Kavanagh reiterates the stricture when discussing seventeenth-century English women: 'their memory has been dismissed with vague and commonplace eulogy' (250).

Kavanagh's contention here is that biographies of pious women flatten them into repetitive religious exemplars, as if all pious women are the same. What this tendency denies, as well as the women's individuality, is the reality and vitality of their spiritual experience. Rather than being instinctively and straightforwardly devout, as the biographers (and no doubt conservative readers of Kavanagh's day) would have preferred, women had been offered, by the advent of Christianity, access to 'the long-denied world of spiritual knowledge', to '[s]ublime and speculative theories', to the opportunity to meditate 'on questions that had long troubled philosophers in the groves of Academia' (4). Spiritual experience for women was intense, changing, and sometimes mentally challenging, as it was accepted as being for men. Piety and devotion to good works, moreover, were not achieved by women without struggle and without sacrifices that were painful – there was nothing automatic or instinctive about them. In dealing with the prison reformer Elizabeth Fry, for example, Kavanagh pays much attention to Fry's early grapplings with the temptations of pleasure, outings and flirtation, a move which complicates the traditional image of the serenely virtuous and pious Quaker. But '[e]very human being whose story is told', declares Kavanagh, 'has a right to have the tale related even as it befell' (425). Alison Booth has noted that Kavanagh was one of the few nineteenth-century 'presenters of good women' who rejected 'the idea of a unified womanhood', and a case in point is her treatment of Elizabeth Fry, which avoids the straightforward hagiography common in accounts of the celebrated reformer.[24]

Both *Woman in France* and *Women of Christianity* suggest that, like Lawrance and Williams, Kavanagh believed in women's intellectual potential. This is also evident in her works of literary criticism, where she several times draws attention to the deleterious effects of the differences in education between the sexes. Whereas boys 'are trained to act a part in life, and a part worth acting', she observes in *English Women of Letters*, 'girls are either taught to look on life, or, worse still, told how to practise its light and unworthy arts' (II, 87). Discussing the once-popular late eighteenth-century novelist Anne Radcliffe, she argues that, '[h]ad Anne Radcliffe been John Radcliffe, and received the vigorous and polished education which makes the man and the gentleman', then the resulting novels would have been fewer, but better (I, 255). In *French Women of Letters*, she condemns Molière's ridicule of Mlle de Scudéry and other women of intellectual pretensions (the 'précieuses'), as 'cruel and ungenerous', since 'women were not too learned, as he knew, but too ignorant, and his sarcasms frightened them into further ignorance' (I, 169). Scudéry herself was motivated by a wish to 'improve the moral, social and intellectual condition of women', and realised that pedantry in them could be blamed on too little, rather than too much, knowledge (I, 157, 160).

Much of Kavanagh's literary criticism, however, is devoted to defining the specific qualities which women novelists brought to the development of French and English fiction. One important quality she identifies, recalling Lawrance's comments on Elizabeth Barrett Browning's poetry, is the kind of insight into women's inner lives to which male writers supposedly have no access. Whereas men's novels might exemplify a 'coarse and low ideal of womanhood', primarily as 'the embodiment of beauty and the object of passion', women novelists have 'delighted in the internal woman, that mystery which man has rarely fathomed'. They have 'developed feelings which [a male writer] could only divine, and analyzed, with minuteness and power, that changeable though faithful world

---

[24]   *How to Make it as a Woman: Collective Biographical History from Victoria to the Present* (Chicago and London: University of Chicago Press, 2004), pp. 65, 147ff.

which lies enclosed in a woman's heart' (*English Women of Letters*, II, 198–203). Women writers are also able to expose in their fiction the crudity and contemptuous attitudes to women that they have encountered in real-life men, as is suggested by Fanny Burney's Mr Smith and Sir Robert Floyer, Maria Edgeworth's Sir Philip Baddeley, and Jane Austen's Mr Collins: such figures 'display to our ridicule and scorn the long triumphant insolence with which coarse and ill-bred men choose to treat women' (I, 139).

Mme de la Fayette's *La Princesse de Clèves*, meanwhile, is particularly ground-breaking, as it has influenced, directly or indirectly, all subsequent love-stories in English and French. She showed, says Kavanagh, that 'there was a vein of rich ore in gentle feelings', and could portray 'what we see daily, what we can all understand and sympathise with' (*French Women of Letters*, I, 200–202). In this novel about a woman tempted to commit adultery, Mme de la Fayette deals with 'the perils of our own weakness and our own hearts; the dangers of youth, of love, of beauty, of all that can charm man and woman away from the cold and narrow path of duty'. Thus she reaches 'the centre of all interest – the heart and conscience of a human being', and '[t]he greatest, the finest, domestic novels that have been written since then possess no other' (I, 202, 253). The implication here is that Mme de la Fayette was the model for writers of both sexes for the exploration of the inner psychological life, a characteristic which, by the time Kavanagh is writing, was especially valued in fiction.

In *French Women of Letters*, Kavanagh calls both Mme de la Fayette and her fiction 'delicate' (I, 180, 200); in her subsequent book, she specifically ascribes to women's fiction what she calls 'feminine attributes' – 'delicacy', 'tenderness', 'purity' and 'sympathy' – and argues that women's works always possess at least one of these (I, 5; II, 188; cf. Williams's very similar list). But this premise does lead to some tensions in Kavanagh's discussion. This is partly because 'purity' is not always an asset to women's fiction, while 'delicacy' in *English Women of Letters* becomes a very fluid term as she tries to demarcate women's from men's fiction.

In discussing Sarah Fielding's novel *David Simple*, Kavanagh contends that women cannot write picaresque fiction (such as that readily associated with Sarah Fielding's brother Henry), because 'it exacts close and accurate knowledge of the world's evil ways, and though these need not be shown, they must be known'. She goes on: 'purity must be proved [tested] in the selection, not in the ignorance, of those sad realities' (I, 57–8) – as if women must be kept unaware of vice for fear of harming the said purity. This is obviously a conservative view: proto-feminists of the mid nineteenth century – not least Barrett Browning in *Aurora Leigh*, as we have seen – argued that women could and should be exposed to vice, and that 'virtue' based on ignorance was not true virtue. Certainly Sarah Fielding's novel, according to Kavanagh, is weakened by what she does not know, although Kavanagh apparently does not wish her to have known more.

Ambivalence over 'purity' and all it implies emerges most strongly, however, in Kavanagh's treatment of Aphra Behn. Kavanagh is dubious about Behn's sexual behaviour, condemns the 'inveterate coarseness of her mind' (I, 7), and declares that 'she loved grossness for its own sake', so that she ignored the 'noble' literary examples of Mlle de Scudéry and Mme de la Fayette that were available to her (I, 21). Behn and 'her pupils', rather than 'raising man to woman's moral standard', reduced 'woman to the level of man's coarseness' (I, 22). But Kavanagh's commentary is at least much more nuanced than that of Jane Williams, who expressed embarrassment at having to deal with Behn at all: Behn is only included in *The Literary Women of England* for the sake of comprehensiveness, and because her novel *Oroonoko* was a source for a tragedy by Thomas Southerne. In Williams's view, she is 'the first English authoress upon record whose life was openly wrong, and whose writings were obscene' (*Literary Women of England*, 127–8). Kavanagh concedes the obscenity, but is much less harsh on Behn's supposed sexual misdemeanours. In the Netherlands, Behn may have traded sexual favours for news of Dutch plans to invade England, but Kavanagh fails to condemn her, lambasting instead the men who scorned her information – they were either traitors to their country, or too patronising towards women to credit Behn's serious political agenda (I, 12ff.).

According to Kavanagh, the 'feminine' quality that characterises Behn's *Oroonoko* is sympathy – hence only a woman could have written it, just as, much more recently, only a woman could have produced Harriet Beecher Stowe's *Uncle Tom's Cabin*. While men possess 'the sense of injustice', it is woman who has 'essentially pity for suffering and sorrow' (II, 189). Behn's novel is the story of an indigenous prince of Surinam and the trials that result from his being sold into slavery, and for Kavanagh, she 'never loses an opportunity of displaying his greatness of mind, his sincerity, his lofty trust in human virtue' (I, 37). Oroonoko is reduced to killing his wife to protect her from the colonists, and is overwhelmed by grief: '[t]here is great beauty and tenderness in this failure of a great and noble heart, overcome by love and sorrow on the very threshold of its revenge', declares Kavanagh (I, 43). Ironically, however, just as *David Simple* was weakened by Sarah Fielding's ignorance of the seamy side of life, *Oroonoko* would for Kavanagh be a lesser novel if it had in fact eschewed one kind of 'coarseness' – depictions of physical violence – and had failed to confront racial otherness. She imagines Mlle de Scudéry telling Oroonoko's story, full of 'delicate and graceful thoughts', but in her hands, 'we may be sure that Oroonoko's complexion would have faded a few shades', and although 'he might have been imprisoned, persecuted, and put to death', he would never have been whipped: hence 'he would have lived and died in the attitude of a well-bred man'. The problem is, that in those circumstances, readers 'should have cared very little about him' (I, 46–7) It is the graphic realism of the story which gives it its power, for all Behn's neglect of Scudéry as a literary model. Kavanagh even expresses regret that she cannot quote Oroonoko's death scene in full, since readers of her own day are more squeamish than were Behn's contemporaries of two centuries earlier (I, 43–4).

The paradox, that familiarity with 'coarsening' knowledge might enhance a woman's writing even as it endangered her womanhood, is implicit in Kavanagh's comparison of men's with women's fiction. She has nothing but condemnation for 'that most shameful form of profligacy – that which man writes for man to read' (*French Women of Letters*, I, 25), so that the influence of women has been salutary here. Thus the French précieuses, '[f]or depravity and impure language, both spoken and written … substituted the refinement of virtue and the delicacy of good taste'. But their rigid standards did check 'poetic flow', and 'reduced the national language to the standard of polite conversation' (I, 25–6). In Britain, women's 'delicacy', by which Kavanagh sometimes means refinement or fastidiousness, can mar their work, by offering a version of the world which is 'too sweet, too fair, too good'. This usage recalls Francis Jeffrey's allusions in 1829 to the 'delicacy' which cuts women off from wide areas of experience. Hence, claims Kavanagh, readers now want fiction to be simply 'pleasant', and 'loves, feelings, enthusiasm, such as no one ever saw, are to be accepted as possible realities'. Immorality is not excluded, but is represented in an exaggerated fashion, Kavanagh suggests: it 'takes a hard, a cruel aspect, and loses [its] indecorous freedom' (*English Women of Letters*, I, 5) – as if women writers' ignorance of sexual licence might induce them, ironically, to represent it too luridly. Moreover, women's fiction is characteristically more didactic than men's, and this can also involve a distortion of reality. Maria Edgeworth's writing is praiseworthy in many ways, according to Kavanagh, as she was generally able 'to see truth, to paint it, to impart it'. But her didactic purpose sometimes meant that her leading characters were too black-and-white and her plots artificial: 'life', asserts Kavanagh, 'is more mysterious than Miss Edgeworth has made it' (II, 116, 119, 134–5).

If 'delicacy' means fastidiousness or refinement, as it sometimes does in Kavanagh's literary criticism, the word can imply an evasion of unpleasant realities. But when she comes to discuss Jane Austen's fiction, she widens the term's meaning to the extent that it seems to involve penetrating the truth, rather than avoiding it. It is as if Kavanagh has not found 'tenderness' or 'sympathy' in Austen's writing, and does not think 'purity' an illuminating criterion either (although she hardly accuses Austen of the opposite). That leaves her with 'delicacy', but she has to expand the word's implications to claim Austen for her sex. So here, she means by it, subtlety and discrimination, but beyond that, a power of vision: 'never has character been displayed in such delicate variety as in her tales; never have commonplace men and women been invested with so much reality. She cannot be said to have created or invented; Jane Austen had an infinitely rarer gift – she saw' (II, 189–90).

That is, Austen was a seer, and '[t]o see well is one of the greatest, and strange, too, of the rarest attributes of the mind'. Kavanagh is in part making the point already by 1862 familiar in commentary on Austen, including that of Maria Jane Jewsbury and Sara Coleridge – that Austen was unparalleled in the verisimilitude of her representations of ordinary life, and that she avoided the easier literary terrain of exciting plots, exotic locales and colourful characters. But the stress here is on the 'keenness' of Austen's vision, the unusualness of her powers, and her subtlety: 'the simply good, the dull, the lively, the mean, the coarse, the selfish, the frivolous, she saw and painted with a touch so fine that we often do not perceive its severity' (II, 190). Moreover, Austen possessed an 'equally rare' power, one not necessarily expected in a writer focused on the nuances of detail – 'she knew where to stop, – and this is a great tribute to her tact and judgment' (II, 190–91).

Kavanagh paraphrases and quotes Austen's novels at length, and notes towards the end of her study that, unlike her near-contemporaries Fanny Burney and Maria Edgeworth, Austen has undergone 'no diminution of fame'. This suggests, she goes on, that 'of all the attributes of women, delicacy alone were matchless' (II, 353). But this 'delicacy' is grounded in the perceptions of the 'seer', rather than in the fastidiousness of the woman writer anxious to make everything in her novel seem 'pleasant'. How this 'delicacy' operates is spelt out in Kavanagh's comments on Austen's portrayal of John Dashwood in *Sense and Sensibility*. She summarises the famous early chapter of the novel where Dashwood rapidly abates his proposed generosity to his stepmother and half-sisters from giving substantial sums of money, to vague goodwill of no practical effect, and she quotes other conversations demonstrating how he judges people entirely in monetary terms. He is, she says, 'admirably brought before us, not merely by those successive meannesses, but much more so by his lukewarm goodwill'. He is the epitome of 'respectable baseness' – but this comes across all the more forcibly because Austen does not give him the conventionally 'hard … cruel aspect' characteristic of more fastidious female writers – insolence, brutality and cold indifference (II, 197–8). Hers is a 'delicacy' which fathoms rather than evades truth, anatomising the particular variety of selfishness Dashwood exemplifies.

Kavanagh does express some reservations about Austen's writing. She believes Austen has 'subdued life and its feelings into even more than their own tameness', largely because she generally 'refused to build herself, or to help to build for others, any romantic ideal of love, virtue, or sorrow' (II, 192–3). In this context, Austen's irony is treated ambivalently by Kavanagh. On the one hand, it is testimony to her subtlety and discrimination, as in her portrayal of John Dashwood – which demonstrates Austen's 'command over her really formidable powers' – and in her representation of Marianne Dashwood's naïve illusions (II, 199). On the other, irony apparently betrays an unfeminine insensibility, as Kavanagh calls it 'the parent of much coldness' (II, 193). It is as if there is something unnatural, for a woman writer, in Austen's detachment from her creations.

In this respect, there is one consolation for those seeking a 'feminine' Jane Austen: the last novel, *Persuasion*. This text, according to Kavanagh, shows 'the phase of [Austen's] literary character which she chose to keep most in the shade: the tender and the sad', portraying 'what can be the feelings of a woman compelled to see the love she most longs for, leaving her day by day'. She also recognises this novel as the progenitor of *Jane Eyre*: 'the first genuine picture of that silent torture of an unloved woman, condemned to suffer thus because she is a woman and must not speak, and which, many years later, was wakened into such passionate eloquence' by Charlotte Brontë (II, 230–31).

In 1847, when *Jane Eyre* appeared, Julia Kavanagh had, unsuccessfully, sought to review it for *Chambers' Journal*; three years later, she met Charlotte

Brontë, but without any lasting friendship developing between the two women.[25] Unfortunately, *English Women of Letters* did not include Charlotte Brontë, possibly because Gaskell's 1857 biography was in 1862 so recent and so (apparently) comprehensive. But by the same token, Gaskell's book had revealed to its large readership how Brontë had resisted Austen as a literary model, calling *Pride and Prejudice* 'a carefully-fenced, highly-cultivated garden', with 'ladies and gentlemen, in their elegant but confined houses'.[26] Yet Kavanagh is hinting here, that had Charlotte Brontë read *Persuasion* instead, she may have sensed some affinity with Austen. There is a difference, in that Brontë's heroine expresses more 'passionate eloquence' than Anne Elliot, but for Kavanagh, Jane Austen's understatement is still a strength: '[s]ubdued though the picture is in Miss Austen's pages, it is not the less keen, not the less painful' (II, 231).

Hannah Lawrance, Jane Williams and Julia Kavanagh shared a wish to rescue the achievements of women from neglect, oblivion and misrepresentation – notably their intellectual and literary achievements. In the view of these Victorian writers, women's contributions to history and to literature had been variously forgotten, overlooked, treated carelessly, or subsumed into conventional female stereotypes.

All three women confronted the issue of whether women's actions and writings manifested specifically 'feminine' traits, as these were construed in the nineteenth century, and concluded that they did. Lawrance ascribes to women the 'gentle virtues' of beneficence, sympathy and self-sacrifice, and highlights their role as mothers; Williams argues that women's writing demonstrates 'intuitive fineness of perception, rapidity of apprehension, tenderness, delicacy, and a certain persuasive sweetness'; Kavanagh emphasises the charity and piety of Christian women and, in dealing with writers, echoes Williams in attributing to them 'delicacy', 'tenderness', 'purity' and 'sympathy'. A female writer, moreover, can offer something to literature which a male writer cannot: both Lawrance and Kavanagh locate in women's writing a special kind of insight – an understanding of women's inner life, which counters masculine literary stereotypes. For Kavanagh, too, it was women, in particular Mme de la Fayette, whose fiction gave to the modern novel its characteristic focus on human feelings and psychological conflict.

Ultimately, however, the three critics did not define women's achievement entirely with reference to specifically 'feminine' traits. The corollary of Williams's argument is apparently that on account of their limited repertoire, women's poetic contribution to English literature is very much subordinate to that of men, but the details of her study implicitly challenge this view; similarly, Kavanagh in practice identifies the benefits to women's writing gained from eschewing 'purity' in the conventional sense, and extends the usual meaning of 'delicacy' to accommodate

---

[25] Amanda J. Collins, 'Grave Duties of the Caretaker in the Lives of Charlotte Brontë', pp. 18ff., 59.

[26] *The Life of Charlotte Brontë* (1857), ed. Linda H. Peterson, vol. 8 of *The Works of Elizabeth Gaskell* (London: Pickering & Chatto, 2005), p. 225. The comment is in a letter from Brontë to G.H. Lewes of 12 January 1848.

what she clearly sees as Jane Austen's remarkable literary achievement. Lawrance's work, which covers the widest sphere of female activity, conveys the impression that although women often manifested, very efficaciously, traits seen as feminine, they were capable, when circumstances arose, of demonstrating qualities usually considered masculine, such as intellectual powers and political acumen. That is, the distinctiveness of women's contribution to history and literature is attributable not just to innate qualities but to the range, or the limits, of the opportunities afforded to them.

Lawrance puts much emphasis on women's intellectual potential and the learning that can result when they are given the chance to develop it: as we have seen, she wrote about remote periods partly so as to suggest how retrogressive later trends in this arena had been. She welcomes the recent achievement of Barrett Browning as exemplifying women's potential for intellectual strength, scholarship, and a powerful imagination, and is adamant that Charlotte Brontë was right in ultimately rejecting Southey's advice about literary careers for women. Williams and Kavanagh also express conviction about women's capacity for showing intellectual prowess when given the right education, and they point to many women writers whose work has proven their mental attainments. For all three critics, intellectual endeavour on the part of women is not at all incompatible with domestic life or affections, or with the feminine virtues. While championing 'feminine' qualities in women's lives and writing, the critics are also loath to accept that there is anything that a woman, simply because she is female, cannot achieve.

Lawrance and Williams, I would argue, also show that they have learned something from the women they have studied about how to represent their own literary ventures, especially as ventures overtly produced by women, rather than published anonymously. Just as Lawrance's queens mostly concentrated their energies on influencing their sons and practising good works, but often revealed talent in the masculine sphere, Lawrance herself focuses on the 'feminine' genre of memoir, while slipping into her books substantial coverage of political, military, diplomatic and ecclesiastical matters. Williams observes how Felicia Hemans and Letitia Landon geared their writings to convey a publicly palatable version of femininity, and how the learned Anna Letitia Barbauld disarmed criticism through her unthreatening demeanour. Accordingly, Williams herself, dealing mainly with women's achievements in the elite genre of poetry, represents their contribution as unthreateningly minor, and therefore positions herself as making only modest claims as a writer – whereas the overall content of her book implies that women's literary output has been significant, and thus that her own study is a major enterprise in rescuing it from neglect and prejudice. Kavanagh takes a different tack, focusing on the less esteemed literary genre of fiction, but one to which women's contribution has been considerable, and which has exemplified powers in them not ultimately definable according to narrow notions of women's potential. For better or worse, too, the novel, rather than poetry, is 'the great feature of modern literature', and for many people, their main moral guide.

Chapter 4
Anne Mozley

In 1863, surveying George Eliot's fiction to date (up to *Romola*), Richard Simpson takes issue with Julia Kavanagh's then-recent identification of 'delicacy' as a distinctive trait of English women's fiction – he believes that she is deceiving herself. 'It is an hallucination in Miss Kavanagh', he declares, 'to suppose that we owe to [women] writers the importation of delicacy into English romance': rather, many of them 'saturate the female characters with passion and sensuality'. He produces quite a roll-call (albeit not all who feature are actually English): 'Mrs Aphra Behn, Mrs Centlivre, Madame de Staël, George Sand, the Countess Hahn-Hahn, Mrs Inchbald, Currer Bell, Mrs Norton, and George Eliot'.[1]

George Eliot, a writer who was (as still living), outside the scope of Kavanagh's *English Women of Letters*, is nonetheless a more complex case for Simpson. This is because she has taken up a masculine role: for Eliot, he asserts, '[t]he direct power and the celebrity of authorship may obscure and replace the indirect influence and calm happiness of domestic feminine life'. As a result, 'the male ideal becomes hers – the ideal of power'. But since Eliot still possesses a 'feminine heart and intellect', this 'ideal' manifests itself in her fiction as 'the supremacy of passion in the affairs of the world'. Because of her essential femaleness, this passion is sometimes sexual, but because of her masculine position, her fiction features the 'male passion of justice' as well.[2]

Although he disagrees with Kavanagh, Simpson, like her, tries to spell out what is distinctive in women's fiction. As far as George Eliot's work is concerned, he grapples with what appears to him as masculine, and he concludes that it was not due to innate traits, so much as the consequence of her unusual social circumstances. Anne Mozley, the subject of this chapter, also dealt with the potentially gender-related qualities of Eliot's writing, but with different results. In 1859, before the sex of the person writing as 'George Eliot' was known, Mozley's review of *Adam Bede* suggested, on the basis of internal evidence, that the author was a woman. Here the characteristics she commented on were, as she presented them, partly innately feminine, and partly the result of women's usual social position. Mozley's articles and reviews often discuss women's lives and women's writing, the extent to which both differ from men's, and how far such differences are innate. In so

---

[1] 'George Eliot's Novels', *Home and Foreign Review*, 3 (October 1863): 522–49, repr. in Stuart Hutchinson (ed.), *George Eliot: Critical Assessments* (4 vols, Mountfield: Helm Information, 1996), vol. 1, *Biography, Nineteenth-Century Reviews and Responses*, pp. 576–600, at p. 593.

[2] Ibid., pp. 592–3.

doing, they draw on the lives and writings of Jane Austen and Charlotte Brontë, as well as those of George Eliot. She does nevertheless present the three novelists as distinct from each other in their salient qualities.

Anne Mozley, born in 1809, was part of a large and upwardly mobile family which moved from Gainsborough (Lincolnshire) to Derby in 1815. Her father Henry Mozley ran a bookselling, publishing and printing business, and became a leading citizen of the town. Not surprisingly, the household had a very good library, which was continually expanded – it included the works of historians, divines, poets, discoverers, essay-writers and novelists, plus magazines and reviews.[3] Henry's wife, née Jane Bramble, was not well-educated when she married at 17, but strove to become more so. Having had to take up the family business at 15, Henry aspired to good educations for his sons, and with his encouragement, three of them took degrees at Oxford and became clergymen – according to the eldest of these, Tom, the father attached more value to the liberal professions than to more financially lucrative careers. One son, James, eventually became Regius Professor of Divinity at Oxford. Two others, John and Charles, were bred to the family business, expanding its publishing side, while the eldest became a coroner.

There were also several daughters, and Anne would recall that the eldest child, Jane, was the 'star' of the family among friends, with her 'clear bright intellect, love of study, and ready powers of argument, eager temperament, social charm, and grace of person and manner'.[4] This sister was apparently interested in writing, as Tom Mozley remembered that she had described for a school magazine the family's performance of 'Pyramus and Thisbe'. Jane died young (in 1833), but was no doubt one model of female authorship available to Anne – like Maria Jane Jewsbury's sister Geraldine, Anne Mozley had in her adulthood the memory of a literary sister no longer present in the flesh. But Jane's experience was also possibly a warning to Anne about prejudices against women writers: her schoolmistress disapproved of women writing for publication.[5]

Anne was the next sister in age to Jane; there were at least three surviving younger sisters, Maria, Fanny and Elizabeth. None of them married, and they stayed living in the family home until the mother's death in 1867, whereupon Anne and Elizabeth moved to Barrow-on-Trent. In her eighties, her eyesight having failed, Anne returned to Derby to live with her surviving sisters and a niece. Census records suggest that she and her sisters, like many single women of their class, lived on income from investments – Anne did not need to work or to write for money.

Anne Mozley's early literary activities were such as might be expected from an educated woman in the provinces with religious interests. She edited three volumes

---

Rev. Tom Mozley, *Reminiscences Chiefly of Towns, Villages and Schools* (2 vols, London: Longmans, Green, & Co., 1885), vol. 1, 58ff.

Letters of the Rev. J.B. Mozley, D.D. (London: Rivingtons, 1885), p. 24.

Rev. Tom Mozley, *Reminiscences Chiefly of Towns, Villages and Schools*, vol. 1, p. 339.

of devotional poetry published by the family firm and by High Church London publisher James Burns: *Passages from the Poets* (1837), *Days and Seasons* (1845) and *Poetry, Past and Present* (1849). A couple of years after Burns established a children's periodical in 1842, *Magazine for the Young*, she became its editor, a role she continued for about 30 years.[6] In 1846 she produced the novel *The Captive Maiden, A Tale of the Third Century* (published by J & C. Mozley), and *Tales of Female Heroism* (published by Burns).

Tales of Female Heroism, though not a study of writers, has something in common with Jane Williams's *The Literary Women of England* (which postdates Mozley's work by 15 years) – in that the tenor of its framing discourse differs somewhat from the overall impression conveyed by its detailed contents. Mozley's preface claims that the work's aim is 'to show the fortitude of which women are capable, rather in a feminine and domestic aspect than a brilliant one, and to exhibit acts of courage and presence of mind in characters distinguished by their conscientious fulfilment of the quiet, unobtrusive duties of every-day life'. The book concentrates on British women of the English Civil War period through to the early nineteenth century, with some attention to women from Europe. Certainly many of them are notable for their devotion to family members, especially husbands, but their arena is for the most part public life, and especially times of strife. Some too distinguished themselves by aiding public figures – such as Lady Morton (Queen Henrietta Maria), Lady Elizabeth Erskine (the Marquis of Montrose), Jane Lane (the fugitive future Charles II), and Flora MacDonald and Miss Mackay (the Young Pretender).

The poetry anthologies Anne Mozley edited demonstrate a broad knowledge of poetry from the sixteenth to the nineteenth century, a knowledge which was to bear fruit also in her later periodical publications. The High Church affiliation is also significant, not only because it inflects much of Anne Mozley's writing, but because of the intellectual world with which it brought her into contact – an intellectual world that extended far beyond the social circles of Derby.

When Anne's elder brother Tom (b. 1804), went up to Oxford, he fell under the influence of the charismatic John Henry Newman, who became his tutor at Oriel in 1826. Like many Oxford men of his generation, Tom Mozley became caught up in the High Church 'Oxford Movement' (he gained an Oriel fellowship in 1829), and his family, including Anne, got to know the Newman family. Generally too, according to Anne, the Mozley family were writers of copious letters,[7] so those back in Derby were kept abreast of developments in Oxford. Eventually, in 1836, Tom Mozley married one Newman sister, Harriette, while his publisher brother John married the other, Jemima.

Newman's conversion to Roman Catholicism in 1845 affected his relationships with his sisters and their Mozley husbands, and contact became more sporadic.

---

[6]   Ellen Jordan, 'Sister as Journalist: The Almost Anonymous Career of Anne Mozley', *Victorian Periodicals Review*, 37/3 (2004): 315–41, at 319.

[7]   *Letters of the Rev. J.B. Mozley, D.D.*, p. 2.

That Anne Mozley retained Newman's goodwill, however, is shown by the fact that, in 1884, he asked her to edit the letters covering his pre-conversion period, and these appeared in 1891, shortly after both of their deaths. This was because she had brought out a series of editions of the sermons, essays and letters of her brother James (d. 1878) – editions which had impressed Newman, accustomed as he was to controversy swirling around him, with their impartiality.[8]

Unlike her earlier publications, Anne Mozley's editions of her brother's and Newman's works came out under her own name, so that, rather as in Sara Coleridge's case 40 years earlier, such public profile as she had was as an editor of the works of distinguished relatives. What had existed, however, in the years between her works of the 1830s and 1840s and the editions for which she become known many years later, was a prolific career as a contributor to leading intellectual periodicals. Anne Mozley's association with High Church figures had not only produced the editions of James Mozley and Cardinal Newman's works; it had also given her the entrée to periodicals published outside Derby, and read far beyond her own social circle.

Anne Mozley's work as a periodical contributor was disclosed only after her death, when her sister Fanny brought out a selection of her essays from *Blackwood's Edinburgh Magazine*, together with the review of *Adam Bede* which had appeared in the short-lived *Bentley's Quarterly Review*; in conjunction with the sisters' nephew Frank (son of Jemima Newman and John Mozley), Fanny wrote a biographical memoir for the collection, which revealed that from 1847 to 1880, Anne had contributed variously not only to *Blackwood's* and *Bentley's*, but also to the *Christian Remembrancer* and the *Saturday Review*. Fortunately the *Blackwood's* and *Bentley's* contributions can be fully identified from the *Wellesley Index*, but those in the *Christian Remembrancer* and the *Saturday Review* can only be attributed in part. According to Fanny and Frank Mozley, Anne contributed to the *Saturday* from 1861 to 1877, but the only articles that can be positively identified are those that were republished in 1864 and 1865 (anonymously, but disclosed as Anne Mozley's by her relatives after her death), in two volumes called *Essays on Social Subjects From the Saturday Review*.[9] It is unfortunate that a third volume that she proposed to John Blackwood in 1870 did not go ahead, since she planned to include extracts from her *Christian Remembrancer* articles: 'some complete passages which would read much like a Saturday Review article of which one may say they never met the eye of the general reader though certainly as good

---

[8]   See Fanny and Frank Mozley's 'Memoir' of Anne in *Essays from 'Blackwood'. By the Late Anne Mozley* (Edinburgh and London: William Blackwood and Sons, 1892), pp. xii–xiii, and Anne Mozley (ed.), *Letters and Correspondence of John Henry Newman During His Life in the English Church, With a Brief Autobiography* (2 vols, London: Longmans, Green, and Co., 1891), vol. 1, p. 5.

[9]   (Edinburgh and London: William Blackwood and Sons).

as any I ever wrote'.[10] As it is, with the publishers' records not having survived, the only clear attributions in the *Remembrancer* have been on the part of W. Robertson Nicoll, who identified as Anne Mozley's the reviews of Charlotte Brontë's *Villette* (April 1853) and Gaskell's *Life of Charlotte Brontë* (July 1857).[11] Thanks to the efforts of the members of the Centre for Literary and Linguistic Computing at the University of Newcastle in Australia, who use computer analysis of commonly used words in a writer's known works in order to suggest further attributions, it looks likely that several other articles can be identified as Anne Mozley's. Those that I will discuss here are 'Female Occupation and Influence' (June 1858) and 'Our Female Novelists' (October 1859).[12] Moreover, an 1866 article which reviews Margaret Oliphant's novel *Miss Marjoribanks* contains comments that are so similar to those Anne Mozley made in a letter to John Blackwood around the same time, that it is very probable that she was responsible for it ('Youth as Depicted in Modern Fiction', July 1866).

Anne Mozley would have had access to the pages of the *Christian Remembrancer* through her brother James, who co-edited it from 1844 to 1855: it was also published by the Mozley firm. It was a High Church organ with a strongly theological emphasis, and much of what Anne Mozley publishes there has some kind of theological dimension. Her letter to Blackwood in 1870 shows her awareness of its narrow readership, and at the point when she seeks republication of her extracts, it had been defunct for two years. She would have gained a wider audience in the *Saturday*, to which she was quite possibly introduced by James's co-editor in the *Remembrancer*, William Bell Scott, who had been one of the weekly's founders back in 1855. Its contributors included a very wide array of people in a wide variety of fields, overwhelmingly male, most of them distinguished in their respective areas, and it assumed a highly educated readership. Its tone, according to its historian Merle Mowbray Bevington, was often condescending, as well as audacious and irreverent towards the pet enthusiasms of earnest Victorians, and its style had an 'epigrammatic directness'.[13] These characteristics were however less evident in Anne Mozley's contributions which, as far as is known, consisted of 'middles' – essays inserted between the lead articles and the reviews proper: these considered, reflectively but concisely, social mores and the quirks of human behaviour, plus general literary issues. The topics she covered included 'Busy People', 'Snubbing', 'Ignorance', 'False Shame', 'Contempt',

---

[10] Letter to John Blackwood, 2 February 1870, MS 4265, National Library of Scotland.

[11] 'Charlotte Brontë and Anne Mozley', *Brontë Society Transactions*, 29 (March 1919): 255–64.

[12] See Ellen Jordan, Hugh Craig and Alexis Antonia, 'The Brontë Sisters and the *Christian Remembrancer*', *Victorian Periodicals Review*, 39/1 (2006): 21–45.

[13] *The Saturday Review 1855–1868: Representative Educated Opinion in Victorian England* (New York: Columbia University Press, 1941, repr. New York: AMS Press, 1966), pp. 47–8, 321.

'Study of Character', 'The Uses of Pathos', 'Uncritical Readers', 'Cheerfulness', 'Grumblers', 'Talking and Reading', 'Small Economies', 'Taste', 'Social Truth', 'The Plain Style', 'Letters' and 'Ladies' Letters'.

Anne Mozley's literary strategies as a periodical writer suggest that she welcomed dissemination of her work beyond a specialised readership, and, in the case of her *Saturday* contributions, in a more lasting form than was likely if they remained wholly within the pages of a weekly periodical. In order to get her essays from the *Saturday* published, too, she did not take the straightforward option of using the family firm: referring in a letter to a book published by the firm in the 1820s, she noted that it 'fell still born as they say from the press', since 'it was published in the country'.[14] Instead, she approached John Blackwood, who both agreed to take the volumes, and accepted her as a contributor to *Blackwood's Edinburgh Magazine*. She had already published one article there, in August 1861 ('On Manners'), but from April 1865 ('Dress'), until October 1880 ('Memory') – by which time her work on her brother James's posthumous publications was no doubt occupying her – she published regularly in the magazine, her contributions amounting to 25 articles.

Although Anne Mozley made efforts to increase the readership of some of her work, she always chose outlets where the convention of anonymity prevailed. Even when, from the 1860s onward, some new periodicals, such as the *Fortnightly Review* and *Macmillan's Magazine*, were adopting the policy of signature, there is no evidence that Anne Mozley sought to publish in any of them. Rather, she was anxious to maintain her anonymity, and for reasons which had much to do with her awareness of the possible consequences of disclosing her sex. Like Maria Jane Jewsbury in her *Athenaeum* contributions, Anne Mozley was happy for her publications to be known, but not her own identity as their author. She argued, in the *Blackwood's* article which discussed the book of the 1820s that had been 'still born' – a book by a woman lamenting her trials as a governess – that prejudice against women writers had diminished since then.[15] But it was strong enough for Mozley to wish to hold on to what she had called, in a letter to John Blackwood in 1864, the 'ease & freedom of expression' which anonymity gave her.[16] She regrets to him in 1865 that in reviewing her second volume of *Essays on Social Subjects*, the *Athenaeum* had expressed 'the suspicion of a lady's pen'.[17] The following year, she proposes to him an article on the divergences of opinion revealed by the recent publications of various Catholic converts, but stresses her need to conceal her identity: 'Of course you will feel the importance of not allowing the name & *sex* of the writer to transpire – I mean on your editorial account as well as my own'. This is because '[p]eople don't generally suspect ladies of writing on such

---

[14]   Letter to John Blackwood, 20 January 1868, MS 4237, National Library of Scotland.

[15]   'Clever Women', *Blackwood's Edinburgh Magazine*, 104 (October 1868): 410–27.

[16]   Letter of 20 April 1864, MS 4191, National Library of Scotland.

[17]   Letter of 7 June 1865, MS 4725, National Library of Scotland.

subjects': any suspicion of female authorship could devalue the article in readers' eyes.[18] In alluding to the reception of women's writing in her review of *The Life of Charlotte Brontë* back in 1857, she had referred to 'that gallantry and patronizing tenderness which is commonly bestowed upon women' – critics' frequent refusal to accord texts by women the same intellectual respect that they gave men's works.[19] Although her discussions of both 'Currer Bell' and George Eliot suggest that Anne Mozley shared the widespread curiosity about the people behind those male pseudonyms, she would have had some sense of the reasons that Charlotte Brontë and Marian Evans adopted them.

Not only does Anne Mozley strive to conceal her sex by preserving her anonymity – she sometimes adopts an overtly masculine voice, one which implies that both she and her readers are male. This stratagem is evident in some of her *Saturday Review* pieces: after all, the weekly's prospectus had declared that its intended audience was 'the educated mind of the country', that is, 'serious, thoughtful men'.[20] For example, the article on 'The Uses of Pathos' laments the decline of appeals to the pathetic in literature, and presents as one consequence that '[n]obody need be afraid of the red eyes of which our boyhood used to be so ashamed'. But literary pathos should not be scorned – weeping over it can 'in no degree shame our manhood'.[21] More subtle, however, are the techniques Mozley uses, not only to affect a male voice, but to accommodate what she implies to be common male attitudes. Sometimes she makes claims for women, especially women's intellectual and literary capacities, in the body of her articles, but frames them by acknowledging, and even purporting to share, more conservative attitudes. She is also, of course, in contributing to the *Remembrancer*, the *Saturday* and *Blackwood's*, writing for periodicals which had a socially conservative orientation.

In an article for the *Christian Remembrancer* for June 1858, Mozley discusses a range of texts which inspire the title, 'Female Occupation and Influence', but concentrates on *A Woman's Thoughts About Women*, by the established novelist Dinah Mulock Craik. Here Mozley adopts an overtly male persona from the outset, and begins and ends her discussion by expressing traditional ideas about the limitations of women's nature and role. She opens by declaring that '[t]he question of the condition of women and their station in the social economy is not likely to lose its hold on popular interest when once fairly started', and then goes on to acknowledge, in a male voice, that the question 'is one naturally to excite mistrust if not disgust amongst the conservative portion of our sex, who are so far

---

[18] Letter of 12 April 1866, MS 4725, National Library of Scotland (Mozley's emphasis).

[19] '*The Life of Charlotte Brontë*', *Christian Remembrancer*, 34 (July 1857): 87–145, at 136. Subsequent references to this review will be included parenthetically in the text.

[20] Quoted in Merle Mowbray Bevington, *The Saturday Review 1855–1868*, p. 19.

[21] *Essays on Social Subjects from the Saturday Review*, vol. 1 (1864), pp. 266–75, at p. 267.

satisfied with things are they are, and with women as they are, that they regard any change, as such, as an unmitigated evil'.[22] At the end, she stresses woman's primary role as a helpmeet for man, and, giving her argument a religious emphasis in keeping with the orientation of the *Remembrancer*, declares that women will be 'always in subordination; always in obedience to the first laws; "for Adam was first formed, and then Eve"' (484).

On the other hand, the article's discussion of Mulock Craik's book expresses frustration with the limitations on women's lives which it seems to endorse. In treating women's existing occupations, Mulock Craik holds women to a more elevated standard of duty and seriousness than men, while failing to advocate new occupational opportunities: by demanding higher levels of fitness for both governessing and creative endeavours, Mulock Craik implicitly denies these occupations to most women, without suggesting alternatives (444–5). For Mozley this view is unreasonable since, as far as literature as an occupation is concerned, male writers usually don't have a high-minded sense of 'responsibility' as the 'depositories of peculiar gifts'. According to Mozley, Mulock Craik exaggerates the differences between the sexes: she examines women 'with a daguerreotype eye for weaknesses and failings' whereas 'we [men] are exhibited in the grand style', being attributed with 'great virtues and faults, but no foibles'. For example, men, for Mulock Craik, 'lie with greater grandeur than women: wilfully, because they have a purpose: women quite involuntarily, from mere weakness of nature' (445–6) – a view which Mozley, purporting to be a man, finds amusing. 'He' is also amused by Mulock Craik's demand that women be brought up to support themselves should they need to. The reason for the quizzical attitude here, however, is not that women are incapable of such training, but that Mulock Craik has not taken account of male self-interest:

> Every man – we may be charged with speaking selfishly – finds the convenience of wife and daughters being able to *leave* what they are about, and take up his interests, and do his errands, carry out his plans, at a moment's notice. He prefers, it is true, not being interrupted himself, and his wife respects his habits; but he would not like not to be able to interrupt his wife. (440–41; Mozley's emphasis)

If articulated in a female voice, this commentary may have seemed an overt complaint against male self-centredness; coming supposedly from a man, it ostensibly defends male interests while allowing readers to register the underlying egotism.

Finally, and most importantly for this discussion, Mozley demystifies any overstrained sense of the differences between the sexes by pointing to the

---

[22] 'Female Occupation and Influence', *Christian Remembrancer*, 35 (June 1858): 436–87, at 436. Subsequent references to this article will be included parenthetically in the text.

contemporary proliferation of female writers. She implies that this development represents a healthier situation than obtained in the past, when readers accepted isolated female figures with pretensions to inspired genius, while not crediting the sex in general with literary potential. But nowadays, she says, 'women write under the ordinary uninspired conditions in which most men write, from no stimulus of genius, but mere exercise of reason and intellect, and the cultivation of such powers as they possess': what represents progress, this suggests, is that women are now credited with 'reason and intellect'. Hence '[t]he public now accepts many women amongst its authorized instructors without doubt, or cavil, or sense of wounded pride', and if some of them may be 'heavily sensible, and reasonably prosy', then this fact simply 'brings any woman into fair comparison with many highly esteemed authors of the sterner sex'. Therefore 'it is a great advance in the popular estimate of women's intellect, when they can write dull books with as complete and entire impunity as men can' (436–7).

The opening up of writing as a career for women, a development Mozley locates in the nineteenth century, is also at stake in her article for *Blackwood's* which deals with the governess's reminiscences from the 1820s. In this 1868 article, 'Clever Women', Mozley's ventriloquising of a male critical voice enables her to make confident claims for women, while taking account of traditional conservative attitudes.

Here in her male persona, Mozley initially endorses some conventional notions about the disadvantages of 'cleverness' in women, notions based on a belief in significant intellectual differences between the sexes. The article contrasts the 'clever woman' with the 'ideal woman': although the latter 'does not reason', because 'her processes of thought are intuitive', yet 'we [men] bow to conclusions formed on no conscious data, with nothing like argument to back them, because in her own province, though she cannot reason, she is apt to be right'. But outside her own province, on questions of art, literature, politics, religion, and all public issues, she submits to masculine guidance. In contrast, '[c]lever women … throw intuition over and aim at logic', cultivating the 'analytical faculty' – with the result that they lose the capacity to use instinct 'to serve their personal needs', and sacrifice the 'subtle power' of tact to 'intellectual exercises'.[23]

Most of the rest of the piece, nevertheless, asserts the advantages of women's increasing access to writing, both as an occupation and as a means of earning a living. It expresses relief that far distant now are the days when Swift attacked learned women, and when people advised young women against 'any exercise of mind' for fear of discouraging potential marriage prospects. Having already assured readers, with quasi-masculine authority, as to her acceptance of fundamental differences between the sexes, Mozley can now make the 'meat' of her article – the governess's book – more palatable. The book, *Dependence*, consists of the young woman's letters to her young clergyman fiancé, and emphasises her sufferings: she has no desire to be a governess, and finds both the way she is

---

[23]   'Clever Women', 411–13.

treated in her employers' families and her state of dependence itself galling, but she has no other way to support herself until her fiancé can afford to marry her. Mozley's article is very sympathetic to the writer, and she uses copious quotations to illustrate both the woman's trials and the literary talent which she may have put to other uses, had she been born a generation later. For '[o]ur age can boast of not a few works composed by women which are marked by such grasp of thought, subtle depth of observation, and original force and grace of expression, as not only rank them among the highest literature of the day, but must secure them a lasting reputation'.[24]

But, as in 'Female Occupation and Influence' several years earlier, Mozley's peroration here, like her opening, reassures her readers that she is not advocating a radical change in the social role of women. After having attributed 'grasp of thought' and 'force' to some women's writing, she backtracks, to explain that the kind of writing she is promoting can be carried out by 'the ordinary domestic type of woman'. Moreover, rather than being comparable to men's writing – great or mediocre – the writing she is commending is really a kind of new but unthreatening female accomplishment: such women write, just as 'skilful women of old spun gossamer thread, or made exquisite lace or embroidery, or exercised themselves in any other graceful art where delicate fingering, a soft touch, and quick perception found an appropriate field'.[25] That is, their work exemplifies traditional feminine traits such as softness, delicacy and female intuition, rather than strength and intellectual acumen.

That Mozley was accommodating here the character of *Blackwood's*, is suggested by her experience of reviewing J.S. Mill's *The Subjection of Women* in it. Here, again adopting a male persona, she asserts that women's physical weakness in comparison with men implies 'a natural law of subordination', and that they are certainly not intellectually equal to men. Far from women having the potential to participate in public life, she argues that only 'one woman in a million' would be capable of being Chancellor of the Exchequer, a Parliamentary debater, a railway builder, a designer of cathedrals, or a barrister conducting an intricate lawsuit.[26] This is partly because, although women possess 'a greater aptitude to catch the tone of thought about them without direct instruction, than in men', they have 'less power of sustained attention and concentration of the mind on a given subject'.[27] But there is evidence that Anne Mozley was under pressure here from John Blackwood to take a hostile attitude to Mill and his book, so that she is ventriloquising the *Blackwood's Magazine* line. Blackwood found her first

---

[24]   Ibid., 436.

[25]   Ibid., 437.

[26]   'Mr Mill on *The Subjection of Women*', *Blackwood's Edinburgh Magazine*, 106 (September 1869): 309–21, at 315–16.

[27]   Ibid., 314.

version of the article 'too dry', and wanted her to 'scourge' Mill,[28] so she returned
a revised proof, claiming to have expressed 'a strong opinion of [Mill's] insolence
& the insult his book is not only to men but women'.[29] She may indeed have
recalled an earlier letter, from 1868, when Blackwood had declared that it was
'really accomplished women' such as George Eliot, Margaret Oliphant and herself,
who were 'least disposed to swagger about the Rights of Women', and had had
patronage at the ready for those female swaggerers: 'The rights of Women papers
that I see are almost invariably badly composed as doubtless their unfortunate
husbands' dinners are cooked.'[30]

In her writing for the short-lived *Bentley's Quarterly Review*, Mozley had
not felt the need to adopt either an overtly male voice or a strategy of clearly
accommodating conservative ideas. This periodical lasted only four issues, over
1859–60, since times were not propitious for new quarterlies, the demand now
being for periodicals that appeared more frequently and hence responded more
immediately to events and publications. (The success of the *Saturday*, which
began in 1855, was a case in point.) *Bentley's* aimed to be independent and various
in its views, and was so for as long as it lasted,[31] for all that it had as its first
editor William Bell Scott of the *Saturday* and the *Remembrancer*. (Since Mozley's
Saturday contributions began in 1861, Scott conceivably took her on for *Bentley's*,
and then invited her to contribute to the *Saturday* when *Bentley's* folded in 1860.)
Mozley wrote an article for each of *Bentley's'* four issues: one was the review of
Adam Bede, but the first was a survey article on Bulwer-Lytton's fiction.

Although this article is not wholly critical of the novelist's output, its strictures
both foreshadow the criteria Mozley brought to bear on Eliot's novel, and fault
the old-fashioned attitudes to women that Bulwer-Lytton's fiction betrays.
Mozley argues that the novelist errs in his strongly-asserted assumptions that his
fiction is true-to-life in either plot or characterisation. Rather, it is fundamentally
flawed: Bulwer-Lytton lacks what she identifies as 'the novelist's crowning
gift – the delineation of the passions and deeper emotions of human nature in
action and by example'.[32] Moreover, although he may claim to 'yield to no one
in chivalrous devotion to woman's merits, her charms, and influence', his tone
is too condescending, and allusions to their 'charming babble' would hardly be

---

[28] Mrs Gerald Porter, *John Blackwood*, vol. 3 of *Annals of a Publishing House: William Blackwood and His Sons, Their Magazine and Friends* (Edinburgh and London: William Blackwood and Sons, 1898), p. 104.

[29] Letter to John Blackwood, 16 August 1869, MS 4251, National Library of Scotland.

[30] John Blackwood to Anne Mozley, 25 January 1868, MS 30362, National Library of Scotland.

[31] Walter E. Houghton (ed.), *The Wellesley Index to Victorian Periodicals*, vol. 2 (Toronto: University of Toronto Press, 1972), p. 5.

[32] 'Novels by Sir Edward Bulwer-Lytton', *Bentley's Quarterly Review*, no. 1 (March 1859): 73–105, at 89.

welcomed by women who 'are accustomed to be listened to, and replied to as equals'. Bulwer-Lytton treats any sign of intellect in women as a 'misfortune', and advocates in them a kind of mindless devotion to men that is reminiscent of dogs. Mozley also draws attention to the sexual double standard in Bulwer-Lytton's works: women characters who fail to behave with 'unreasoning fidelity' are visited with 'a sort of *lash* of indignation', but his '*men* are not equally bound' to constancy. One development that had fostered changes in attitudes to women, moreover, was the advent of 'the august band of female novelists', who had established 'counter ideals from the old, soft, submissive, gentle type – women who can stand alone, reason, lead, instruct, command', and these heroines have been 'wrought out with such power that they take hold on men's minds'.[33]

In her periodical contributions of the 1850s and 1860s, then, Anne Mozley asserted that women's intellects, women's literary capacities, and women's writing practices, had all garnered greater respect than they had enjoyed earlier in the century. But her own writing strategies – her concealment of her identity, her sometime adoption of an overtly male persona, and her accommodating of traditional attitudes to women – suggest that she was not convinced that either women's intellects or women's writing were yet consistently treated in an unprejudiced way. So how did this paradox inflect her treatment of Jane Austen, Charlotte Brontë and George Eliot?

Anne Mozley never produced an extended, freestanding discussion of Jane Austen. That she would have liked to, is suggested by a letter to John Blackwood of 1 November 1869, where she proposes reviewing the *Memoir of Jane Austen* by the novelist's nephew James Edward Austen-Leigh that was about to appear. She tells Blackwood: 'I have always been a great admirer of her; an admiration that does not cool'.[34] Moreover, Tom and Harriette Mozley had been friendly in the 1830s with the Wiltshire clergyman Mr Fowle, and were aware that he had known Jane Austen, his aunt Mary Lloyd having married her eldest brother James (and thus, incidentally, become the mother of Austen-Leigh). In 1838, Harriette reports to her sister Jemima in Derby some of Fowle's recollections of Jane Austen, and concludes, 'I tell you all this for Anne who will like to hear about Miss Austen'.[35] During the 1850s and 1860s, the Mozley firm brought out some of the novels of Fanny Caroline Lefroy, Jane Austen's great-niece.[36] In 1869, Blackwood eventually gave the *Memoir* to Margaret Oliphant to review, but back in 1857 at least, Anne Mozley had taken a cue from Charlotte Brontë's criticisms of Austen, revealed in Gaskell's biography, to develop an insightful comparison between the two novelists, as will be discussed below. Passing allusions to Austen's works, too

---

[33]   Ibid., 91ff. (Mozley's emphasis).

[34]   MS 4251, National Library of Scotland.

[35]   Letter of 2 November 1838, quoted in Dorothea Mozley (ed.), *Newman Family Letters* (London: SPCK, 1962), pp. 78–9.

[36]   Kathryn Sutherland, *Jane Austen's Textual Lives: From Aeschylus to Bollywood* (Oxford: Clarendon Press, 2005), p. 259.

– as well as to those of Charlotte Brontë and George Eliot – are found in several of Mozley's periodical contributions: they are evidently all writers whose output she knew well and who came to mind readily.

As far as Austen is concerned, for example, in 'Clever Women' Mozley evokes the trials of governesses by alluding to the 'immortal Mrs Elton' in Austen's *Emma*, who patronises Jane Fairfax by expatiating on the supposed 'prizes' of the governess's life.[37] The same novel is praised in another *Blackwood's* article, on 'Prolixity': *Emma* is said to demonstrate (through a character like Miss Bates), 'how tedious, pointless chat, rendered with absolute truth of delineation, may be made to serve the aims and needs of the novelist, amuse the reader whom the original would bore to death, and, by chance touches, tell the author's story'.[38] In writing on 'Illustration', by which she means figures of speech, Mozley includes Austen among the writers who seldom use such, because of 'a certain concentration in the matter in hand – the scene, the situation'.[39] Reading Austen's works (among others), indeed, is recommended as enhancing women's intellectual development: in a *Blackwood's* article, 'On Fiction as an Educator', she argues that many women

> would have been pleasanter and so far better members of society if once in their girlhood they had read a good novel with rapt attention – one of Walter Scott's, or Miss Austen's, or … Sir Charles Grandison – entering into the characters, realizing the descriptions, following the dialogue, appreciating the humour, and enchained by the plot.[40]

By concentrating on something outside themselves, their faculties would have been 'nerved and tightened by the tonic, not for the time only, but with lasting results'. As it is, many women are 'desultory, restless, incorrigible interrupters, incapable of amusing themselves or of being amused by the same thing for five minutes together'. Novel-reading, far from an idle pastime, could be a means of mental development – and Mozley's lament here for the current mental state of many women suggests that even as late as 1870, their intellectual potential had often not been realised because of a deficient education.

The publication of Elizabeth Gaskell's *Life of Charlotte Brontë* in 1857 brought into the public domain the private criticisms of Jane Austen that Charlotte Brontë had made in her correspondence with George Henry Lewes, who had suggested Austen to her as a literary model, and prompted her to read *Pride and Prejudice*. To Lewes, Charlotte Brontë described Austen's novel, in a passage quoted by Mozley in her review, as:

---

[37] 'Clever Women', 416.

[38] *Blackwood's Edinburgh Magazine*, 109 (May 1871): 610–26, at 623.

[39] *Blackwood's Edinburgh Magazine*, 110 (December 1871): 754–70, at 754.

[40] *Blackwood's Edinburgh Magazine*, 108 (October 1870): 449–59, at 457.

> An accurate daguerrotyped portrait of a common-place face; a carefully-fenced, highly-cultivated garden, with neat borders and delicate flowers; but no glance of a bright vivid physiognomy, no open country, no fresh air, no blue hill, no bonny beck. I should hardly like to live with her ladies and gentlemen, in their elegant but confined houses. (136)

Further on, Brontë declares that, if Austen lacks 'sentiment' or '*poetry*', as Lewes had conceded, then she may be 'sensible, real (more *real* than *true*)', but 'cannot be great' (137, Brontë's emphasis).

Whereas Julia Kavanagh had tried to relate the two novelists to each other, Anne Mozley takes the opportunity here to define what she sees as the fundamental difference between them, and how this manifests itself in their novels. Austen, she argues, 'described life as she saw it, genteel, decorous, every-day domestic life'; in addition, '[h]er disciplined mind and easy temper saw in this aspect of existence all that satisfied the wants of her nature', and she was a participant in the kind of society she describes, 'fortunate in a pleasing person, agreeable address, and friends in the sphere of society she depicts'. Hence Austen 'knew perfectly how people acted in the intercourse of every day', her imagination could 'work in such decorous, veiled excitement as "society" gives room for', and so she was unparalleled in her portrayal of '[t]he happy stir of domestic love, the thrill of a reciprocal passion, the trials of unrequited tenderness in a chastened, well-regulated nature – all this, as disciplined by the will or by the conventionalities of society'. What is represented in her fiction is thus 'human nature precisely as she heard and saw it', albeit she shows awareness of the 'deeper currents of feeling' experienced by the members of the society she knows and depicts (137).

Charlotte Brontë also wrote about what she knew, but in relation to Jane Austen, according to Mozley, 'their education, training, and experience of life were so absolutely different, that no chord in harmony could be struck between them'. Because of the life she lived, Charlotte Brontë had no understanding of 'society, technically so called', and this was 'because she never saw it, never was in it, and knew nothing about it', since '[s]hyness and selfconsciousness kept her apart from her fellows'. She never viewed people 'as united by one social bond, as acting upon one another in a certain acknowledged and received relation'; hence her characters are 'independent of any social code', and 'expatiate in a freedom which persons once feeling themselves members of a body cannot attain to' (137). That is, she had her characters verbalise the 'deeper emotions' of their hearts, so that in *Shirley*, for example, characters express what they think, what is plausible as the genuine feelings that might be disclosed in soliloquy, but 'perfectly out of the question from one human being to another'. So Brontë, according to Mozley, is in fact right in claiming that Austen is 'more *real* than *true*' (138).

The contrast between Austen and Charlotte Brontë that Anne Mozley makes here foreshadows to some extent a recent commentary by Pam Morris. The modern critic points to how 'the precision and security of Austen's voice derives from her sense of addressing the known community of civil society, whose perspective, values, and cultural assumptions she largely shares', whereas 'Brontë speaks to no such known community'. The difference between Morris's view and Mozley's however, is that Morris identifies Charlotte Brontë's contrasting narrative stance as deriving from social changes that have occurred since Austen's day: she is addressing in *Shirley* 'a public sphere that has become much more heterogeneous', such that she 'has to make guesses as to her readers' perspectives, and she expects that miscommunication, misunderstanding, and misrepresentation will result'.[41] For Mozley, the problematic aspects of Charlotte Brontë's take on society result from the novelist's own unusual character and circumstances.

The view of Charlotte Brontë that Mozley expresses here is evidently drawn from the version of the woman offered by Gaskell's biography as much as from her novels. Like most reviewers of the biography, Mozley found that it explained the aspects of the fiction that many had found strange or disturbing. What some of these aspects are emerges in her earlier article on Brontë, her review of *Villette* back in 1853. But it is also notable here that in discussing this novel in a conservative periodical, Mozley is, as in other articles, accommodating readers' possible reservations about Charlotte Brontë and her fiction.

Mozley begins her extended discussion of Brontë and her novel by recalling *Jane Eyre*, pointing to

> the outrages on decorum, the moral perversity, the toleration of, nay, indifference to vice which deform her first powerful picture of a desolate woman's trials and sufferings – faults which make Jane Eyre a dangerous book, and which must leave a permanent mistrust of the author on all thoughtful and scrupulous minds.

In this first work, the novelist had come across as 'soured, coarse, and grumbling; an alien, it might seem from society, and amenable to none of its laws'.[42] Near the end of the review, too, Mozley adopts a very overtly masculine voice, and lambasts Charlotte Brontë's heroines:

> We want a woman at our hearth; and her impersonations are without the feminine element, infringers of modest restraints, despisers of bashful fears, self-reliant, contemptuous of prescriptive decorum; their own unaided reason, their individual opinion of right and wrong, discreet or imprudent, sole guides of conduct and rules of manners, – the whole hedge of immemorial scruple and habit broken down and trampled upon. (442)

---

[41]   Pam Morris, *Imagining Inclusive Society in Nineteenth-Century Novels: The Code of Sincerity in the Public Sphere* (Baltimore and London: Johns Hopkins University Press, 2004), p. 61.

[42]   'New Novels by Lady G. Fullerton and Currer Bell', *Christian Remembrancer*, 25 (April 1853): 401–43, at 423. Subsequent references to this review will be included parenthetically in the text.

As we have seen, in criticising Bulwer-Lytton's portrayal of women in a different periodical several years later, Mozley would contradict this view, commending contemporary women writers' heroines 'who can stand alone, reason, lead, instruct'. Here, however, Mozley also, as 'he', not only attacks the independent spirit of Brontë's heroines, but affects dismay at the apparent revelation about women that has emerged since 'our fair rivals wield the pen': that women 'often give away their hearts unsought', such that the besieged castle of womanhood has been 'all the while wanting a commander, the heart an owner'. She denies the likelihood of this disclosure, however, since the 'restless heart and vagrant imagination' of Charlotte Brontë 'can have no sympathy or true insight into the really feminine nature' (443). The implication being that a 'man', like the reviewer, is a better authority on womanhood than an atypical woman like Charlotte Brontë!

On the other hand, the review overall is quite positive about *Villette*. After expressing reservations about *Jane Eyre*, Mozley reassures her readers that 'in many important moral points "Villette" is an improvement on its predecessors', since 'the author has gained in both amiability and propriety' (423). Brontë is then commended for several aspects of the novel, including unconventional aspects: for example, she makes the Belgian school, a very unusual setting for a novel, compelling from her 'clear, forcible, picturesque style' (424). In particular, Mozley praises Brontë for eschewing a 'standard hero' in favour of M. Paul Emmanuel. The 'standard hero' would be someone like protagonist Lucy Snowe's first love-interest, Dr John Graham Bretton: a 'less discriminating observer' would perceive him as 'an uncommonly fine fellow', but the novel allows us to recognise in him

> a kind of worldliness as well as subtlety, an insight into his own interests, and a gift at securing them, which would render it impossible in him to commit what the world would consider an imprudence, and which makes him fortunate at the expense of magnanimity. (434)

M. Paul, by contrast, is 'a character in the highest degree fresh and original' (434), and the scenes featuring him are notable for Brontë's

> accuracy and truth of detail, the bright playful enjoyment of her own success, her power of seizing the point, of bringing minds in contact, of showing what vivid moments there are in scenes apparently trivial, if only a quick eye and graphic pen can catch the evanescent spirit, and give it consistency. (436–7)

The qualities the review commends in *Villette* stand out in stronger relief, too, when the discussion of Brontë's novel is read after Mozley's long and testy account of Lady Georgiana Fullerton's fictional effort, *Lady Bird*. The contrast is established at the outset, before Mozley goes on to deal with *Lady Bird*, then *Villette*. Since Fullerton 'has been educated in the consciousness of rank and station' and is part of 'a brilliant courted, envied society', this is 'the medium through which she has seen the world': hence the 'embarrassments, sins, sorrows' evident in her fiction are 'born of excitement, luxury, and a superabundance of leisure'. Brontë, on the other hand, 'has looked upon life under less agreeable, but perhaps more truth-telling circumstances': unlike Fullerton, she has known 'neglect' and 'the struggle with adverse fate' (401). And whereas Fullerton's characters 'too often think and feel out of one common stock of thought and sentiment', Brontë makes hers 'each speak and act according to their individual nature' (403).

For all the review's commendations of *Villette*, however, Charlotte Brontë herself was perturbed by the implication that she had been 'an alien, it might seem, from society, and amenable to none of its laws'. She wrote to the *Christian Remembrancer* in July 1853, invoking her reviewer (not surprisingly) as male, and declaring that 'no cause of seclusion such as he would imply has ever come near [her] thoughts, deeds, or life'. Her 'seclusion', she explained, was that of 'a country parsonage'; and now, as the last survivor of six children, and with a father in delicate health and threatened with blindness, her 'place consequently is at home'. In the October issue, the editor (W.B. Scott or James Mozley?) acknowledged the letter, saying that the reviewer's comments had been written 'in entire ignorance of the author's private history, and with no wish to pry into it'; he is now pleased to learn that the main reason for Charlotte Brontë's seclusion is 'devotion to the purest and most sacred of domestic ties'.[43]

In her correspondence with her publisher's deputy W.S. Williams, nonetheless, Charlotte Brontë showed that she had registered the mixed messages of the review, though she interpreted them as the result of conflicted responses, rather than as rhetorical strategies. She imagined her opponent as a High Church ecclesiastic, compelled against his will to keep reading *Villette*:

> He snarls, but still he reads. The book gets hold of him he curls his lip, he shows his teeth, he would fain anathematize; excommunicate the author; but he reads on, yes – and as he reads – he is forced both to *feel* and to *like* some portion of what is driven into his hostile iron nature. Nor can he … altogether hide the involuntary partiality; he does his best; he still speaks big and harsh, trying to inflict pain, striking at hazard, guessing at weak points, but hoping always to hit home.

She herself claims to feel 'content and thankful' – but apparently as 'Currer Bell', since she asserts of herself in the third person, 'when an enemy [the reviewer] is so influenced – he has not written in vain'.[44] Both Brontë and Mozley feel less vulnerable posing as men; by the time of *Villette*, however, Brontë is known to be female, and indeed writes to the *Remembrancer*'s editor as 'C. Brontë' in disclosing her true circumstances. Charlotte Brontë assumed of Anne Mozley's review, as she had of Elizabeth Rigby's review of *Jane Eyre* in 1848, that the perpetrator was male.

---

[43]   Quoted in Juliet Barker, *The Brontës* (London: Weidenfeld, 1994), p. 733.

[44]   Letter of 8 April 1853, quoted in Lyndall Gordon, *Charlotte Brontë: A Passionate Life* (London: Chatto & Windus, 1994), p. 285, Charlotte Brontë's emphasis.

Gaskell's biography of Charlotte Brontë was written partly to counter negative impressions of the novelist arising from such elements as the strong passions and independent thinking of her heroines which Mozley had criticised, as well as the behaviour and language sometimes blamed as 'coarse'. In reviewing the biography, Mozley made some criticisms of the Brontë sisters' responses to their circumstances, and confessed to some residual perplexity after reading it, saying of Charlotte: 'Who can sum up such a character? who can reconcile its contradictions, account for its eccentricities, nicely discriminate and mark out its good and evil, bring the whole nature into harmony?' (144). But she accepts that Gaskell's work explained much about the woman, and, quoting Charlotte Brontë's letter to the *Remembrancer* in response to the *Villette* review, expresses regret that lines from the review had 'caused her undesigned pain' (134–5). In addition, as the comparison Mozley makes between Austen and Brontë suggests, she believes that the content and tone of the writers' respective novels reflect their characters and their social circumstances.

Mozley certainly expresses doubts about the spiritual state of Charlotte Brontë, as it is implied by her life and writings: a focus on such an issue might in any case have been expected by readers of the *Christian Remembrancer*. Although both biography and novels show that Charlotte Brontë possessed a 'sense of divine presence … a need of God's help, and dependence on Him as of the dread Power on whom our happiness depends', for her this 'Deity' was 'a fate to be feared, a Power to be propitiated, a Master to be obeyed', an all-pervasive influence – but seldom 'a Father and a Friend' (91–2). Correspondingly, for all her knowledge of scriptural language and her fulfilment of the duties of a clergyman's daughter, Brontë lacked both a sense of the meaning of Christ and an upward spiritual yearning: a sense of being 'one with Him, hidden with Him, bought with a price, and therefore no longer our own', such that she must seek 'the things *above* – the second birth – the indwelling of the Spirit – mysteries – sacraments' (91, Mozley's emphasis). As a result of failing to achieve 'faith, nor joy and peace in believing', Charlotte Brontë was characterised by 'a clinging to time and sense', plus 'a low standard of excellence in others, and bitterness of spirit, narrow sympathies, and harsh judgments' (89). Moreover, her circumstances were made worse by her tendencies for a self-sacrifice which was often ultimately pointless: principally her (and her family's) toleration of and sacrifices for her brother Branwell, but also her overloading herself with housework so as to cover the inadequacies of the ageing servant Tabby (112ff.). Hannah Lawrance, as we have seen, also criticised the indulgence of Branwell Brontë revealed by the biography, but presented Charlotte as a victim of her brother and father, rather than as wilfully colluding in the subordination of her own life and interests to Branwell's.

On the other hand, Mozley accepts that much can be accounted for by the Brontë children's upbringing, as described rather luridly in the biography. They were neglected by their widowed father, allowed to develop only their intellects and their sense of household duty, and denied '[n]ourishing food, tender maternal watchfulness, the attentions and cares of the nursery, plenty of playthings' (96).

Their surroundings and experience, too, explain the wild and crude male characters in their novels: in Charlotte's case, she produced Mr Rochester because '[s]he thought real men were all that sort of thing, – selfish, somewhat grovelling, with no guiding principle, but redeemable through their purer affections' (124).

There is also for Mozley here an impressiveness about Charlotte Brontë which exists in spite of – but also partly because of – the strange circumstances of her life which the biography emphasises. She declares that 'Charlotte Brontë lived with a reality and clearness which throw busier careers into mist and shade', with the 'thought, feeling, passion' all heightened because of 'being confined in the narrowest range', and so her life teaches 'what small external aids' can serve to 'expand thought, to concentrate feeling, to intensify emotion'. Her very limited experiences 'furnished training enough for the acute intellect, taught the secrets of the human heart, and fed the vivid imagination – the faculty which glorifies every great idea, stamps every congenial fact indelibly on the brain, and gives significance to every encounter with the outer world' (87–8). Mozley is more confident than Sara Coleridge had been about women's potential to possess the transformative power of the imagination.

There is thus a close match for Mozley between Charlotte Brontë's life and works, as there is in Jane Austen's case. 'All her actuating principles influenced her works', Mozley argues: 'She and her works are identical', with her strength lying 'in analysis, in looking deep down into the heart' (92). But Brontë had no understanding of abstract ideas or of people in the mass: 'Things and persons must have entered into her brain through her heart, feelings, and sympathies, and been thus incorporated into her own being, for her to have a judgment upon them, or, we may add, a conscience about them' (94).

Mozley does discuss Charlotte Brontë explicitly as a woman writer – but with some inconsistency in her argument. Like Lawrance, she deals with Southey's famous letter which told Charlotte Brontë that '[l]iterature cannot be the business of a woman's life, and it ought not to be'. Unlike Lawrance, however, Mozley does not blame Southey for the letter, pointing out that what Brontë had sent him back in 1837 was only '*tolerable* verses', so he could not have registered her remarkable potential as a novelist. Yet she does assert that 'a vivid imagination and a forcible style – be they gift of man or woman – are given them for use' (116, Mozley's emphasis), following Gaskell's own line of argument. Mozley's view here is also consistent with those expressed in her other discussions of women's writing: one great advance during the nineteenth century has for her been the acceptance of women's writing on similar terms to men's. Also consistent, however, is her reservation about Charlotte Brontë's own belief that she could write only out of inspiration (140–41): in dealing with Mulock Craik's book the following year, Mozley would argue that women, like men, could write 'from no stimulus of genius, but mere exercise of reason and intellect'. The notion that writing had to be 'inspired' tended, in Mozley's opinion, to foster the belief in occasional female geniuses, at the expense of crediting substantial numbers of women with literary ability.

On the other hand, Mozley sometimes fudges nature and nurture in her account of Charlotte Brontë. One reason for sympathising with Charlotte Brontë, Mozley claims, is that she was subject to a conflict between mind and body, and she presents this conflict in gendered terms. Charlotte Brontë's mind was 'masculine, vigorous, active, keen, and daring', while her body was 'feeble, nervous, suffering under exertion' – that is, presumably feminine (89). But Mozley's discussion as a whole implies that this conflict resulted from nurture rather than nature: Patrick Brontë's childrearing methods starved the body and developed the intellect. Similarly, as Mozley presents it, what comes across as 'masculine' in Brontë's novels, such as the style and the presentation of the male characters, is identifiably the outcome of her unusual upbringing and range of experience. Mozley also blames Patrick Brontë for stymying his daughters' potential for enjoying 'trifles' and 'amusements': she argues that 'woman's nature' possesses a 'cheerful power … of extracting and imparting pleasure from little things – exercising wit and ingenuity on airy nothings' (117). But if women do manifest such a tendency, might not this be because women's lives are, in this period, more focused on 'airy nothings' and 'little things' than are men's?

Ultimately, however, Mozley, taking Gaskell's lead, plumps for a version of Brontë which is, despite all the novelist's unconventionality, recognisably feminine. Her case, Mozley says, shows that 'the boldest, most fearless style, may emanate from a nature which has its sensitive, shrinking, timid side' (136), while the scenes of *Jane Eyre* 'are all seen through woman's eyes', with 'an identification of the author with the heroine which could not be assumed' (124). Although the novels express in many ways the strange, warped creature that was the 'true' Charlotte Brontë, the woman herself was ultimately more feminine than her writing. Mozley herself was of course aware that masculinity in writing could be a performance.

Mozley also gives some attention to Emily and Anne Brontë, but in ways that make Charlotte's strengths and virtues stand out – she is more normal than Emily, and more gifted than Anne. Mozley's portrayal is consistent with but also extends Gaskell's own presentation of the younger sisters. She perceives Emily as exemplifying in an extreme, even inhuman way, the Brontë family's intense self-preoccupation, such that she had no meaningful human ties outside the family, and lacked concern for even its members (106). But the information about her provided by Gaskell does serve to explain for Mozley how Emily could have written *Wuthering Heights*: her strongest feelings were for dogs, rather than for people, and so the characters of the novel were comprehensible if imagined in canine terms. Mozley is not being facetious here: she argues at length that '[j]ust such instinctive, soulless, savage creatures as compose a pack of hounds, form the *dramatis personae* of this unique story' (128).

By contrast with Emily, Anne Brontë was 'not unnatural', while she was also more truly Christian (in Mozley's terms) than Charlotte: her death was 'illuminated by the Christian's peace and hope', as she 'placed her full, deliberate trust in her Redeemer's merits' (129). Yet for Mozley, her novel *The Tenant of Wildfell Hall*, though inflected with the moral purpose that *Wuthering Heights* clearly lacks, can only be testimony to the baneful effects of Anne's prolonged exposure to Branwell and his vices. It possesses 'coarseness of manners and unfathomable vulgarity of tone', brutal men and offensive women, such that even the supposed hero (Gilbert Markham) is '[v]iolent in his temper, rude in his impulses, fickle in his attachments, ungrateful, sullen, vain and loutish' (130–31). The novel has less 'force or swing' than *Wuthering Heights*, while Anne's lack of the imaginative power possessed by both her sisters means that it would actually fail to have the morally improving effect intended. Mozley's judgment of *The Tenant* here betrays a narrowness on her part, but it also suggests that it was not necessarily straightforward for her to find consistency between a woman writer's personality and her works.

One appeal of the *Life of Charlotte Brontë* in 1857, as Mozley acknowledges at the beginning of her review, was that it seemed to offer a partial solution to a mystery – what kind of woman was behind the novels of 'Currer Bell'? Two years later appeared a novel that made a great impact, as *Jane Eyre* had done in 1847, and created another mystery: who was behind the pseudonym, 'George Eliot'. As was her wont, Anne Mozley tried to link writer and text, hypothesising as to the character of the author of *Adam Bede*. She was not of course unusual in doing this, but she was unusual in identifying the author as female, on internal evidence. Again her assumptions about women and women's writing are salient.

As noted in the Introduction, Anne Mozley begins by briefly tracing the expansion of novel-reading among those who claim serious interests, a development she attributes to the increasing variety and richness of fiction from Scott onwards (she adduces Dickens, Thackeray, Kingsley, Charlotte Brontë, Gaskell, Bulwer-Lytton and Yonge). But the culmination of this trend has been *Adam Bede*, 'a story which we believe has found its way into hands indifferent to all previous fiction, to readers who welcome it as the voice of their own experience in a sense no other book has ever been'.[45]

If *Adam Bede* is the voice of readers' experience, this in Mozley's view is largely because it impresses them as the hard-won fruit of the author's own. The novel's evocations of country life suggest 'constant familiar interactions with its details', coexisting with a high level of education. Although, like most reviewers of the novel, Mozley writes at length about its recreations of the recent past, and what could by the 1850s be called its realism (a term Eliot herself had pioneered), she also focuses on the wisdom that seems to pervade it. The writer, she says, comes across as 'one who has learnt from experience, and, we must believe, real contact with trouble': all the novelist's views 'are clearly arrived at by a process of thought', and 'the weight of calm conviction gives value to every sentiment whether we agree or not'. This novel (unlike Bulwer-Lytton's fiction as Mozley had represented it in the previous issue of *Bentley's*), is the product of 'hard-won knowledge, with ample space to look back upon the conflict, to mature thought

[45] '*Adam Bede* and Recent Novels', *Bentley's Quarterly Review*, no. 2 (July 1859): 433–72, at 433–4. Subsequent references to the review will be included parenthetically in the text.

out of transient pain' (435–6). Whether strictly autobiographical or not, Mozley is convinced that it shows that 'the author has witnessed, perhaps experienced, all the deeper, more powerful feelings so truthfully portrayed' (436).

This author, too, she opines, is female, and in dealing with this question, Mozley both accepts that there are subjects outside women's range, and makes significant claims for that range. So, she acknowledges, 'there are subjects and passions which will always continue man's inalienable field of inquiry', but she assures her readers that *Adam Bede* does not impinge on them – without actually spelling out what they are. For some women, moreover, 'a wide range of human nature lies open to their comprehension', and '[t]he time is past for any felicity, force, or freedom of expression' to rule female authorship out of court. As with her treatment of Charlotte Brontë, Mozley does not clearly distinguish what comes from women's 'nature' and what from their habitual way of life, but the emphasis here is on the latter. So the 'full, close scrutiny of observation exercised in scanning every feature of a bounded field of inquiry' recalls the conventional belief that women had a better eye for detail than understanding of wider concepts – but such a talent might also be developed from their habitually circumscribed lives. Similarly, the novel's strong focus on clerical doings might not betray a clerical hand (the Warwickshire clergyman Joseph Liggins had been claiming authorship), so much as a woman's, since for women 'the politics of a parish, its leaders and party divisions' are 'the most stirring bit of public life that comes under their immediate eye' – a circumstance evidently the consequence of women's social position. Mozley has it both ways, saying that 'women are by nature and circumstance the great clerical sympathisers' (437).

Most interesting as an insight into the novel's narrative perspective, is the comment that 'the position of the writer towards every point in discussion is a woman's position, that is, from a stand of observation rather than more active participation'. Yet neither a woman author's supposedly circumscribed life nor her stance as an observer weakens a novel where her experience has yielded such wisdom. In addition, her sex actually gives her some insights less available to men. The novel's male characters fail to register the shallowness and self-centredness of Hetty Sorrel, because of her sheer physical appeal, and this circumstance, according to Mozley, discloses on the novelist's part 'a feminine insight into men's weakness for grace and beauty, and their utter blindness to what may lie underneath a fair outside' (444–5). This point foreshadows Julia Kavanagh's observation in 1862 of how some male characters in the fiction of Burney, Edgeworth and Austen illustrate women's more negative experiences of men's behaviour and judgments.

As with Mozley's reviewing of *Villette* in tandem with Lady Georgiana Fullerton's *Lady Bird*, the importance she gives to *Adam Bede* stands out in strong relief when we are aware that she reviews four other novels in her article, but devotes over 23 of her 40 pages to *Adam Bede* alone. Next in importance is the latest effort from Anthony Trollope – *The Bertrams*, which is discussed in six pages just after the treatment of *Adam Bede*. But whereas 'George Eliot' is one of 'the loftier race of novelists', those who aim to 'show us the universal brotherhood of human kind', Trollope's fiction, if engaging, is simply part of contemporary 'light literature' (456). Eliot herself, who disliked reviews, called this one 'on the whole the best we have seen' in Britain, and arranged for the author to be sent a copy of her next novel, *The Mill on the Floss*. Paradoxically, she attributed the review to the kind of male and clerical authorship that had been often ascribed to *Adam Bede* itself, having heard it was by 'a Mr Mosely a clergyman and a writer in the "Times"' – a confusion, on the part of her informant, with Tom Mozley, who was indeed both of those things.[46]

One of the reasons for *Adam Bede*'s popularity, according to Anne Mozley, was that it dealt with religious issues from a non-sectarian viewpoint, and she observed that reviewers had all identified in the novel a tone on such questions which was 'orthodox and serious, but viewed rather in their moral than doctrinal aspect'. Readers had welcomed the novel's implicit strictures on narrow sermons and 'the war of doctrine waged in this polemical age' (434–5). But it had not occurred to Mozley, any more than to other reviewers, that the hard-won experience from which the novel had emerged had entailed a severance from the Christian belief system, at least in its theological aspects: a rejection of belief in God, in Christ as a semi-divine entity, in the Bible as divinely inspired, and in a supernatural realm to which human beings could aspire after death.

Some time shortly after writing the *Adam Bede* review, Mozley evidently heard reports as to who George Eliot really was, since she comments on these at the end of another account of recent fiction, this time in the *Christian Remembrancer*. (This article reviews another Mulock Craik effort, *A Life for a Life*, and two now-forgotten novels.) Here she maintains the view that *Adam Bede* is 'a work of genius' which, if written by a woman, 'places woman's aptitude for this form of composition in some points higher than it has ever stood before – fairly side by side with man'.[47] It is also a work which demonstrates 'a profound realization of certain great moral principles as the key to man's nature and moral government', and which comes from the heart. But if it is the work of the figure known for her translations of books that challenged Christian orthodoxy (D.F. Strauss's *Life of Jesus* and Ludwig Feuerbach's *The Essence of Christianity*), and also for her non-marital cohabitation with George Henry Lewes, then it perplexes Mozley. The author may be a woman, as she had guessed, but there is no fit between *Adam Bede* and this particular woman – and this is 'an enigma which interposes itself and confuses our critical powers when we attempt any analysis'. Mozley cannot reconcile the novel's apparently honest and 'deep religious sentiment', with the religious scepticism evident in the known works of the purported author. If the

---

[46]   Letter to Charles Bray, 25 November 1859, in Gordon S. Haight (ed.), *The George Eliot Letters* (6 vols, New Haven and London: Yale University Press, 1954), vol. 3, pp. 213–14, Fanny and Frank Mozley, 'Memoir' in *Essays from 'Blackwood'. By the Late Anne Mozley*, p. x.

[47]   'Our Female Novelists', *Christian Remembrancer*, 38 (October 1859): 305–39, at 338–9.

novelist is who she is rumoured to be, then 'there is nothing in "Adam Bede" so surprizing as its authorship'.

How Mozley responded to Eliot's gift of *The Mill on the Floss* is not recorded, but she seems to have enjoyed the Dodson sisters, to judge from incidental references in other articles. In a piece on 'Contempt' for the *Saturday Review,* she mentions them as despising 'all who were not Dodsons',[48] and in an article for *Blackwood's* where she is discriminating between unreasonable and reasonable behaviour among women, she cites a scene where Mrs Glegg interrupts a conversation between her husband and the packman Bob Jakin by claiming that packmen can be murderers. Although this accusation seems unreasonable, Mrs Glegg herself is not, since she achieves her purpose of breaking up a conversation in which she is not involved.[49] Mozley does not make the point herself, but perhaps this scene implies that there can be aspects of women's behaviour which cannot be pigeonholed as the product of either feminine intuition or masculine intellect?

Anne Mozley did not review any of Eliot's other novels, but her comments in 1868 to John Blackwood (Eliot's publisher as well as her own) about Eliot's poem, *The Spanish Gypsy*, suggest that she continued to grapple with the implications of the other writer's now notorious repudiation of Christianity as a theological system. She commends the poem, saying that it demonstrates Eliot's 'overpowering interest in the subtler workings of the mind', and – recalling *The Mill on the Floss* again – acknowledges that novel's evidence that 'the gypsy race has been an interest to her mind from early childhood'. But Mozley suspects that now 'gypsies are attractive to her as having no religion & therefore fit subject for experiment'. Zarca, the gypsy who reveals to the protagonist Fedalma her gypsy heritage and her consequent racial destiny, Mozley sees as 'a sort of Moses, only without any external inspiration'. Foreshadowing what has often been said since about the relationship between Eliot's teaching and Christianity, Mozley observes that '[t]he book could not have been written without Christian training, the morality as far as we go with it is Christian morality; but still it is a resolved effort to dissociate morality from religion & even to assert a morality higher, more self-sacrificing than Christianity teaches'. (Contemporary reviews of the poem did not discuss it in a Christian framework.) The Christian Anne Mozley, as in 1859, still finds it hard to credit George Eliot's rejection of Christianity, and notes in the poem 'a constant effort to contract the great unseen world into this visible one'. She also respects Eliot's honesty, but thinks the poem reveals the baneful consequences of abandoning Christianity: 'the very severity the terrible demands she makes on self-renunciation strike us as harsh; if indeed this life is all'. Mozley herself cannot believe that 'human beings are constituted either to excessive austere virtue & absolute self abnegation without hope in a future, or to endure the contemplation

---

[48]   *Essays on Social Subjects from the Saturday Review*, vol. 1 (1864), pp. 58–68, at p. 61.

[49]   'Vapours, Fears and Tremors', *Blackwood's Edinburgh Magazine*, 104 (February 1869): 228–37, at 236.

of it in others'. She goes on: 'Pain and suffering are not good in themselves. We *must* desire our own felicity and surely ought to aim at it', and she thinks too that the severe moral of the poem will injure its popularity.[50] As she had argued with respect to Charlotte Brontë's own self-denial, self-sacrifice is only valuable if animated by an inner sense of Christ and the hope of a future life.

It is difficult to judge how different Mozley really believed the two sexes were in their natures and their writing – how far her assertions of difference emerged from personal (including religious) belief, and how far from a felt need to accommodate the views of conservative readers. Her appraisals of Austen, the Brontës and Eliot do imply, nonetheless, that whatever women's writing is like, it is by no means homogeneous: there are significant divergences among the outputs of various women writers. But her treatment of them suggests too that, in both gender-related and other ways, she expects novels to bear the signs of their authors' characters. So when her brother James and his wife, while visiting the Blackwoods in 1867, met with another prominent *Blackwood's* writer, Margaret Oliphant, Mozley reported back to John Blackwood that '[w]hat he said of her answered very well I thought to what such a writer ought to be'.[51]

There is no surviving evidence to suggest that Anne Mozley and Margaret Oliphant ever met in person. But since the letters of both to the Blackwood publishing firm are extant, plus some of the responses to both from members of the firm, it is clear that they were interested in each other's work. It seems that the firm did not disclose Mozley's identity to Oliphant, in keeping with her known wishes, whereas Mozley could recognise Oliphant's style, even when her fiction and criticism was published anonymously. (Mozley was also able to recognise the author of the anonymous novel *Nina Balatka* as Anthony Trollope, despite its being set in Eastern Europe.[52])

On the other hand, Mozley initially found it difficult to credit that so many and such diverse works could all be by Oliphant. She asked John Blackwood in March 1865 to confirm or deny a rumour she had heard that the *Chronicles of Carlingford* series were 'by the Mrs Oliphant who wrote Miss Margaret Maitland & a host of similar novels'.[53] The current *Chronicles* novel, *Miss Marjoribanks*, is, she believes, far superior to *Margaret Maitland*, 'a surprising performance, a photograph of a mind with wh. the artist has not the least sympathy … wonderfully true as well as amusing'. John Blackwood obviously sent the letter to Oliphant, identifying its author as a writer for the hard-hitting *Saturday Review*, and Oliphant for her part found an incongruity between the letter and its *Saturday* connection – telling Blackwood, 'it is incredible that a Saturday Reviewer should write such

---

[50] Letter of 25 June 1868, MS 4237, National Library of Scotland (Mozley's emphasis).

[51] Letter of 23 September 1867, MS 4244, National Library of Scotland.

[52] Letter to John Blackwood, 7 September 1866, MS 4312, National Library of Scotland.

[53] Letter of 2 March 1865, MS 4725, National Library of Scotland.

a pretty hand!'.[54] Oliphant's response was that the difference in her books was 'natural enough when you reflect that the first one was written when [she] was twenty, and the others some the work of a "troubled" life, not much at leisure', so that '[i]t is only to be expected that one should do a little better when one has come to one's strength'. Blackwood then confirmed to Mozley Oliphant's authorship of all the novels she had found so uneven, and reported back her comments on the issue. He had wanted Mozley's praise of *Miss Marjoribanks* to lift Oliphant's spirits following the loss of her only daughter, part of her 'troubled' life.[55]

Mozley discussed *Miss Marjoribanks* at some length in her *Remembrancer* article of July 1866, 'Youth as Depicted in Modern Fiction', and the parallels between her argument here and what she says to John Blackwood in letters identify the review as hers. (The identification is also borne out by the tests of the Centre for Literary and Linguistic Computing at the University of Newcastle.) The closest verbal parallel is between the article's comment on how often Oliphant uses 'to be sure' and 'naturally' and a targeting of the same tendency in the letter already quoted.[56] As the letter had done, the article also deals with the sheer number and variable quality of Oliphant's works; both it and a later letter identify her most impressive characterisations (apart from Lucilla Marjoribanks) as Mr Tozer and Phoebe Tozer, also from the *Chronicles*, and comment on the writer's apparently increasing sympathy for Lucilla as *Miss Marjoribanks* (which *Blackwood's* was serialising) goes on.[57]

Mozley's review and letters are all very positive about the characterisation of Lucilla Marjoribanks, but in the review she criticises the implausibility of the plot – attributing the problem to a limitation of some women writers, as well as to Oliphant's own necessarily rapid composition. It is not convincing, according to Mozley, that Lucilla is 'so royally potent for ten years of actual life', with 'all Carlingford thronging to her "Thursdays", and under her control, and occupied generally with Lucilla for ten years'. This 'absurdity', she says, results from 'the especial infirmity of female writers, otherwise very acute discerners, to reason from too bounded a view, to make great things hang on small occurrences … to stretch nine-days' wonders into historical events, and to draw into the vortex of the plot and stimulate with its interests numbers on whom it can have no personal bearing'.[58] That is, Mozley draws on the traditional notion that women can understand the minutiae of domestic life, its 'airy nothings', without being able to grasp its larger context.

---

[54]   Letter of 8 March 1865, MS 4202, National Library of Scotland.

[55]   Letter of 31 March 1865, MS 30361, National Library of Scotland.

[56]   'Youth as Depicted in Modern Fiction', *Christian Remembrancer*, 52 (July 1866): 184–211, at 201.

[57]   'Youth as Depicted in Modern Fiction', 198, 201; Anne Mozley to John Blackwood, 1 April 1865, MS 4201, National Library of Scotland, and 3 March 1866, MS 4725, National Library of Scotland.

[58]   Ibid., 199.

Moreover, Oliphant's rapid composition means that for Mozley her fiction, unlike the novels of Charlotte Brontë and George Eliot – the latter of whom at least grasps larger social contexts – does not always come across as a grappling with actual experience. In her weaker texts, Oliphant seems to be 'writing as in a dream, working from a mere reflection of a mirror, like the lady of Shalott, and never lifting her eyes to see the real life which passes by', and there are recurrent themes throughout her fiction whose repetition in the stronger work mars its effect.[59]

Margaret Oliphant, as is well-known, needed to write for money, and this fact emerges strongly when her correspondence with the Blackwoods is considered in tandem with that of Anne Mozley. Mozley suggested topics that interested her, and never published more than three *Blackwood's* articles in the one year; Oliphant was an extremely prolific contributor, and constantly suggested topics for coverage. Oliphant also often asked to be sent books, not only for review, but as background reading: she sometimes had to 'get up' her subjects.

A related contrast is that between Mozley's sense of belonging to an intellectual community – even if one that did not always give women's intellect and writings the respect they deserve – and Oliphant's sense of herself as outside the intelligentsia, even as she struggled to support her two sons at Eton and then Oxford. For example, while visiting Oxford in 1879, Oliphant writes to John Blackwood that 'intellectualism like any other *ism* is monotonous', and that young intellectuals are 'so much afraid of committing themselves or risking anything that may be found wanting in any minutiae of correctness', such that '[s]cholarship is a sort of poison tree and kills anything.' But her own name on a text 'seems to be sufficient warrant for all manner of accusations of inconsistencies, from all the whippersnappers of *young* scholars'.[60]

The contrast between the two women comes to the fore when Oliphant, in her 'New Books' column in *Blackwood's* in December 1872, reviews Augustus Hare's *Memorials of a Quiet Life*. The following month, Mozley remonstrates to John Blackwood that Oliphant (whose voice she recognises) had treated the book cruelly, partly from not having read it carefully enough. She notes that it 'has excited a great deal of interest among people whose opinion has weight', and that the Hares 'are names still remembered in both universities'.[61] Blackwood clearly passed the comments on to Oliphant, who said in riposte that the book's success was attributable to something she was 'anxious to struggle against – the fictitious reputation got up by men who happen to be "remembered at the universities"'.[62] Oliphant had in turn been critical of Mozley's article 'Clever Women', registering

---

[59] Ibid., 198.

[60] Letter of 16 March 1879, MS 4396, National Library of Scotland (Oliphant's emphasis).

[61] Letter of 31 January 1873, MS 4308, National Library of Scotland.

[62] Letter of 6 February 1873, quoted in Mrs Harry Coghill (ed.), *Autobiography and Letters of Mrs Margaret Oliphant* (1899), intro. Q.D. Leavis (Leicester: Leicester University Press, 1974), p. 241.

the condescending aspect of its narrative voice (although not its authorship), and writing to John Blackwood:

> Who is your friend who is so smartly patronizing to women in the last number? It is very comforting to be told that we may write for a living without being monsters – but isn't it a trifle out of date to say so just at this particular moment?[63]

No reply survives to reveal whether Blackwood disclosed to Oliphant anything about the critic. By 1868, Oliphant herself had been publishing for nearly 20 years, and her periodical contributions from the 1850s onward will be one focus of the next chapter.

---

[63]   Letter of 1 October 1868, MS 4238, National Library of Scotland.

Chapter 5
Margaret Oliphant and Mary Augusta Ward

Margaret Oliphant

Margaret Oliphant was a regular reviewer for *Blackwood's Edinburgh Magazine* for over 40 years, from the mid-1850s till her death in 1897, writing on multifarious authors female and male, past and present, British and Continental. She also reviewed, more sporadically, for other major periodicals such as the *Edinburgh Review*, *Fraser's Magazine* and the *Contemporary Review*. Oliphant's work as a literary critic, and also as a commentator on the 'Woman Question', has received welcome attention in recent years.[1] But as a way in to discussing her career as a critic of women's writing, I wish to consider first of all an article which, because it concerned the canonical male author Thomas Hardy, has long been known to scholars.

This is 'The Anti-Marriage League', published in *Blackwood's* for January 1896, as a review of Hardy's *Jude the Obscure* and Grant Allen's *The Woman Who Did*: long after Oliphant's death, Hardy was to describe it as 'the screaming of a poor lady in *Blackwood*'.[2] Since it attacked the prominence of sexual feeling in the two novels, the review has been interpreted as an outburst of old-fashioned Victorian prudishness – and certainly a comment such as that 'nothing so coarsely

---

[1]   Elisabeth Jay, *Mrs Oliphant: 'A Fiction to Herself' A Literary Life* (Oxford: Clarendon Press, 1995); Valerie Sanders, *Eve's Renegades: Victorian Anti-Feminist Women Novelists* (Houndmills, Basingstoke and London: Macmillan; New York: St Martin's, 1996); John Stock Clarke (comp.), *Margaret Oliphant (1828–1897): Non-Fictional Writings: A Bibliography* (St Lucia, Brisbane: Department of English, University of Queensland, 1997). See also Joan Bellamy, 'Margaret Oliphant: "mightier than the mightiest of her sex"', in Joan Bellamy, Anne Laurence and Gill Perry (eds), *Women, Scholarship and Criticism: Gender and Knowledge c.1790–1900* (Manchester: Manchester University Press, 2000), pp. 143–58, and 'A Lifetime of Reviewing: Margaret Oliphant on Charlotte Brontë', *Brontë Studies*, 29 (2004): 37–42; Barbara Onslow, *Women of the Press in Nineteenth-Century Britain* (Houndmills, Basingstoke and London: Macmillan; New York: St Martin's, 2000); George Worth, 'Margaret Oliphant and Macmillan's Magazine', in Elizabeth James (ed.), *Macmillan: A Publishing Tradition* (Houndmills, Basingstoke: Palgrave; New York: St Martin's, 2002), pp. 83–101; Anne M. Scriven, 'Margaret Oliphant's "Marriage" to *Maga*', *Scottish Studies Review*, 8 (2007): 27–36.

[2]   'The Anti-Marriage League', *Blackwood's Edinburgh Magazine*, 159 (January 1896): 135–49. Thomas Hardy, Postscript (1912) to the Preface to *Jude the Obscure* [1895], ed. Cedric Watts (Peterborough, Ontario and Orchard Park, NY: Broadview, 2004), pp. 41–2.

indecent as the whole history of Jude in his relations with Arabella has ever been put in English print'[3] comes across that way, although Oliphant does qualify the assertion by the words, 'that is to say, from the hands of a Master'. But there is more than disgust at sexualised conversation and behaviour behind the disquiet that Oliphant expresses here. There is a sense that the bond between men and women, potentially comprising many aspects, such as 'the perfect friendship of joy and sorrow, of interests and of hopes, of mutual help, support, and consolation',[4] has been debased in Hardy's novel to one biological urge. Moreover, by offering in Arabella Donn and Sue Bridehead two central women characters who differ much from each other while still having a damaging effect on his hero's life, Hardy was for Oliphant betraying a reductive and offensive attitude to women. She sees Arabella as appallingly crude and sex-obsessed, and Sue as self-willed and manipulative, but both as defined in the novel predominantly by their sexual behaviour. In her view, the novel aims to 'show after all what destructive and ruinous creatures [women] are, in general circumstances and in every development, whether brutal or refined'.[5] As we shall see, Hardy was for Oliphant hardly unique among male writers in his reductive approach to women's potential.

This review was unusual in Oliphant's output, in that it was more or less signed: she initialed it at the end, and it was attributed to 'Mrs Oliphant' in the table of contents. She seems to have wanted to write here overtly as a woman – she is defending her sex against what she sees as the insulting stereotyping visited on it by Hardy and Allen. But she was uncertain, even after a literary career of over 40 years, known for her many novels and monographs if not for her periodical contributions, whether she had the public literary stature to launch an effective attack. 'The evil is very great', she wrote to Archibald Blackwood – 'I only doubt if my voice is authoritative enough to denounce it'.[6]

Although her volume publications often appeared under her own name, Oliphant supported the convention of critical anonymity in periodicals. In her *Literary History of England in the End of the Eighteenth and Beginning of the Nineteenth Century*, she argued that 'the verdict of an important publication … is more telling as well as more dignified than that of an individual, whose opinion, in nine cases out of ten, becomes of inferior importance to us the moment we are acquainted with his name'.[7] That is, she endorsed the traditional belief that the identity of a periodical transcended that of any individual contributor. Even in the other one case out of 10, as she contends a few years later in memorialising the career of a notable *Blackwood's* reviewer, the Rev. W. Lucas Collins, anonymity

---

[3]   'The Anti-Marriage League', 138.

[4]   Ibid., 144.

[5]   Ibid., 139.

[6]   Letter of 28 November 1895, MS 4635, National Library of Scotland, quoted in Joan Bellamy, 'Margaret Oliphant: "mightier than the mightiest of her sex"', p. 148.

[7]   (3 vols, London: Macmillan, 1882), vol. 2, p. 59.

frees the reviewer from 'the embarrassing difficulties of holding the literary balance steady when treating friends or acquaintances'.[8]

Oliphant's concern in writing 'The Anti-Marriage League' under her own name was about the strength of her own reputation, but Hardy's characterisation of the review as 'the screaming of a poor lady in *Blackwood*' suggests that patronising treatment because of her sex was another risk. There have been valuable recent studies focusing on Oliphant's gendering of her reviewing voice. As well as being discussed by Elisabeth Jay and Valerie Sanders, this was one emphasis in the articles by Ann Heilmann and Sandra Spencer in the special issue of *Women's Writing* devoted to Oliphant in 1999, which examined her writings in *Blackwood's* on the legal and political rights of women.[9] Both J. Haythornthwaite and Joanne Shattock have explored the gendering (or lack thereof) of the voices in Oliphant's journalism over her career as a whole, and Solveig C. Robinson has discussed the overtly masculine personae she adopted in her late-career *Blackwood's* contributions as the 'Looker-On' and the man in 'The Old Saloon'.[10] In this context, it is notable that when writing as a woman in 'The Anti-Marriage League', Oliphant claims not to know the works of Emile Zola, the only novels she considers likely to have come close to the 'indecency' of *Jude the Obscure*, whereas an earlier 'Old Saloon' piece in a male voice, although critical of contemporary French fiction, makes it clear that the writer is familiar with it.[11]

What I wish to emphasise at this point, however, is not so much the gendering (or sometime lack of gendering) of Oliphant's reviewing voices, as her recurrent concern with the lack of respect with which women, including women writers, are often treated, compared with men. In her published work, this is particularly evident in her review of George Meredith's *The Egoist*: Meredith, although not popular, is, she says, 'a favourite with people who are supposed to know much better than the multitude', such that '[n]ot to know Mr Meredith is to argue yourself unknown', and *The Egoist* is a book which 'claims to represent to us the leading qualities of

---

[8]   'Rev. W. Lucas Collins', *Blackwood's Edinburgh Magazine*, 141 (June 1887): 734–6, at 735.

[9]   Ann Heilmann, 'Mrs Grundy's Rebellion: Margaret Oliphant Between Orthodoxy and the New Woman', and Sandra Spencer, 'Words, Terms, and Other "Unchancy" Things: Rhetorical Strategies and Self-Definition in "The Laws Concerning Women"', *Women's Writing*, 6/2 (1999): 215–37, 251–9.

[10]   J. Haythornthwaite, 'Friendly Encounters: A Study of the Relationship Between the House of Blackwood and Margaret Oliphant in her Role as Literary Critic', *Publishing History*, 28 (1990): 79–88; Joanne Shattock, 'Work for Women: Margaret Oliphant's Journalism', in Laurel Brake, Bill Bell and David Finkelstein (eds), *Nineteenth-Century Media and the Construction of Identities* (Houndmills, Basingstoke: Palgrave, 2000), pp. 165–77; Solveig C. Robinson, 'Expanding a "Limited Orbit": Margaret Oliphant, *Blackwood's Edinburgh Magazine* and the Development of a Critical Voice', *Victorian Periodicals Review*, 38/2 (2005): 199–220.

[11]   'French Novels', in 'The Old Saloon', *Blackwood's Edinburgh Magazine*, 144 (September 1888): 419–42, at 440–42.

the human race in an exceptionally clear and animated way'. But to Oliphant, the novel is 'three huge volumes made up of a thousand conversations, torrents of words in half lines continued, and continued, and continued, till every sentiment contained in them is beaten to death in extremest extenuation, and the reader's head aches, and his bones are weary'. Despite his critical eminence, Meredith is in fact no better than the women novelists 'who are rated in the newspapers about the devices to which they are driven to furnish forth their third volume'.[12] Even where a comparison with the reception of women writers is not made, Oliphant sometimes suggests that there is a sort of literary/critical 'boys' club' which allows some male writers to enjoy an undeservedly elevated prestige not available to their female counterparts. We have already noted her response to Augustus Hare's *Memorials of a Quiet Life*; of Matthew Arnold, she declared in the *St James Gazette* that his 'reputation is very greatly that of a man borne upward on the shoulders of his friends'.[13]

Oliphant could also be acute about the notions underlying some male commentary on women, as we shall see in her treatment of J.W. Cross's *Life and Letters of George Eliot*, and of Austen-Leigh's *Memoir of Jane Austen*. When she submitted the article on Burns in her *Blackwood's* series, 'A Century of Great Poets', John Blackwood edited out much of her criticism of Burns's partner Jean Armour. But Oliphant was far from attributing this to any respect for the woman concerned – rather, she asserted, 'the tolerance you men pride yourselves on arises from contempt, a sentiment which we [women] don't entertain for ourselves'.[14] Less direct, because in print, is her commentary of 1862 on the reasons for the continuing fame of the eighteenth-century figures Mrs Delany and Mrs Thrale. The explanation she ostensibly favours is that 'some national instinct of humanity points out as the perfection of her sex, the appreciative sympathetic woman, whose business it is to comprehend, to perceive, to quicken the eye and ear of society with that bright and sweet intelligence, which, in the most subtle, imperceptible way, leads, and forms, and defines public opinion, and brings genius and excellence into fashion'.[15] This is the kind of woman who draws out and helps to articulate men's ideas, without putting herself forward, the woman who works through influence rather than direct creative or intellectual endeavour. Oliphant's alternative, more cynical, explanation of the long popularity of such women is attributed to 'some fond female fanatics', but it is still spelt out: 'the jealousy of man, which keeps down the gifted among women, gladly compounds by elevating now and then a

---

[12]   'New Novels', *Blackwood's Edinburgh Magazine*, 128 (September 1880): 378–404, at 401–4.

[13]   *St James Gazette*, 9 May 1888, quoted in Elisabeth Jay, *Mrs Oliphant: 'A Fiction to Herself' A Literary Life* (Oxford: Clarendon Press, 1995), p. 79.

[14]   Letter to John Blackwood, 1872, n.d., MS 4295, National Library of Scotland.

[15]   'The Lives of Two Ladies', *Blackwood's Edinburgh Magazine*, 91 (April 1862): 401–23, at 402.

feminine celebrity whose claims can never come into rivalry with his own'.[16] Like Jane Williams (who had published *The Literary Women of England* the previous year), Oliphant registers the appeal to men of the unthreatening literary woman.

Unfortunately, according to Oliphant, a woman of intellectual claims may try too hard to counter conventional assumptions about women. This was the case with Sara Coleridge, whose *Memoir and Letters*, edited by her daughter Edith Coleridge, Oliphant reviewed in 1873. 'By way of revulsion, perhaps, from the frivolity and lightness of character so often attributed to them', women like Sara Coleridge can be 'more pitilessly intellectual' than men of similar attainments. On the evidence of the letters, Sara Coleridge is for Oliphant 'always at the same high level, always thinking, always communicating her thoughts'. She never lapses into 'gossip' or 'personal comment', such that she 'never unbends from the height of reflectiveness, from the serene justice of her moral judgment, and her disposition towards the discussion of intellectual questions'.[17] Oliphant does not here take into account the possibility that Sara Coleridge found private letters a less contentious means of communicating her ideas than publications; more surprisingly, given her scepticism about the biographical accounts of Jane Austen and George Eliot offered by their relatives, Oliphant does not canvass the possibility that Edith Coleridge has edited out personal elements from her mother's letters (as she had).

We have noted that both Hannah Lawrance and Julia Kavanagh ascribed to women writers greater insight into the female character than was possessed by men. Oliphant was certainly scathing about the limitations of some prominent male novelists' apparent understanding of women. Of Thackeray, she observed that he 'does not seem acquainted with anything feminine between a nursery-maid and a fine lady – an indiscriminate idolator of little children and an angler for a rich husband', such that he offers 'tender pretty fools' rather than 'rational creatures'. She declares that 'besides marrying, and contriving opportunities to give in marriage, besides the nursery and its necessities, there are certain uses for womankind in this world of ours'.[18] In an obituary article on Dickens, she commented that Little Dorrit was 'one of those inconceivably and foolishly devoted little persons, mawkishly fond of some disagreeable relation, and delighting in making victims and sacrifices of themselves, who represent the highest type of female character to the author'.[19] Like Hardy's women characters many years later, Thackeray's and Dickens's female figures are in Oliphant's view defined primarily through the way they treat men.

---

[16]   Ibid., 403.

[17]   'New Books', *Blackwood's Edinburgh Magazine*, 114 (September 1873): 368–90, at 370–71.

[18]   'Mr. Thackeray and His Novels', *Blackwood's Edinburgh Magazine*, 77 (January 1855): 86–96, at 90, 95.

[19]   'Charles Dickens', *Blackwood's Edinburgh Magazine*, 109 (June 1871): 673–95, at 691.

But difficulty in representing the opposite sex justly was not for Oliphant a gender-specific problem, to judge from some of her other commentaries: in an earlier article in Dickens, she had remarked that '[v]ague pictures of perfection figure in a woman's novel for the hero, and indistinct visions of beauty and sweetness represent, for the most part, the heroines of a man'.[20] Moreover, Anthony Trollope, a writer whom Oliphant considered had never had his due from critics,[21] did in her view show some insight into women. He 'realises the position of a sensible and right-minded woman among the ordinary affairs of the world', of a 'rational creature[ ]', as is borne out by his portrayal of Mrs Archdeacon (Susan) Grantly in his Barchester series:

> Mrs Grantly's perception at once of her husband's character and of his mistakes
> – her careful abstinence from active interference and her certainty to come in
> right at the end – her half-amused, half-troubled spectatorship, in short, of all the
> annoyances her men-kind make for themselves, her consciousness of the futility
> of all decided attempts to set them right, and patient waiting upon the superior
> logic of events … is a perfect triumph of profound and delicate observation.[22]

Of a different order of insight, and even more impressive, is Samuel Richardson's representation of his heroine Clarissa – the result of Richardson's wide and close acquaintance with women and their points of view, but of something more as well. For Clarissa, claims Oliphant, is a 'virgin–martyr, a poetic visionary being, one of the few original types of art … the highest poetic creation of the age', and ultimately she transcends her creator: 'Nothing can be more unlike Richardson than Clarissa, and yet without Richardson Clarissa had never been.'[23]

Clarissa may have been 'one of the few original types of art', but perhaps because of this, she had no successors. The key heroine of fiction for the nineteenth century was in Oliphant's view Charlotte Brontë's Jane Eyre, and both *Jane Eyre* and Charlotte's other novels reflected the author's gender. *Jane Eyre*, she would recall in 1892, gave Charlotte Brontë 'a sudden and extraordinary fame', and 'took the world by storm'.[24]

---

[20]   'Charles Dickens', *Blackwood's Edinburgh Magazine*, 77 (April 1855): 451–66, at 465.

[21]   See her letter to William Blackwood, 30 April 1897, quoted in Mrs Harry Coghill (ed.), *The Autobiography and Letters of Mrs Margaret Oliphant* (1899), intro. Q.D. Leavis (Leicester: Leicester University Press, 1974), p. 434.

[22]   'Novels', *Blackwood's Edinburgh Magazine*, 102 (September 1867): 257–80, at 278.

[23]   'Historical Sketches of the Reign of George II. No. X The Novelist', *Blackwood's Edinburgh Magazine*, 105 (March 1869): 253–76, at 264, 276.

[24]   Margaret Oliphant, with F.R. Oliphant, *The Victorian Age of English Literature* (2 vols, London: Percival & Co., 1892), vol. 1, pp. 320–21.

Oliphant first published on Charlotte Brontë in her 'Modern Novelists – Great and Small', which appeared in *Blackwood's* for May 1855. As Joanne Shattock has noted, this is one of the cases where the opening paragraphs of Oliphant's reviews are self-consciously masculine in tone, magisterial and unfortunately platitudinous[25] – suggesting that she adopted, rather more clumsily, the ventriloquising of Victorian masculine attitudes we have observed in some of Mozley's articles. Here she opens with the patronising tone towards women that she would later complain of elsewhere:

> *Place aux dames!* how does it happen that the cowardice of womankind is a fact so clearly established, and that so little notice is ever taken of the desperate temerity of this half of the creation? It is in vain that we call to the amazon, as the lookers-on at that famous tourney at Ashby-de-la-Zouche called to the disinherited knight, 'Strike the Hospitaller's Shield – he is weak in the saddle'. While we are yet speaking, the female knight-errant rushes past us to thunder on the buckler of Bois Guilbert, the champion of champions. Where philosophic magnates fear to tread, and bodies of divinity approach with trembling, the fair novelist flies at a gallop. Her warfare, it is true, is after the manner of women: there is a rush, a flash, a shriek, and the combatant comes forth from the mêlée trembling with delight and terror; but the sudden daring of the attack puts bravery to shame.[26]

In proposing the article to John Blackwood, Oliphant had spoken of her wish to write of 'the Jane Eyre school – those books which are so unwomanly that they only could have been written by women', and had promised to 'do [her] best to keep from scratching, and conceal the feminine hand'.[27] Instead of being catty in a (supposedly) female fashion, she has managed in the event to be laboriously arch and condescending, aping a certain kind of critical masculinity.

As the article goes on, however, Oliphant makes less effort to strain for this kind of tone, with the result that, while critical of Brontë, she pays tribute to the power and originality of her fiction. She does pick up on the point in her letter, that the books are 'so unwomanly that they only could have been written by women', declaring that '[t]here is a degree of refined indelicacy possible to a woman, which no man can reach', such that '[t]here are some conversations between Rochester and Jane Eyre which no man could have dared to give – which could only have been given by the overboldness of innocence and ignorance trying to imagine what it could never understand, and which are as womanish as they are unwomanly'.[28] It is this ignorance and lack of tact which expose the woman behind the pseudonym

---

[25]   Joanne Shattock, 'Work for Women', p. 168.

[26]   'Modern Novelists – Great and Small', *Blackwood's Edinburgh Magazine*, 77 (May 1855): 554–68, at 554–5.

[27]   Letter of 1855, n.d. MS 4111, National Library of Scotland.

[28]   'Modern Novelists – Great and Small', 557–8.

'Currer Bell'. Oliphant is of course writing before Gaskell's revelations about Branwell Brontë, but her comment foreshadows Julia Kavanagh's discussion a few years later, of how women never exposed to vice are handicapped in their efforts to portray it.

As in some of Mozley's articles, including her review of *Villette*, the meat of Oliphant's article, despite its opening, is sympathetic to the case being made for women – the 'sudden daring of the attack' on convention in Brontë's works does indeed 'put bravery to shame'. *Jane Eyre* implied, according to Oliphant, that the traditional deference and respect shown as being offered women in earlier novels betrayed the sex's inferiority in men's eyes. It was the suitor who struggled with her, as Rochester struggled with Jane, who was the heroine's true equal. Hence 'this furious love-making was but a wild declaration of the "Rights of Women" in a new aspect'.[29] Women could acknowledge their feelings and express them to the men they desired. Moreover, as Joan Bellamy has emphasised, Oliphant believes that the sheer emotional power of the Brontë novels disarms criticism:

> We feel no art in these remarkable books. What we feel is a force which makes everything real – a motion which is irresistible. We are swept up in the current and never draw breath till the tale is ended. Afterwards we may disapprove at our leisure, but it is certain that we have not a moment's pause to be critical till we come to the end.[30]

Oliphant was nonetheless to express dismay at the legacy of Charlotte Brontë's novels in the highly sexualised heroines of the 'Sensation Fiction' of the 1860s, and ultimately in a figure like Hardy's Arabella Donn. In her well-known *Blackwood's* article 'Novels' of September 1867, she attacked the fiction of writers like M.E. Braddon, Ouida and Rhoda Broughton: what has happened here, she suggests, is that the heroines' sexual desires have raged out of control, even leading them into potential sexual immorality – what she calls 'a very fleshly and unlovely record' of womanhood includes

> [w]omen driven wild for the love of the man who leads them on to desperation before he accords that word of encouragement which carries them into the seventh heaven; women who marry their grooms in fits of sexual passion; women who pray their lovers to carry them off from husbands they hate; women, at the very least of it, who give and receive burning kisses and frantic embraces, and live in a voluptuous dream, either waiting for or brooding over the inevitable lover.[31]

---

[29]   Ibid., 557–8.

[30]   Ibid., 558–9; see Joan Bellamy, 'A Lifetime of Reviewing'.

[31]   *Blackwood's Edinburgh Magazine*, 102 (September 1867): 257–80, partly repr. in Solveig C. Robinson (ed.), *A Serious Occupation: Literary Criticism by Victorian Women Writers* (Peterborough, Ontario and Orchard Park, NY: Broadview, 2003), pp. 146–74, at p. 149.

The typical heroine of these novels, she goes on, is preoccupied with the physical, yearning for 'flesh and muscles, for strong arms that seize her, and warm breath that thrills her through', and manifests an 'eagerness of physical sensation'.

Charlotte Brontë was the pioneer here, not just in *Jane Eyre* but also in her representation in *Shirley* of Caroline Helstone's 'passionate lamentation over her own position and the absence of any man whom she could marry' – yet in Oliphant's view, the novelists of the 1860s, possessing 'no genius and little talent', have gone too far.[32] It is as if these inferior novelists have taken their cue from Charlotte Brontë, but have made of their heroines creatures governed wholly by the sexual impulse. As in her critique of Hardy's Arabella Donn nearly 30 years later, Oliphant's protest here seems motivated not simply by prudishness over what is acceptable to represent in fiction, but also by a sense that the 'sensation' writers have introduced a new type of fictional heroine which does as little to encompass the true complexity of women as any of its predecessors.

By the time of her appraisal of the Brontës in 1897, in her chapter in *Women Novelists of Queen Victoria's Reign*, Oliphant, as Valerie Sanders has noted, seems anxious to dissociate Charlotte Brontë from her fictional successors.[33] She reiterates her point about Charlotte Brontë's heroines being the first in English fiction to express overtly their need for a male partner, and regrets that her novels 'opened the gates to imps of evil meaning, polluting and profaning the domestic hearth' – but Oliphant now asserts that Brontë's followers were wrong in attributing to her a wish for 'emancipation'. What she sought was 'an extended duty', and insofar as her heroines' desires reflected her own, what was being expressed was not sexual yearning, but regret for the loss of the chance of motherhood, a sense of 'the great instinct of her being unfulfilled'.[34] Perhaps Oliphant believed this, but by disclaiming Charlotte Brontë's responsibility for her successors' baneful impact on the 'domestic hearth', Oliphant may also be trying to clear her of any taint, in the pages of a memorial volume produced for Victoria's Diamond Jubilee in which her chapter on the Brontës appeared under her own name.

Oliphant's later writings on Charlotte Brontë also deal with *Villette*, a novel she evidently finds very impressive, especially in its portrayal of the protagonists Lucy Snowe and M. Paul Emmanuel. In *The Victorian Age of English Literature*, she called Lucy 'so astonishingly true to life … the real little proper Englishwoman, with the well-concealed volcano under the primness', and claimed that such was the impact of the novel, that the ambiguous fate of M. Paul 'was debated in a hundred circles with greater vehemence than many a national problem'.[35] *Women Novelists of Queen Victoria's Reign* would extend this discussion, expressing

---

[32]   Ibid., p. 148.

[33]   *Eve's Renegades*, p. 51.

[34]   'The Sisters Brontë', in Margaret Oliphant and others, *Women Novelists of Queen Victoria's Reign: A Book of Appreciations* (London: Hurst and Blackett, 1897), pp. 21–4, 49–50. Subsequent references to this chapter will be included parenthetically in the text.

[35]   Vol. 1, p. 324.

admiration of the impartiality shown in Brontë's treatment of Lucy, her failure to demand the reader's sympathy or approval for 'the hungry little epicure, looking on while others feast, and envying every one of them, even while she snarls at their fare as apples of Gomorrah' (36). With the ambivalence about this rather impersonal approach which had characterised her commentary on Jane Austen in 1870 (discussed below), Oliphant does commend Charlotte Brontë for offering one character who could arouse the reader's 'lively liking, amusement and sympathy' – M. Paul Emmanuel. Recalling Anne Mozley's comparison between M. Paul and the conventional fictional hero represented by Dr John Graham Bretton, Oliphant observes that M. Paul is 'as far from the English ideal as it is possible to imagine', being 'cruel, delightful, barbarous and kind', as well as 'devoid of dignity' and 'contradictory, inconsistent, vain' (38). Hence, no doubt, the fervent reader interest in his eventual fate.

Oliphant's final appraisal of Charlotte Brontë would also return to the paradox of her fiction being limited, yet able to overcome the reader's sense of its limitations through its emotional power. Her novels possess the philosophical maturity of 'a schoolgirl', show almost no 'knowledge of the world', and are 'confused by the haste and passion of a mind self-centred and working in the narrowest orbit' (5). But the flipside of all this is the author's 'absolute untempered force', devoid of 'charity' or 'softness', which had an immense effect on readers. Oliphant also pays tribute to a visionary quality in Charlotte Brontë, a trait which to some extent recalls Julia Kavanagh's view of Jane Austen as a 'seer' but which operates in a very different way. Whereas Austen, according to Kavanagh, had deliberately circumscribed the field of observation reflected in her fiction and had recorded it with extraordinary penetration, Charlotte Brontë was for Oliphant inherently limited in her imaginative capacities, but could represent what she did perceive with great force. She had 'that strange form of imagination which can deal only with fact, and depict nothing but what is under its eyes', and what 'the remorseless lights of this outward vision' portray, comes across all the more strongly for the absence of 'any softening of love for the race, any embarrassing toleration as to feelings and motives' (41). Oliphant's view here recalls that of Anne Mozley, who also paid tribute to Charlotte Brontë's powerful imagination, although for Mozley, the novelist's limitations consisted in her lack of understanding of abstract ideas or of people in the mass.

Oliphant's response to Charlotte Brontë, to judge from her *Autobiography*, was inflected by her sense of how her own career and consequent perspective on life had differed from Brontë's. Reading Gaskell's biography of Brontë in 1864, Oliphant, then a financially-strapped widow with children, reflected that to herself, her writings looked 'perfectly pale and colourless' beside Brontë's – lacking, no doubt, the latter's keen and concentrated, if limited, vision. But she believed she had had 'far more experience and … a fuller conception of life' than Brontë had ever attained. Because of her roles as mother and breadwinner, she had in some ways moved beyond the preoccupations of Brontë's fiction: 'I have learned to take perhaps more a man's view of mortal affairs, – to feel that the love between men and women, and marrying and giving in marriage, occupy in fact so small a portion of either existence or thought'.[36]

Another important novelist against whom Oliphant measured herself in her *Autobiography* was, notoriously, George Eliot. In this case, although she did believe that Eliot outstripped all her female contemporaries as a writer, she surmised that she herself might have written better fiction had she enjoyed Eliot's advantages. In the early 1870s, after her brother had failed in business and inflicted on her the financial responsibility for himself and his family, Oliphant became aware that she might never be free of the need to write prolifically and at speed to fulfil her family obligations. The 'hardest of all' the facts she had to resign herself to, she wrote to John Blackwood in March 1872, was the need to 'do second class work all [her] life for lack of time to do [her]self full justice'.[37] The financial demands on Oliphant did not abate, and the publication in 1885 of *The Life and Letters of George Eliot* by Eliot's widower J.W. Cross threw into strong relief for her the difference between Eliot's circumstances and her own. She recognised that Eliot had garnered 'more praise, and homage, and honour' than herself; moreover, as well as not facing the financial pressures experienced by Oliphant, Eliot had been cosseted by her partner G.H. Lewes, protected by him from exposure to criticism of her works, and thus had lived in a 'mental greenhouse'.[38]

But this is not the whole story as far as Oliphant's response to Eliot is concerned. To begin with, just as Sara Coleridge had found it hard to believe that 'Currer Bell' was female, Margaret Oliphant was very surprised to learn of 'George Eliot's' true sex. On requesting from John Blackwood in 1860 a copy of the newly-published *The Mill on the Floss*, Oliphant asked whether the 'mysterious' author was a woman, saying, 'I shall feel very much humiliated if it is so, seeing I have staked my critical credit on the other side, indeed fear I shall scarcely believe it even if you tell me'.[39] Unfortunately, she does not spell out the reasons for her assumption, and thus articulate her sense of what was distinctive about men's or women's writing. It is hence ironic that a couple of years later, the *Saturday Review* claimed that Oliphant's own series of novels, *The Chronicles of Carlingford*, must be written by or in imitation of George Eliot. So Oliphant declared to Blackwood that 'the faintest idea of imitating or attempting to rival the author of Adam Bede never entered [her] mind';[40] when one of the *Chronicles* was reprinted the following year, she drafted a Preface denying the charge again (albeit both she and Blackwood thought better of publishing it), staking a claim to a fictional world of her own. If, she says, she had 'entered more closely than is usual into the local history of a dissenting church, a subject which has been handled on

---

[36] Quoted in Elisabeth Jay (ed.), *Autobiography of Margaret Oliphant. The Complete Text* (Oxford and New York: Oxford University Press, 2002), p. 10.

[37] MS 4295, National Library of Scotland.

[38] *Autobiography of Margaret Oliphant. The Complete Text*, pp. 15–17.

[39] Letter of 1860, n.d., MS 4152, National Library of Scotland.

[40] Letter of 1862, n.d., MS 4172, National Library of Scotland.

various occasions by the author of *Adam Bede*', this circumstance 'arose simply from the fact that a Dissenting chapel formed a salient feature in the peculiarities of the town of Carlingford', rather than from 'any impulse of imitation'.[41]

Moreover, Oliphant came to register in Eliot's later fiction qualities that she found antipathetic: a rather uncritical admiration for characters who were morally and/or intellectually superior to the general run of mortals, and on the author's part, a corresponding lack of respect for ordinary human beings. Writing to John Blackwood, she was unenthusiastic about Eliot's 1866 novel, *Felix Holt, the Radical*, which she thought an example of what was for Eliot slack writing that betrayed the author's contempt for her public and her critics – she described it, memorably, as like 'Hamlet played by six sets of gravediggers'.[42] Reading *Middlemarch* in December 1871, during its part-publication, Oliphant was repelled by Eliot's 'superior' heroine, Dorothea Brooke, and by her apparent harshness to 'all the mediocrities' – since, as she wrote to Blackwood, 'mediocrity is the rule and only a very few of the human race can be superior'.[43]

In print a few years later, Oliphant discussed *Romola* (1863), the text where for her the rot had set in. She argued that the eponymous heroine was throughout the novel too separated from and contemptuous of ordinary life, possessing 'a narrowness which is fatal to true grandeur' – but it was a narrowness of which Eliot herself seemed unaware. Even after her various travails, Romola is 'visiting like a queen the poor who want caring for, improving all who cross her path, and receiving everywhere a visionary worship, but never once descending into any kind of human equality'. Her love for her husband Tito is superficial, and she relinquishes it with unconvincing suddenness and coolness, 'able to drop him like a stone'. The result is that readers – evidently including Oliphant herself – fail to warm to Romola: '[t]hey are too little and she is too elevated to afford that ground for union which fellow-feeling gives'.[44] And if she never in her own fiction imitated Eliot, she did possibly parody this particular novel: Elizabeth Winston has argued that, not long after *Romola* had appeared in 1863, Oliphant had taken aim at its 'structure, learned style, and tragic mode' in her novel *Miss Marjoribanks* (1866). In particular, Romola's social and spiritual mission is evoked in that of Oliphant's eponymous heroine, but Lucilla Marjoribanks has as her arena a drawing-room and a provincial town, rather than an Italian political centre and a plague-struck village.[45] If parody was the aim, then the novel's attribution of wide

---

41   Letter to John Blackwood, 1863, n.d., MS 4184, National Library of Scotland.

42   Letter of 30 June 1866, MS 4213, National Library of Scotland, quoted by Valerie Sanders, *Eve's Renegades*, p. 42.

43   Letter of 2 December 1871, MS 4280, National Library of Scotland.

44   'Two Cities – Two Books', *Blackwood's Edinburgh Magazine*, 116 (July 1874): 72–91, at 77–81.

45   '"Taking off" the Neighbours: Margaret Oliphant's Parody of *Romola*', in William Baker and Ira Bruce Nadel (eds), *Redefining the Modern: Essays on Literature and Society*

consequences to Lucilla's activities, an aspect of the novel that Anne Mozley had found implausible, was entirely intentional.

On the other hand, George Eliot's literary achievement was particularly impressive in that she showed powers in a woman writer that men could not treat patronisingly. In *The Victorian Age of English Literature*, Oliphant argues that Eliot had proven that a woman writer could be as eminent as a man: 'No man, no critic, could condescend to her, or treat her with that courteous (or uncourteous) superiority which has been the ordinary lot of women.' Although she remained critical of 'ideal' figures like Dorothea Brooke or Daniel Deronda, she had strong praise for *Adam Bede*, describing the novel as '[t]his wonderful transcript of humanity containing so much that is usually undiscovered in life, the movement of the heart and mind, the workings of motive, the extraordinary inadvertencies and misconceptions of existence which mingle with its most common calculations, and balk its schemes and alter its course'.[46]

Moreover, although Oliphant was repelled by the version of Eliot offered by Cross, concluding that 'she must have been a dull woman with a great genius distinct from herself',[47] she was by no means convinced that it represented the woman as she had been. That is, the *Life and Letters* was an instance of a male relative presenting a particular interpretation of a woman writer which might not square with the facts. This is one emphasis of the review of Cross's work that she published in the *Edinburgh Review*.

Oliphant observes in the review the difference between the 'timidity' and 'docility' of Marian Evans the woman and the 'mature and easy force of the style, the command of all her materials' in the fiction of George Eliot, including, in her very first novella *The Sad Fortunes of the Reverend Amos Barton*, her 'freedom and power' in dealing with 'some of the darkest and least attractive features of rural life'.[48] She also notices the divergence in tone between the humourless letters quoted by Cross and the free, strong and penetrating 'comic faculty' of Eliot's early fiction (542–3). All this may be explained by Oliphant's private speculation as to the 'great genius' distinct from the woman – a view after all consistent with her belief that Samuel Richardson's Clarissa transcended her creator. But the review as a whole suggests that another possible hypothesis is that Cross is not presenting a true-to-life picture of his subject.

What Oliphant evidently finds hardest to fathom is how Eliot made two decisions, decisions which potentially had strong repercussions both personally and socially, with the level of equanimity implied by Cross. The decisions were, of course, to repudiate the Christian faith, and to live openly with a man she could not

---

in Honor of Joseph Wiesenfarth (Madison and Teaneck: Fairleigh Dickinson University Press; London: Associated University Presses, 2004), pp. 115–29.

[46]   Vol. 2, 164ff.

[47]   *Autobiography of Margaret Oliphant The Complete Text*, p. 7.

[48]   '*The Life and Letters of George Eliot*', *Edinburgh Review*, 161 (April 1885): 514–53, at 542. Subsequent references to this review will be included parenthetically in the text.

legally marry. According to Cross's account, says Oliphant, Eliot passed through her life without the 'disturbances ... such as ordinary people have, none of the doubts and vacillations, none of the struggles of more common human creatures'. It is as if '[s]he stepped from evangelical faith to philosophical atheism as you would step from one street to another without turning a hair', and when she compounded her transgression by going to live with Lewes, Oliphant wonders, '[d]id she never falter when she turned from all she had been taught to love and reverence in one case, and from all the traditions of strait respectability in which she had been bred in another?' (518–19). Nor does Cross acknowledge any difficulties in the early years of Eliot's life with Lewes (537).

Oliphant does not find Cross's representation of Eliot and her behaviour at all convincing, and speculates as to the reasons for his deficiencies. He could have been uninformed, not having known Eliot in her early years, or he could have been loath to offend the surviving members of her family. Or he could be as timid as he represents Eliot as being – perhaps the book reflects 'the frightened retirement of a man not strong enough to trust to his own judgment from all the risks of frankness and plain speaking?' (525, 519) (To William Blackwood, she observed in a letter, 'Surely Mr. Cross must have cut out all the human parts'.[49]) Whatever the reason, he has presented a figure that 'is large and imposing, but ... lifeless', 'a large image without a broken line or indiscreet wrinkle', such that George Eliot is 'a more completely veiled prophet than ever' (518, 516). Oliphant assumes, like many readers since, that Eliot's *The Mill on the Floss* is autobiographical, and hence for her, it is probably a more reliable source for Eliot's early spiritual and emotional life than Cross's *Life and Letters* (519–21). She had not always resembled some of her later characters (as Oliphant saw them), as a creature superior to the personal vicissitudes of ordinary mortals.

Near the end of her life, Oliphant gained access to material which confirmed her hunch that Cross's presentation of Eliot represented a simplification of the woman. Commissioned to write the history of the Blackwood publishing firm, she was able to read correspondence between Eliot and John Blackwood which Cross either could not access or declined to use. The second volume of her projected three-volume history deals in part with the early years of Eliot and Blackwood's association, from Lewes's submission to *Blackwood's* of 'Amos Barton', in 1857. This volume goes only to 1861, and although she foreshadows further coverage of the correspondence in the succeeding volume, Oliphant did not live to write this.[50]

What Oliphant emphasises is Eliot's sensitivity to criticism. Although John Blackwood's comments on their work were welcomed even by authors as established as Edward Bulwer-Lytton, Eliot possessed an 'extreme sensitiveness ... to any check, however slight' (435), and hence Blackwood had to be careful

---

    [49]   Letter of 1885, n.d., MS 4476, National Library of Scotland.

    [50]   *Annals of a Publishing House: William Blackwood and His Sons, Their Magazine and Friends* (3 vols, Edinburgh and London: William Blackwood and Sons, 1897–8), vol. 2, p. 440. Subsequent references to this volume will be included parenthetically in the text.

about what he said to her. So when Oliphant characterises their correspondence as a succession of 'applause on one side and acceptance of it on the other' (443), she implies that the repetitiveness is due as much to Blackwood's accommodating Eliot's sensitivity, as to the quality of her fiction. Given, moreover, that much correspondence of this ilk had actually been quoted by Cross, it arguably aggravated the lifelessness Oliphant found in his version of Eliot: she says that a reader of the correspondence welcomes the occasional change of tone as 'the interposition of some other human sentiment'.

Not that the changes of tone are entirely to Eliot's credit, from Oliphant's account. While intolerant of criticism, Eliot complains about printer's errors, and takes issue with such strictures as Blackwood ventures (441–2). More damningly, Eliot forcibly rejects Blackwood's initial offer and arrangements for *The Mill on the Floss*, despite the fact that the firm had voluntarily paid her an extra £800 after the success of its predecessor, *Adam Bede* (442–3). Nevertheless this incident, plus her later complaints about insufficient advertising of her works (446–7), do demonstrate that, rather than the timid and protected creature represented by Cross, Eliot was a capable woman of business, operating with the 'clear head and strong intelligence' evident in her fiction (446, 448).

Oliphant's preference for *The Mill on the Floss* over Cross's *Life* as an insight into Marian Evans the woman, recalls Maria Jane Jewsbury's take on Jane Austen: that the novels express more of the personality of the writer than the demeanour of the woman in real life, as described by Henry Austen in his 'Biographical Notice'. Jewsbury's interpretation was that Jane Austen herself restrained in her life aspects of her personality which she gave free rein in her fiction, whereas Oliphant suspects in Eliot's case that Cross may be misrepresenting his wife. When Oliphant had reviewed in 1870 the second biographical account of Jane Austen written by one of her male relatives, her nephew James Edward Austen-Leigh's *Memoir of Jane Austen*, she had also identified an inconsistency between the personality that emerged in the biography and that which was implied by the novels. But, just as in her review of Cross's *Life and Letters of George Eliot*, she had attributed the discrepancy, more definitely in this case, to the biographer rather than to the subject.

On the other hand, Oliphant evidently did not believe Austen and Eliot resembled each other as novelists – rather the opposite, in fact. In the letter to John Blackwood where she commented on Eliot's *Felix Holt*, she mentioned what she saw as the rather lukewarm reviews in the *Saturday Review* and the *Times*, and, in reference to the latter, ridiculed the way in which this review had linked the two novelists: 'the idea of starting with [Austen] for a criticism on George Eliot is the sublime of absurdity'.[51]

What E.S. Dallas had done in the *Times* review was to hail Eliot as the successor and superior to Austen: Austen has until now 'had the honour of the first place among our lady novelists', but now has been surpassed by 'a lady who in grasp of

---

[51] 30 June 1866, MS 4213, National Library of Scotland.

thought, in loftiness of feeling, in subtlety of expression, in fineness of humour, in reach of passion, and in all those sympathies which go to form the true artist has never been excelled'.[52] Austen is 'still pre-eminent among women' in 'the art of weaving a narrative': everything in her plots seems 'natural', and she says neither 'too much' nor 'too little'. But this is because she 'scarcely ever gets out of the humdrum of easy-going respectable life', and hence can 'well afford to be calm and neat in arranging every thread of the narrative she has to weave'. George Eliot falls short in this art, admittedly – but only because 'she has to deal with subjects far more difficult … with wilder passions, with stronger situations, with higher thoughts': Eliot 'play[s] with torrents where Miss Austen played with rills'.

Oliphant picks up on Dallas's discussion of Austen, and expresses to John Blackwood 'pure exasperation at the way in which that respectable woman's name is shoved down all our throats on any occasion'. What precisely she is objecting to here is not spelt out, but her words seem to express frustration at Austen's being held up as some sort of model for women writers. She would have known, of course, of Charlotte Brontë's expressions of similar annoyance at G.H. Lewes's exhortations for her to adopt Austen as a literary exemplar. She may also be 'exasperated' that women novelists are habitually yoked together in critical discourse, however dissimilar the women's writings may be, rather than being dealt with in a gender-neutral context. She tells Blackwood that her 'exasperation' might produce from her 'a paper one of these days on Miss Austen', and four years later, she did indeed publish on the novelist. What she had to say, moreover, implied that she considered Austen more clever and subtle than the modest miniaturist she was often seen as being.

Like Jewsbury's, Oliphant's perspective on Austen the woman would presumably have been hampered by a lack of information, other than that supplied by her relatives. The only pre-1869 sources on her life were still the versions of Henry Austen's brief 'Biographical Notice'. Oliphant concludes, nonetheless, that Austen-Leigh was imperceptive about his aunt, and finds evidence for this in his response to the now-celebrated exchanges between Jane Austen and the Rev. James Stanier Clarke, the Prince Regent's librarian, which first saw the light in Austen-Leigh's *Memoir*. Clarke had suggested to Jane Austen that she 'delineate in some future work the habits of life and character and enthusiasm of a clergyman … fond of, and entirely engaged in literature, no man's enemy but his own'.[53] Jane Austen dealt with this proposal by disclaiming the level of learning needed for such a project – knowledge of science and philosophy, plus 'quotations and allusions' unfamiliar to her, and summed up by declaring that she was 'the most

[52]   *Times*, 26 June 1866, repr. David R. Carroll (ed.), *George Eliot: The Critical Heritage* (London: Routledge & Kegan Paul; New York: Barnes & Noble, 1971), pp. 263–70, at p. 263.

[53]   James Edward Austen-Leigh, *A Memoir of Jane Austen and Other Family Recollections*, ed. Kathryn Sutherland (London and Oxford: Oxford University Press, 2002), pp. 94–6.

unlearned and uninformed female who ever dared to be an authoress'. Undaunted, Clarke wrote again to propose she write an 'historical romance, illustrative of the history of the august House of Coburg'. According to Oliphant, 'Mr. Collins himself could not have done better' than Clarke, and Jane Austen 'exults over him; she gives him the gravest answers, and draws her victim out'.[54] Austen's Mr Collins was evidently a favourite of Oliphant's: back in 1862, when John Blackwood had mentioned his contributor the Rev. W. Lucas Collins (whose obituary Oliphant would later write), she had joked: 'Your Mr Collins is *not* related to the Revd. Mr. Collins in *Pride and Prejudice* I presume? – though somehow Miss Austen's man haunts one in hearing the name – '.[55]

Oliphant can see very clearly that Jane Austen's claims about her limitations are not to be read literally, however confident Austen was that Clarke himself would take them at face value. Her further point, however, is that Austen-Leigh takes her assertions seriously: he 'does not seem to see the fun, but comments gravely upon it', as he observes that 'Mr. Clarke should have recollected the warning of the wise man, "Force not the current of the stream"' – a response which Oliphant sees as 'scarcely less amusing than the preceding narrative' (305).

The main problem for Oliphant in Austen-Leigh's representation of his aunt is that it conveys no sense of her unusualness: '[n]ot Jane Austen only, but hosts of sweet women beside her, might have sat for the picture', and his text is for her 'much trellis-work and leafage' which offers only 'brief and slight' glimpses of its subject (290). This complaint of Jane Austen's being reduced to a stereotype recalls Julia Kavanagh's regrets over the reductive approach taken to 'women of Christianity' by their biographers. But according to Oliphant, Austen-Leigh's lack of comprehension of his aunt reflects a wider obliviousness on the part of the Austen family, some of whom would have known her better than her nephew. Jane Austen, in Oliphant's view, was overshadowed by her brothers' 'more noisy claims', in that 'the boys' settlement in life, their Oxford successes, their going to sea, their early curacies, and prize-money, filled everybody's mind'. Meanwhile the only other daughter, Cassandra, whose fiancé died young, 'filled up every corner vacant from the boys in the tender heart of the Steventon vicarage'. By contrast, Jane 'gave nobody any trouble', was just 'one of the creatures evidently born to marry and be the light of some other home', and when that failed to happen, 'the change was so soft and slight as scarcely to count' (290). Insofar as the family registered that Jane was a writer, the hints about novel-writing they gave her which she paraphrased in her parodic 'Plan for a Novel' suggest that they believed she 'was very much the same as other people, and not a person to be any way afraid of' (306). In other words, like Mrs Thrale and Mrs Delany in an

---

[54] 'Miss Austen and Miss Mitford', *Blackwood's Edinburgh Magazine*, 107 (March 1870): 290–313, at 305. Subsequent references to this review will be included parenthetically in the text.

[55] Letter to John Blackwood, 1862, n.d., MS 4172, National Library of Scotland (Oliphant's emphasis).

earlier period, Jane Austen could be seen as unthreatening. In her *Literary History of England in the End of the Eighteenth and Beginning of the Nineteenth Century* of 1882, Oliphant would be even more scathing about the Austen family, whom she called '[a]n excellent ordinary strain of honest gentlefolks, peaceably tedious and undistinguished, and anxious to make it apparent that their Jane knew nothing of literary people, and was quite out of any possibility of association with such a ragged regiment'.[56]

Although for Oliphant Austen the individual was little like the woman her relatives portrayed, she believed that Austen's perspective as a writer was affected by her circumstances, and specifically her circumstances as a woman. She was a gentlewoman, so free of the need to write from financial necessity – but also, as a very clever person, and a female to boot, she was unlikely to make much impact on the less intelligent people around her. Hence Austen was given to inflecting her fiction with what Oliphant calls a 'fine vein of feminine cynicism':

> It is something altogether different from the rude and brutal male quality that bears the same name. It is the soft and silent disbelief of a spectator who has to look at a great many things without showing any outward discomposure, and who has learned to give up any moral classification of social sins, and to place them instead on the level of absurdities. (294)

This learnt habit of observing without criticising results from female powerlessness, and the attitude which emerges is a way of coping with this predicament. So Austen the narrator 'is not surprised or offended, much less horror-stricken or indignant, when her people show vulgar or mean traits of character, when they make it evident how selfish and self-absorbed they are, or even when they fall into those social cruelties which selfish and stupid people are so often guilty of, not without intention, but without realising half the pain they inflict'. Her response is that she 'stands by and looks on, and gives a soft half-smile, and tells the story with an exquisite sense of its ridiculous side, and fine stinging yet soft-voiced contempt for the actors in it'. Meanwhile the victims of all this stupidity and selfishness are protected from harm, by sharing their creator's sense of superiority, a 'gentle disdain of the possibility that meanness and folly and stupidity could ever really wound any rational creature' (294). This perspective is the direct outcome of the tendencies fostered by the leisured gentlewoman's life, and because she is unable to influence others directly, Jane Austen develops a certain fatalism, which according to Oliphant comes out in her fiction:

> A certain soft despair of any one human creature ever doing any good to another, of any influence overcoming those habits and moods and peculiarities of mind which the observer sees to be more obstinate than life itself, a sense that nothing is to be done but look on, to say perhaps now and then a softening word, to make

---

[56] (3 vols, London: Macmillan), vol. 3, p. 226.

the best of it practically and theoretically, to smile and hold up one's hands and wonder why human creatures should be such fools. (296)

The approach to life Oliphant identifies here in Jane Austen resembles that which she had recognised in Trollope's (fictional) Susan Grantly. But whereas Mrs Grantly practises 'half-amused, half-troubled spectatorship' and 'careful abstinence from active interference' in her men-folks' misguided doings, while expecting that the 'superior logic of events' will still make things come right, Oliphant's Jane Austen, in adopting a similar stance, feels no hope that anything will change.

Whereas Julia Kavanagh had found the ironic detachment from her characters which she identified in Austen's fiction troubling, because she considered it cold and therefore unfeminine, Oliphant here attributes the same quality specifically to habits of mind which, while not innate in women, might result from the circumstances of their lives. Such women persuade themselves to accept folly, selfishness and stupidity, and downplay the capacity of these traits to do lasting damage, taking refuge in the sense of being superior 'rational creatures'.

Kathryn Sutherland has discussed the evidence now available about the *Memoir*'s genesis and the reasons for its shortcomings. Austen-Leigh and his sisters, children of Jane's eldest brother James, had limited personal knowledge of Jane Austen, especially of her early life, and did not have access to all available letters, notably most of those Jane wrote to her sister Cassandra, her closest confidant.[57] It was also an era where complete frankness about the private life of biographical subjects, or revelation of information possibly embarrassing to living people or their descendants, was not considered normal or desirable.

This reticence was something of which Oliphant herself claimed to approve, and her engagement in the notorious Froude–Carlyle controversy in the early 1880s is pertinent here. When James Anthony Froude challenged biographical conventions of reticence in his publications about Thomas and Jane Carlyle (1881–4), Oliphant expressed outrage. Commenting in the *Contemporary Review* on Froude's three-volume edition of Jane Carlyle's letters, she lambasts him for misinterpreting his subject and for exposing her, such that 'her whole existence has been violated, every scrap of decent drapery torn from her, and herself exhibited as perhaps never modest and proud matron was before to the comments of the world'.[58] This is also a signed article, where Oliphant is defending a fellow woman, and fellow Scotswoman, against what she sees as an appallingly intrusive male.

Moreover, Oliphant's scepticism about the versions of distinguished women offered by male relatives in particular had also been evident in what she wrote on Froude's first Carlyle-related publication. This was his 1881 edition of Thomas Carlyle's *Reminiscences*, some of which focused on Jane Carlyle as interpreted

---

[57]   See her introduction to her edition of Austen-Leigh's *Memoir of Jane Austen and Other Family Writings*, and her *Jane Austen's Textual Lives: From Aeschylus to Bollywood* (Oxford and New York: Oxford University Press, 2005), 61ff.

[58]   'Mrs. Carlyle', *Contemporary Review*, 44 (May 1883): 609–28, at 611.

by Thomas in the aftermath of her unexpected death in 1866. Overcome by remorse at what he saw as his own callous and negligent treatment of his wife, Thomas Carlyle represented her as a paragon – but it was a representation which Oliphant questioned as a mere stereotype of conventional femininity. Reviewing the *Reminiscences* in *Macmillan's Magazine*, again under her own name, Oliphant accepted Thomas Carlyle's version of Jane as the understandable outpourings of a distraught and recent widower, rather than as a deliberate misrepresentation, but she still considered it unfortunate, and best left unpublished. (She had known both the Carlyles personally, and says so.) Surrounding Jane with 'the love-halo of their youth', Thomas ignores her 'swift caustic wit, her relentless insight, and potent humour', and gives her 'the pretty air of a domestic idol'.[59] The view of Jane Carlyle transmitted via Froude's publications on the Carlyles was therefore for Oliphant both distorted, and the outcome of unwarrantable intrusiveness. Her reservation about Austen-Leigh's text, then, was that it conveyed little sense of Jane Austen's personality or of her 'feminine cynicism', did not portray the kind of woman the novels' tone implies – not that it should have delved into her private life.[60]

Oliphant's discussion of Austen is not entirely laudatory, any more than is her commentary on Charlotte Brontë or George Eliot. In her article she is also reviewing a memoir of Mary Russell Mitford, and she claims to prefer the world of Mitford's *Our Village* to that of Austen's novels. Mitford's work, unlike Austen's, includes the poor as well as the rich, and her 'genial blue eyes' show 'a kindly sympathy over all the world', one which includes haymakers, shopkeepers, cobblers, 'a world twice as full as Miss Austen's' and one with 'a breadth and atmosphere' beyond hers (293, 296). Oliphant warms more to Mitford's 'sweet flowery picture', although she recognises that it represents an idealised view of Mitford's life and surroundings (297).

But the article makes it clear that Oliphant's preference for Mitford's works over Austen's is an emotional rather than an aesthetic judgment. (She no doubt identified personally more with Mitford, whose profligate and extravagant father made her a literary drudge most of her life, a predicament to which Oliphant devotes much space.) Austen confines herself to the class she knows 'with an extraordinary conscientiousness'. This in itself discloses that hers 'is not the simple character it appears at the first glance, but one full of subtle power, keenness, finesse, and self-restraint' (293–4) – a description which recalls Kavanagh's identification of Austen's distinctive qualities. Like Kavanagh, too, Oliphant seeks something in Austen's work which mitigates the effect of her 'feminine cynicism'. She finds

---

[59] 'Thomas Carlyle', *Macmillan's Magazine*, 43 (April 1881): 482–96, at 486–7. See also D.J. Trela, 'Margaret Oliphant, James Anthony Froude and the Carlyles' Reputations: Defending the Dead', *Victorian Periodicals Review*, 29/3 (1996): 199–215; Oliphant, when researching her biography of Edward Irving (1862) had learned from Jane Carlyle of her abortive engagement to him, but was not given permission to use the information.

[60] Kathryn Sutherland also makes this distinction in *Jane Austen's Textual Lives*, pp. 85–7.

it, not, as Kavanagh had done, in the lovelorn Anne Elliot, but in the portrayal of Miss Bates in *Emma*, where Austen can 'touch the region of higher feeling by comprehension of the natural excellence that lies under a ludicrous exterior' (295) – a capacity, we recall, that she could not see in the later novels of George Eliot. In the years between *Pride and Prejudice* and *Emma*, '[t]he malicious, brilliant wit of youth has softened into a better understanding of the world' (303).

For Margaret Oliphant, all three of the major nineteenth-century women writers she discusses in her published criticism have significant limitations, in each case concerning the comprehensiveness of her material and her treatment of it. Charlotte Brontë focuses too much on love and courtship, and her understanding of the world is narrow and immature. George Eliot comes to have too uncritical an admiration for 'superior' characters, and to lose touch with the minds and priorities of ordinary mortals, both inside and outside her texts. The limitations of Jane Austen's work are to some extent more consciously chosen – she exercises intelligent discrimination in confining her novels to her own social class – but her outlook is too cynical. George Eliot and Jane Austen differ, according to Oliphant's appraisal of them, in that Eliot's fiction became more narrowly focused later in her career, whereas Austen's broadened in its scope. That is, while Eliot's early fiction had shown remarkable insight into the inner and outer forces affecting human conduct in general, her works from *Romola* onwards eschewed this complexity to concentrate on less plausible, and more simply conceived, remarkable figures. On the other hand, while Austen's early novels are brilliant but rather heartless, the later ones show a broader understanding of human experience.

Of the three novelists, Oliphant wrote most extensively on Charlotte Brontë, and saw her as the most significant literary figure. Despite her reservations about Brontë's scope, Oliphant recognised in her writing an emotional power which disarmed criticism. She also registered the tremendous impact her heroines, particularly Jane Eyre, had on subsequent writers. She felt uneasy about these developments, and it is notable that in her last discussion of Brontë, she dissociates her from her successors, whom Oliphant had come to see as obsessed with female sexuality.

Oliphant read Gaskell's and other accounts of Charlotte Brontë's life (Clement Shorter's *Charlotte Brontë and her Circle* came out in 1896, just before Oliphant's chapter in *Women Novelists of Queen Victoria's Reign*); she also reviewed the accounts of George Eliot's and Jane Austen's lives published by their male relatives. She was ambivalent about the level of probing into the personal lives of authors which was justifiable in biographies. Of the three authors, Brontë was the one who attracted greatest public speculation about her life, and Oliphant expressed reservations about how far this should go, criticising Gaskell for her revelations about Branwell Brontë, and later writers for surmises about Charlotte Brontë's romantic life. In the cases of Austen and Eliot, however, her concern was with the discrepancy between the images of the writers offered by the male relatives and the personality that was suggested by the novels. Eliot seemed from Cross's account to be dull, humourless and timid, while her novels expressed vitality, a comic spirit, and daring. Moreover, given that the facts of Eliot's abandonment of religion and liaison with Lewes were publicly known, her biographer in Oliphant's view should throw some light on how she experienced these significant transgressions – but Cross's version of the impact on Eliot of her life-changing decisions was implausible. In Austen's case, her nephew had presented a sweet and commonplace figure, very different from the personality suggested by the novels. This personality was inflected by Austen's experience as a formidably intelligent but powerless woman, and for Oliphant, the Austen family's imperceptiveness had contributed to her powerlessness while she lived, and to the misrepresentation of her after her death.

Ironically, although Oliphant herself was experienced at projecting various personae, including male personae, in her criticism, she assumes that there is some link between the narrative persona of a novelist and the actual person behind it. She is like Anne Mozley in both these tendencies. For her, a biographer should illuminate this link, not obscure it, and both Cross and Austen-Leigh have failed in this respect. In both cases, moreover, the deficiency in their representation relates partly to specifically female experience: George Eliot must have been affected by violating religious and sexual conventions which weighed more heavily on women than on men, and the outlook on life expressed in Jane Austen's novels reflected her position as an insightful woman who could only observe rather than act on events. These experiences had a direct effect on the women's writing, Oliphant implies, but the accounts of the writers' male relatives do not register them. On the other hand, female biographers were more reliable: while Oliphant censured Gaskell's frankness, she trusted Gaskell's version of her close friend, just as she gave credence to Edith Coleridge's representation of her mother Sara.

Mary Augusta (Mrs Humphry) Ward

The publication of Austen-Leigh's *Memoir of Jane Austen* was a watershed in the reception history of the novelist. On the one hand, the wide critical attention it attracted meant that there were more articles devoted to Jane Austen in the two years from 1870 than in the preceding half-century since her death, and Bentley, who had published the *Memoir* and had been reissuing the novels since 1833, brought them out again in his 'Favourite Novels' series in 1870.[61] But as B.C. Southam and Kathryn Sutherland have amply demonstrated, the *Memoir* projected a particular version of Austen that was to have baneful consequences for the images of the woman and her novels which became prevalent in writing directed at the general public, and this is an aspect of the context in which Mary Augusta (Mrs Humphry) Ward came to publish on Austen in 1884.

One significance of Oliphant's review was that it was unusual in expressing scepticism about Austen-Leigh's version of his aunt. Oliphant attributed what

---

[61]   Ibid., pp. 1–3.

she saw as the text's failings to the Austen family's imperceptiveness about the brilliant woman in their midst, an imperceptiveness heightened by their greater valuing of males than of females. But the *Memoir* can now be recognised, partly because more information has come to light about its genesis, as not only based on limited information, but also as the product in part of a fairly deliberate exercise in image-making. Although it does give attention to her writing, it is concerned to highlight Austen's womanliness, and the pre-eminence of family and domestic duty in her life. As Southam observes, 'the *Memoir* evokes a comfortable, approachable figure who put down her needlework to pick up her pen – who wrote in the odd moments snatched from the daily round, who scribbled to please herself and entertain the family'.[62]

The result of this emphasis was to make the novels themselves seem rather cosy and comfortable, perfect in their way, but limited in their scope, and full of gentle humour, rather than possessing any satirical dimension or critical distance from the society they treat. Although this view was also current in some pre-1869 writing on Austen, the *Memoir* extended it, while also sentimentalising the novelist and imbuing her life with a nostalgic aura. Since much nineteenth-century fiction since Austen's had dealt with obvious social, industrial and political ills, or had featured 'sensational' plots full of crime and illicit sex, Austen's novels came to be presented as a sort of healthy antidote to these kinds of writing.[63] The details of bygone family and domestic life Austen-Leigh offered, meanwhile, were inflected with a sense of regret for a lost and simpler way of life, apparently free of the kinds of problems this later fiction had articulated. Austen-Leigh had also made Hampshire, where Jane Austen spent most of her life, seem more of a backwater than it had been in her lifetime,[64] so that it represented, in Kathryn Sutherland's words, 'a quintessential England, whose gentle scenery mapped an ideal creation, untouched by the upheaval, squalor, and class tension of industrializing society'. Hence Austen's 'occlusion within nature and family served a mythographic interest; in her case, the literary reconstitution of the lost English "village geography" we each carry in our hearts', and this kind of image-making served to give Austen's novels an escapist quality.[65] The otherworldly impression of Jane Austen's environment was also fostered, as Emily Auerbach has shown, by Austen-Leigh's tendency to edit out from the letters of Austen's that he quotes, some of her allusions to the Napoleonic Wars, other countries and politics, plus comments out of keeping with the respectable spinster he is striving to project, such as that on 'some naked Cupids over the Mantlepiece'.[66]

---

[62] B.C. Southam (ed.), *Jane Austen: The Critical Heritage*, vol. 2 *(1870–1940)* (London: Routledge & Kegan Paul; New York: Barnes & Noble, 1987), p. 4.

[63] Ibid., pp. 8–11.

[64] Kathryn Sutherland, *Jane Austen's Textual Lives*, pp. 67–8.

[65] Ibid., p. 69.

[66] Emily Auerbach, *Searching for Jane Austen* (Madison, WI: University of Wisconsin Press, 2004), pp. 9–11.

The outstanding reviews, as Southam highlights, were those of Oliphant and Richard Simpson,[67] and they could be seen as foreshadowing two important strands of criticism that were to emerge in the twentieth century. Simpson, writing in the *North British Review*, deals with the *Memoir* by giving it only perfunctory attention, and concentrates on the novels, analysing Austen's technique, and particularly the subtlety of her characterisation. Unlike in his discussion of George Eliot a few years earlier, he does not concern himself with gendering Austen's writing – as if he is impatient with the sentimental approach of other reviews, and/or does not construe Austen (unlike Eliot) as formidably 'masculine'. In addition, rather than treating her as a writer who transcribes directly from life (as was habitual), Simpson presents her as using other literature as a way of testing her perceptions: 'Miss Austen schooled herself into an unimpeachable conformity to nature, not by direct imitation of nature, but by looking through, and amusing herself with, the aberrations of pretended imitators'.[68] Like Oliphant, Simpson also identifies cynicism in Austen, expressed for him in the way she takes a 'humourist's view' of the belief in '[t]hat predestination of love, that preordained fitness, which decreed that one and one only should be the complement and fulfillment of another's being' – treating it as 'mere moonshine', while, on account of literary convention, 'found[ing] her novels on the assumption of it as a hypothesis'.[69] What is emphasised here is an Austen absorbed, not in bucolic domestic life, but in other people's writing, good and bad – she is a woman informed about, and responding to, literature.

Like Kavanagh and Oliphant, Simpson stresses Austen's deliberate crafting of her work. By downplaying the content of the *Memoir* and relating Austen's novels to a host of other writers of both sexes, he succeeds in treating Austen without condescension, taking her as seriously as he might an eminent male writer. Hence his work foreshadows the trend that emerged with Mary Lascelles' *Jane Austen and Her Art* in 1939 and continued through the 1940s in the writing of critics such as F.R. Leavis and D.W. Harding, where Austen's novels ceased to be seen as the exquisite but limited product of an inoffensive proto-Victorian spinster. Meanwhile Oliphant's interpretation, by demystifying the image created in the *Memoir* and pointing to ways in which Austen's writing may have been inflected by her powerlessness as a woman, foreshadows the approaches to Austen provoked by the 'second-wave' feminist movement of the 1970s, inaugurated by Sandra M. Gilbert and Susan Gubar's *The Madwoman in the Attic: The Woman Writer and the Nineteenth-Century Literary Imagination* (1979) – approaches which foregrounded her situation as a woman and investigated the impact this had on her writing.

---

[67]　*Jane Austen: The Critical Heritage*, vol. 2, 17ff.

[68]　'*Memoir of Jane Austen*', *North British Review*, 52 (April 1870): 129–52, repr. in *Jane Austen: The Critical Heritage*, ed. B.C. Southam (London: Routledge & Kegan Paul; New York: Barnes & Noble, 1968), pp. 241–65, at p. 243.

[69]　Ibid., p. 246.

As Southam laments, however, twentieth-century critics often had no awareness of the valuable perceptions offered by such predecessors as Kavanagh, Oliphant and Simpson.[70] The sentimental image of the *Memoir* persisted for decades. It was also fostered by the next significant publication by a member of the Austen family, the *Letters of Jane Austen*, edited with an introduction and critical remarks by Edward, Lord Brabourne, and published by Bentley in 1884. Among its reviewers was Mary Augusta Ward, whose 'Style and Miss Austen' appeared under her own name in *Macmillan's Magazine* in December 1884.

Lord Brabourne was one of a number of Jane Austen's collateral descendants who launched into print either in her wake, or as writers about her. James Austen-Leigh's half-sister Anna Austen (later Lefroy) had been a budding novelist in her aunt's lifetime, and the most extended surviving commentary by Jane Austen about novel-writing is found in letters of advice she wrote to Anna about the latter's novel, *Which is the Heroine?*, letters published in the *Memoir* and in Lord Brabourne's collection. This particular novel never appeared, but in 1834 Alaric Watts' *Literary Souvenir*, which had published early work by Maria Jane Jewsbury, brought out her *Mary Hamilton*, as 'By a Niece of the late Miss Austen'. Anna's daughter Fanny Caroline Lefroy published a number of novels in the 1850s and 1860s, some with the Mozley family firm, albeit without exploiting the Jane Austen connection.[71] More opportunistic was Catherine Anne Hubback née Austen, daughter of Jane's brother Frank, who in 1850 published *The Younger Sister*, a continuation of Jane Austen's fragment *The Watsons*, dedicated 'To the Memory of her Aunt, the Late Jane Austen'. Her later novels appeared as by 'Mrs. Hubback, niece of Jane Austen', and in 1871, following the publication of the *Memoir*, she announced to her son that she would henceforth have her name printed as 'Mrs. C. Austen Hubback', and pretend that the 'A.' in her name stood for 'Austen'.[72]

The efforts of Jane Austen's nieces to capitalise on her name suggest that it had a cultural cachet at least from the 1830s, but one that was enhanced following the publication of the *Memoir*. Her great-nephew Edward, Lord Brabourne, was the representative of the most upwardly mobile branch of the Austen family: his mother had been Fanny Knight, another niece close to Jane Austen as Anna had been, and the eldest child of Edward Knight, the Austen brother who had inherited the estate of a childless couple and had taken their name. Fanny Knight had become Lady Knatchbull, and Edward, her eldest son, was raised to the peerage. The bulk of the material he published had not been available to Austen-Leigh: they were letters from Jane Austen to her sister Cassandra which Cassandra had bequeathed to Fanny Knatchbull and which Brabourne had turned up after her death. He offered them to Bentley, and his edition of them came out in two volumes, dedicated to Queen Victoria.

---

[70] *Jane Austen: The Critical Heritage*, vol. 2, pp. 125–32.
[71] Kathryn Sutherland, *Jane Austen's Textual Lives*, pp. 258–9.
[72] Ibid., pp. 259–64.

Mary Ward's review of the letters was scathing, partly because she saw Brabourne as a very inept editor, and partly because she saw their publication as evidence of a contemporary tendency on the part of the families and friends of the famous to rush their letters into print, however private – or however uninteresting – the contents. Like Oliphant, she targets the most notorious offender, J.A. Froude, whose 'seven volumes' on the Carlyles, she says, 'would have been a scandal' in Jane Austen's day.[73] Such people cannot persuade themselves 'that the world could possibly do without information which it is in one's power to give it', and the distinction between public and private life which obtained in Austen's time has been 'rapidly swept away during the last generation' (256). Ward also hints that the motives for such publications may be mercenary: '[t]aste is laxer, the public easier to please, and book-making more profitable' (256–7). As far as Brabourne himself is concerned, she is percipient. Some of his diaries and correspondence with George Bentley over the publication are extant, and have been published by Deirdre Le Faye. A diary entry of 24 February 1884 reads, '[r]ead my mother's aunt Jane Austen's Letters & settle to see if I can publish or sell them', and three days later he writes both to George Bentley and to a book-dealer. Bentley agreed to the publication, and Brabourne's diary entry of 7 March notes that he is to get two-thirds of the profits of the first publication and three-fifths of that from any second or cheap edition.[74]

Ward also – quite rightly – sees Brabourne's editorial work as slapdash. It includes 'family pedigrees of which [Jane Austen] would have been the first person to feel the boredom and incongruity, and literary criticisms of a kind to have set that keen wit of hers moving in its most trenchant fashion' (256). The letters themselves are swamped by Brabourne's own 'ponderous' material, his 'endless strings of names and wandering criticisms on the novels' – for Ward, this is lazy, irresponsible work (257).

Ward was not alone in her criticisms of Brabourne. The critic in *The Times* – writing anonymously, unlike Ward – makes similar points, but with more scorn: this writer also believes that Jane Austen herself 'would have been tickled by the ludicrous absurdity of much that Lord Brabourne writes about herself in a style bearing a close resemblance to that of the Rev. William Collins', and finds the collection lacking in really helpful annotations. Thomas William Lyster in *The Academy* also finds Brabourne's own material heavy-going, while his 'critical remarks' are 'of as little value as the critical remarks of average school girls', and the reader is inconvenienced by the absence of an index.[75]

---

[73] 'Style and Miss Austen', *Macmillan's Magazine*, 51 (December 1884): 84–91, repr. in Solveig C. Robinson, *A Serious Occupation*, pp. 254–68, at p. 256. Subsequent references to this review will be included parenthetically in the text.

[74] Deirdre Le Faye, 'Lord Brabourne's Edition of Jane Austen's Letters', *Review of English Studies*, ns 52 (February 2001): 91–102, at 92–3.

[75] *Times*, 6 February 1885: 3; Thomas William Lyster, *'Letters of Jane Austen'*, *Academy*, 22 November 1884: 334–5.

Both Ward and some other reviewers, moreover, are dubious about the value of the letters themselves. The reviewer in *The Times*, as well as those for the *Athenaeum* and the *Gentleman's Magazine*, believe it would have been preferable to publish only a selection of the letters, as they are mostly not inherently interesting or especially well-written; G. Barnett Smith in the *Gentleman's Magazine* also claims that they add 'very little knowledge of a personal character to that we already enjoyed'.[76] Ward agreed with Barnett Smith, saying that 'the newly-discovered correspondence threw practically no fresh light on Miss Austen's personality' (257). Her focus, however, more so than that of other reviewers, is on Jane Austen as a novelist. Some of the early letters, written when Jane Austen was in her early twenties and drafting her earliest novels, she does think worth publishing, but because their tone 'reminds one of an older and shrewder Catherine [Morland], and the ways of seeing and describing to which they bear witness are exactly those to which we owe the unflagging liveliness and gaiety of the two famous books in which the adventures of Catherine and of Elizabeth Bennett [*sic*] are set forth' (257–8). And as *Northanger Abbey* underwent less revision before publication than did *Pride and Prejudice*:

> It is in the story of Catherine Morland that we get the inimitable literary expression of that exuberant girlish wit, which expressed itself in letters and talk and harmless flirtations before it took to itself literary shape, and it is pleasant to turn from the high spirits of that delightful book to some of the first letters in this collection, and so to realise afresh, by means of such records of the woman, the perfect spontaneity of the writer. (258)

But according to Ward, the later letters 'had become the mere ordinary chit-chat of the ordinary gentlewoman, with no claims whatever to publication or remembrance beyond the family circle'. This was partly because Austen was 'practically a stranger to … the world of ideas', and her letters also show almost no interest in the public events of 'the stormiest period of modern European history' (261–2). To this extent, Ward accepted the view of Austen fostered by the *Memoir*. But she also recognised possible constraints on letter-writing, recalling in her comments Maria Jane Jewsbury's view that Jane Austen expressed in her fiction elements of herself that she had to constrain in private life:

> The graphic portraiture of men and women seen from the outside, in which she excelled, was not possible in letters. It required more freedom, more elbow-room than letters could give. Jane Austen, in describing real people, found herself limited by the natural scruples of an amiable and gentle nature. (263)

---

[76] G. Barnett Smith, 'More Views of Jane Austen', *Gentleman's Magazine*, 258 (January 1885): 26–45, at 38; *Athenaeum*, 8 November 1884: 585–6.

Ward could not have known that Brabourne and Bentley, like Austen-Leigh, had altered and omitted parts of the letters, so as to enhance the image of Jane Austen as possessing 'an amiable and gentle nature'. For example, they cut from one a comment on a Mrs Tilson, 'but poor Woman? how can she be honestly breeding again?',[77] and in another, changed Austen's quip, 'I was as civil to them as their bad breath would allow me', so that 'bad breath' was replaced by 'circumstances'.[78] Brabourne had also emulated his cousin in stressing the domesticity of Jane Austen's existence: 'In truth, the chief beauty of Jane Austen's life really consisted in its being uneventful: *it* was emphatically a home life, – *she* the light and blessing of a home circle'.[79] Ward's conclusion in any case is that 'broadly speaking, the whole *yield* of Jane Austen's individuality was to be found in her novels' (261–2, Ward's emphasis), and it is the special quality of these that she goes on to discuss.

For Ward, recalling points made by Kavanagh and Oliphant, the distinctive literary trait of Jane Austen's fiction was its concentration, the sense it conveyed that she knew what to omit. She saw this characteristic as foreshadowing the concern in contemporary writing to 'avoid commonplace and repetition', such that the modern writer's mind 'will never describe if it can suggest, or argue if it can imply', and '[t]he first condition of success in letters is nowadays to avoid vapouring, and to wage war upon those platitudes we all submit to with so much cheerful admiration' in eighteenth-century writers. 'Condensation in literary matters', in which Austen excelled, she goes on, 'means an exquisite power of choice and discrimination – a capacity for isolating from the vast mass of detail which goes to make up human life just those details and no others which will produce a desired effect and blend into one clear and harmonious whole'. It also means 'the determination to avoid everything cheap and easy – cheapness in sentiment, in description, in caricature', plus 'the perpetual effort to be content with one word rather than two, the perpetual impulse to clip and prune rather than expand and lengthen'. According to Ward, Jane Austen possessed as well 'the imagination which seizes at once upon the most effective image or detail and realises at a glance how it will strike a reader', and, this, combined with her literary self-restraint, makes her fiction demonstrate 'that wrestle of the artist with experience which is the source of all the labours and all the trials of art' (265–7).

To illustrate her argument, Ward compares a passage from *Marriage*, by Austen's near-contemporary Susan Ferrier, with one from *Persuasion*. The latter describes Anne Elliot's renewed hopes of reaching an understanding with Captain Wentworth:

---

[77] Deirdre Le Faye, 'Lord Brabourne's Edition of Jane Austen's Letters', 99 n10.

[78] See Edward Lord Brabourne (ed.), *Letters of Jane Austen* (2 vols, London: Richard Bentley and Son, 1884), vol. 1, p. 243; Deirdre Le Faye (ed.), *Jane Austen's Letters*, 3rd edn (Oxford and New York: Oxford University Press, 1995), p. 61; Emily Auerbach, *Searching for Jane Austen*, p. 5.

[79] Edward Lord Brabourne, *Letters of Jane Austen*, vol. 1, p. 5 (Brabourne's emphasis).

How she might have felt had there been no Captain Wentworth in the case was not worth inquiring; for there was a Captain Wentworth, and be the conclusion of her present suspense good or bad, her affection would be his for ever. Their union, she believed, could not divide her more from other men than their final separation. Prettier musings of high-wrought love and eternal constancy could never have passed along the streets of Bath than Anne was sporting with from Camden Place to Westgate Buildings. It was almost enough to spread purification and perfume all the way. (267–8)

Of this passage, Ward remarks, '[h]ow terse it is, how suggestive, how free from vulgarity and commonplace!' (268). On the other hand, the musings of Susan Ferrier's Gertrude in a similar situation are 'all conventional, traditional, *hearsay* in fact', with 'nothing intimate or living' in them, and are hence potentially interminable (266–7, Ward's emphasis): Ferrier would have 'embroidered' Anne Elliot's thoughts with 'what raptures, what despairs, what appeals to heaven'. Similarly, in *Pride and Prejudice*, although there is very little actual description of Darcy's Pemberley estate, 'every stroke of the pen is so managed that any reader with ordinary attention may realise, if he pleases, the whole lie of the park, the look of the house, as Elizabeth surveyed it from the opposite side of the ravine above which it stood, the relative positions of the lawns, stables, and woods'. For all this, 'there is no effort, no intention to describe, nothing but a clear and vivid imagination working with that self-restraint, that concentration, which is the larger half of style' (268). In English literature, Austen's work embodies 'those drier and more bracing elements of style in which French literature has always been rich, and our own perhaps comparatively poor' (268). Like Kavanagh and Oliphant, Ward recognises that Austen is more than a transcriber of social minutiae – that what she omitted, she omitted deliberately, and to good effect.

Elsewhere, Ward situated Austen in an historical context. In her obituary of Anthony Trollope in the *Times* back in 1882, she had identified his fictional world as 'the heir of Miss Austen's', paying tribute again to Austen's 'style': 'Miss Austen drew the middle class of the England of Napoleon's day; her country squires, her fashionable ladies, above all her clergymen, are as real as they can be made by the most delicate observation, expressed in a style which for its mixture of crispness, pliancy, and a kind of rippling gaiety has no rival in English'. On the other hand, neither she nor Trollope is among the 'great novelists of the century' – these are 'Scott, Balzac, Dickens, Georges Sand, George Eliot, Charlotte Bronte, Thackeray, Turguenieff'. Together with Elizabeth Gaskell, Austen and Trollope are 'at the head of the second order', and this is because they lack 'certain rare and in-born gifts of genius which as it were take the heaven of our praise by force and conquer for themselves a place apart whenever they appear'.[80]

At the turn of the twentieth century, Mary Ward wrote a series of introductions to a collected edition of the Brontë novels put out by Smith Elder (the Brontës'

---

[80] *Times*, 7 December 1882: 9.

publisher and her own). In describing the strengths of Charlotte and Emily Brontë (she was lukewarm about Anne), she suggests one version of what she had meant by the 'gifts of genius which … take the heaven of our praise by force and conquer for themselves a place apart'. Characteristic of each of Charlotte and Emily is that she 'touches the shield of the reader; she does not woo or persuade him; she attacks him'.[81] Ward's article on Jane Austen had indeed identified as a flaw in the latter's work its lack of '[e]motion, inspiration, glow, and passion' (268). It is a deficiency of emotional power in her fiction, then, that makes Jane Austen a novelist of the second rank only.

I shall return to Ward's extensive treatment of the Brontës themselves in more detail below. I would note here, however, that in her introduction to *Jane Eyre*, she sketches for Charlotte a place in a continuum of women's fiction, between Jane Austen and George Eliot. Austen was the 'gentle and witty successor of Miss Burney and Richardson', and Charlotte Brontë stands between her and George Eliot. Whereas Charlotte Brontë's fiction was inflected by French Romanticism, Eliot's influences were 'German, critical, scientific'.[82] As Beth Sutton-Ramspeck has noted, Ward points also to the greater acceptability of fiction as a medium for female artistic endeavour in the nineteenth century than other genres, such as poetry, so that women 'have been poets in and through the novel'. Whereas in other fields, women are still trying to discover how best 'to appropriate traditions and methods not created by women, in the novel they are accepted as being 'among the recognized "masters of those who know"'. In this context, Ward again identifies the specific traits of particular women novelists. The 'Cowper-like poets of the common life' are Austen, Gaskell – and, interestingly, Oliphant – while George Sand and Charlotte and Emily Brontë are 'romantic or lyrical artists'. On the other hand, George Eliot is one of the 'Lucretian or Virgilian observers of the many-coloured web'.[83]

This account of Eliot both echoes a key image used by the narrator in *Middlemarch* to describe that novel's scope, and aligns Eliot herself with Lucretius and Virgil, eminent Roman practitioners of philosophy and epic respectively. But Ward's published views on Eliot were not always so positive. In an earlier article,

---

[81]   *The Life and Works of the Sisters Brontë*. Haworth Edition, introductions by Mrs Humphry Ward (7 vols, London: Smith, Elder, 1899–1903), vol. 5, *Wuthering Heights by Emily Brontë (Ellis Bell) and Agnes Grey by Anne Brontë (Acton Bell)* (1903), p. xii. Subsequent references to this Introduction will be included parenthetically in the text.

[82]   Introduction to *Jane Eyre*, vol. 1 of *The Life and Works of Charlotte Brontë and Her Sisters* (1899), pp. xxxvii–xxxviii. Subsequent references to this Introduction will be included parenthetically in the text.

[83]   Introduction to *Villette*, vol. 3 of *The Life and Works of Charlotte Brontë and Her Sisters* (1900), xxv–xxvi, quoted in Beth Sutton-Ramspeck, 'The Personal is Poetical: Feminist Criticism and Mary Ward's Reading of the Brontës', *Victorian Studies*, 34/1 (1990): 55–75, at 60. Subsequent references to this Introduction will be included parenthetically in the text.

written for adolescent girls in a series 'English Men and Women of Letters of the 19th century' and focusing on Elizabeth Barrett Browning, Ward had identified 'the great literary Englishwomen of the century, names familiar and dear to us all' as 'Miss Austen, Charlotte Brontë, George Eliot, Mrs. Gaskell, Mrs. Browning'. Her brief discussion here suggests again why she ranked Austen's achievement below that of Charlotte Brontë – for the latter expressed 'much less perfectly things better worth the trying', and Ward ultimately values content over technique. But what is notable too is the very lukewarm view of George Eliot: Eliot possesses 'far greater general power and competence' than either Austen or Charlotte Brontë, but she is 'subject in compensation to more aggressive faults'.[84]

Ward's stance in relation to George Eliot is paradoxical. Writing in *Macmillan's* in 1884 on 'Recent Fiction in England and France', she presents English fiction as in need of renewed vitality following the deaths of the last two generations of novelists. For her own contemporaries, 'Romola and Dinah Morris, and Esmond, and Jane Eyre and Anne Elliot, are ghosts of a past far off from us'.[85] Here she is of course evoking Eliot, Thackeray, Charlotte Brontë and Jane Austen. These are the departed great – but given that Eliot had died only in 1880, long after the others, and had published her final novel as recently as 1876, Ward is relegating her to a more distant past than seems warranted.

In a sense, Eliot is for Ward the strong precursor whose importance the later woman writer strives to deny. As for Oliphant, Ward's own novel-writing career is relevant to her response to Eliot. Unlike Oliphant, Ward published all her fiction and most of her criticism after Eliot's death, but she tried to distance herself from Eliot while capitalising on the potential links between them. As William S. Peterson has shown, when preparing for publication what was to be her landmark novel, *Robert Elsmere* (1888), she emulated the publication format of Eliot's landmark novel, *Middlemarch* – the green covers, the chapters numbered consecutively rather than by volume – while the two-volume format recalled Eliot's most popular novel, *Adam Bede*. On the other hand, Ward would later claim to find Eliot hopelessly old-fashioned. In a letter of 1896 to her publisher George Smith, she disclosed that she had abandoned an article on Eliot because of her frustration with *Adam Bede*, and in 1898 she would politely decline an offer from Eliot's publisher Blackwood's to write a monograph on her.[86] She told Smith she felt she would have to approach Eliot 'wholly or even mostly on my knees', although she felt terribly bored with *Adam Bede*. The reason for the boredom, moreover, was Eliot's narrow old-fashionedness:

> What a prig is Adam, & what a Sunday school tone much of it has! The Hale [*sic*] Farm, Mrs. Poyser, Hetty, Dinah – these remain; but the whole handling of

[84]   'Elizabeth Barrett Browning', *Atalanta*, 1 (September 1888): 708–12, at 708.
[85]   *Macmillan's Magazine*, 50 (August 1884): 250–60, at 250.
[86]   William S. Peterson, *Victorian Heretic: Mrs Humphry Ward's 'Robert Elsmere'* (Leicester: Leicester University Press, 1976), pp. 102–3.

the seduction, compared to what Turgieneff or Tolstoy would have made of it, seems to be superficial & conventional.[87]

For Ward, Eliot's approach to human sexuality and the issues it raised had been superseded, at least by the great Russian masters, but the younger English woman novelist would still be expected to defer to her. Yet in venturing into print with *Robert Elsmere*, a self-conscious claim to intellectual 'power and competence', steeped in the German scholarship so familiar to her predecessor, Ward seems to have deliberately raised the memory of George Eliot.

Whatever Ward's intentions, moreover, comparisons with Eliot were plentiful in the responses garnered by *Robert Elsmere*. James Knowles, the editor of the *Nineteenth Century* wrote to Gladstone (who was to produce an article on the novel), that Ward reminded him of George Eliot, such that 'she gives the impression of wishing to be Elisha to George Eliot's Elijah'. That is, Ward sought to be a prophet who was the designated successor to another prophet.[88] In the published criticism, meanwhile, analogies between Ward's novel and Eliot's works became commonplace, to the extent that the *Pall Mall Gazette*, not long after the novel's publication, could refer cynically to the 'log-rolling fraternity' who hailed Ward as 'greater than George Eliot'.[89] *Robert Elsmere* was immensely popular in both Britain and the United States, but Ward never achieved a like success in fiction, although she published novels right up to her death in 1920. It could be argued that, after tapping into the theological concerns of the 1880s, her work became intellectually rather old-fashioned. In addition, her conservative stance on women's role – shown in her public anti-suffrage activities as well as in her fiction – would also come to seem dated.

If Ward considered herself, however ambivalently, a successor to George Eliot, she certainly had a strong professional investment in Charlotte Brontë as well. Ward's response to the latter has been discussed in detail by Beth Sutton-Ramspeck and by Amanda Collins.[90] Ward was President of the Brontë Society for five years from 1912, and in her valedictory address in 1917 she draws an implicit parallel between her first visit to Smith Elder, the publishers she shared with Charlotte Brontë, and the famous occasion when Charlotte and Anne Brontë came to London to disclose the identities of the mysterious 'Bells' to George Smith.[91] On the other hand, when she emphasises in her treatment of Charlotte Brontë's

---

[87]   Ibid., p. 102.

[88]   Ibid., p. 103.

[89]   Ibid., p. 171.

[90]   Beth Sutton-Ramspeck, 'The Personal is Poetical'; Amanda J. Collins, 'Grave Duties of the Caretaker in the Lives of Charlotte Brontë' (PhD thesis, Sydney: University of Sydney, 2004), 245ff.

[91]   'Some Thoughts on Charlotte Brontë', in Butler Wood (ed.), *Charlotte Bronte: 1816–1916: A Centenary Memorial* (London: T. Fisher Unwin, 1917), pp. 13–38, quoted in Amanda J. Collins, 'Grave Duties of the Caretaker in the Lives of Charlotte Brontë', p. 250.

novels the primacy of feeling over form, emotional over intellectual content, Ward is implicitly defending her own fiction, according to Sutton-Ramspeck, in that her writing both 'aimed to move its readers emotionally and challenge them intellectually'.[92] Conceivably she thought of her own novels as combining the strengths of Charlotte Brontë and George Eliot.

As Sutton-Ramspeck stresses, Ward's discussion of Charlotte Brontë's work is mostly positive. With fewer provisos than Oliphant, Ward celebrates the emotional power of her fiction. In defending this power, Ward is also grappling with the public tendency, in the wake of the Gaskell biography, to conflate the Brontë sisters' works with their lives, even to manifest more interest in the compelling story of the idiosyncratic and ever-struggling sisters, than in anything they wrote. Ward's friend Henry James, whose views she respected, believed that such a tendency encouraged a diminished critical rigour in dealing with the actual literary output of the Brontës, and thus an overrating of their work.[93]

In reviewing Lord Brabourne's edition of Jane Austen's correspondence, Ward saw no value in publishing biographical material about authors for its own sake – to be worth publishing, it needed to demonstrate aspects of the author that were relevant to their writing. Some years after this article, Ward reviewed a substantial new biographical work on Charlotte Brontë, Clement Shorter's *Charlotte Brontë and Her Circle*. Again, she criticises the publication of material which contributes nothing to our knowledge of the author or her works – in his case, Charlotte's letters to her teacher Miss Wooler, written with 'a certain constraint', and discussion of her reactions to Haworth curates which show an immaturity she outgrew. Like Oliphant, Ward also condemns bringing too much of a subject's private life into the public domain, exemplified in Shorter's book by letters about Charlotte Brontë's courtship and married life, plus comments on people still living.[94]

But Ward welcomes some of the new letters, including those to George Smith's colleague, William Smith Williams, and new ones to Ellen Nussey. This is because they express Charlotte Brontë's personality, and are also very well-written. For Ward, the two traits go together: both Charlotte Brontë's letters and her novels are a manifestation of her character; by the same token, since writing was so central to her life, the same literary qualities are evident in her personal correspondence as in her fiction. So her letters express 'the Brontë temperament, with its sincerity, its passion, its swiftness to anger or to love', its freedom from 'pretence' or 'pedantry'. Moreover, 'Charlotte, even in her most intimate letters, hardly ever keeps down the artist': 'the search for the telling, the poignant phrase is instinctive', such that 'emotion, even the most primitive and passionate, cannot be satisfied without it'.

Ward's conviction is that Charlotte Brontë's fiction is autobiographical in its feeling, if not in its narrative details. In this respect, the novelist is not alone among English writers. In reviewing Walter Pater's *Marius the Epicurean* in 1885,

---

[92] 'The Personal is Poetical', 70.
[93] Ibid., 56ff.
[94] *Times*, 23 October 1896: 10.

Ward identified a paradox in recent English literature: overtly autobiographical writing possesses 'a touch of dryness and reserve', whereas 'what is deepest, most intimate, and most real' in nineteenth-century English writers' experience is not found in avowed autobiographies, so much as in books like *Marius*, plus earlier works such as Carlyle's *Sartor Resartus*, J.A. Froude's *The Nemesis of Faith* or Charles Kingsley's *Alton Locke*.[95] It is the sense of personal emotional and spiritual experiences these texts express that gives them their impact, not any precise correspondence with the lives of their authors.

Ward's response to Charlotte Brontë's fiction, articulated in detail in her Introductions to the Haworth edition of the Brontë novels at the turn of the century, recalls Oliphant's earlier comments about how the emotional power of her writing disarms criticism. But, despite acknowledging the implausibility of *Jane Eyre*'s plot and some of its characterisation, she is more laudatory than Oliphant about the value of the fiction's emotional force. 'The main secret of the charm that clings to Charlotte Brontë's books is, and always will be', she declares, 'the contact which they give us with her own fresh, indomitable, surprising personality – surprising above all' (xx). It is Charlotte Brontë's 'strong, free, passionate personality' which 'is the sole but the sufficient spell of these books' (xxi). Her linking of the life and work recalls Mozley's, but Ward's admiration is less equivocal. Of *Villette*, Ward asserts that '[f]rom beginning to end it seems to be written in flame', such that 'there is nothing in the book but what shares in this all-pervading quality of swiftness, fusion, vital warmth' (xix–xx). Such a quality emerges in the portrayal of Lucy Snowe, which, like Oliphant, Ward admires, but (unlike Oliphant), considers partly autobiographical, praising 'Lucy's hungering nature, with its alternate discords and harmonies, its bitter-sweetness, its infinite possibilities for good and evil, dependent simply on whether the heart is left starved or satisfied, whether love is given or withheld' (xxii). Like Oliphant and Mozley, Ward relished the portrayal of M. Paul Emmanuel: 'what variety, what invention, what truth, have been lavished upon him!' (xxi).

In *Shirley*, admittedly, she finds such power less consistently evident. Charlotte Brontë is still present, with different aspects of her personality distributed among the three main female characters, Caroline Helstone, Shirley Keeldar and Mrs Pryor, but the middle section of the novel lacks momentum and style, with its concentration on Shirley's charitable plans, the school-treat, the curates, and the old maids. For Ward, Charlotte Brontë's forte was 'the play of personal passion' – the representation of 'country and clerical life' was better handled by writers such as Jane Austen, Elizabeth Gaskell, George Eliot and Anthony Trollope.[96]

For Oliphant, the passion evident in Charlotte Brontë's fiction was a problematic trait, particularly in its legacy to later novelists. She also considered the novels as a whole narrow in scope, overemphasising the importance to life of 'the love between

---

[95]   '*Marius the Epicurean*', *Macmillan's Magazine*, 52 (June 1885): 132–9, at 134.

[96]   Introduction to *Shirley*, vol. 2 of *The Life and Works of Charlotte Brontë and Her Sisters* (1899), xviff.

men and women'. By contrast, Ward pinpointed Charlotte Brontë's treatment of love as a distinctive strength of her writing, and as something especially enabled by her being a woman. Women have been deprived of many kinds of opportunities open to men, she argued, and this has limited the source-material for their fiction – but they have always known love, and love as felt by their sex. Ward's case here recalls Julia Kavanagh's highlighting of women writers' portrayal of their sex's take on love as part of their distinctive contribution to the novel. For Ward, echoing Kavanagh, women's 'peculiar vision, their omissions quite as much as their assertions, make them welcome' (Introduction to *Villette*, xxvi). Men's novels, more broad-ranging, may satisfy the modern wish for knowledge, but, Ward contends, 'the craving for feeling is at least as strong, and above all for that feeling which expresses the heart's defiance of the facts which crush it, which dives … into the inner recesses of man, and brings up, or seems to bring up, the secrets of the infinite' (xxvi–xxvii). Charlotte Brontë, and other women writers, have delved into specifically female feelings and insights, and succeeded in representing these in fiction, not only as revelations of women's inner lives, but so as to tap into the deep-seated needs of both sexes.

If Charlotte Brontë's fiction was for Ward both an expression of her temperament and a manifestation of insights specific to her sex, neither her personality nor her writing emerged *sui generis*. Brontë's character was the product of both her heritage and her environment, while the particular qualities of her writing were enhanced by her exposure to French Romanticism. She was neither totally idiosyncratic, nor an untutored genius: her personality may have been 'surprising', but it was by no means inexplicable. More than most commentators, including Lawrance and Mozley, Ward goes beyond the specifics of Charlotte Brontë's family dynamics to interpret her.

It is in the Introduction to the first volume of the Haworth edition, *Jane Eyre*, that Ward spells out the elements of the Brontës' personal and literary background. The aspect of the Brontë heritage that she highlights is its Celtic dimension: the siblings were the offspring of an Irish father and Cornish mother. Drawing on her uncle Matthew Arnold's theories about the Celtic temperament, articulated in his *On the Study of Celtic Literature* (1866), Ward attributes to Charlotte Brontë what she calls 'the main characteristics of the Celt' – 'disinterestedness, melancholy, wildness, a wayward force and passion, for ever wooed by sounds and sights to which other natures are insensible' (xxii). Hence her work, as well as Emily's, possesses:

> Idealism, understood as a life-long discontent; passion, conceived as an inner thirst and longing that wears and kills more often than it makes happy; a love of home and kindred entwined with the very roots of life, so that homesickness may easily exhaust and threaten life; an art directed rather to expression than to form – ragged often and broken, but always poignant; always suggestive, touched with reverie and emotion. (xxii)

The 'Celtic vision' is also one that 're-makes the world, throws it into groups and pictures, seen with a magical edge and sharpness' (xxix). Existing in tandem with all these qualities, according to Ward, are 'the Celtic pride, the Celtic shyness, the Celtic endurance', and, together with passion, they are 'writ large' in Charlotte's novels: hence these traits '*are* Jane Eyre and Lucy Snowe', and 'supply the atmosphere, the peculiar note, of all the stories' (xxiv–xxv, Ward's emphasis).

Yet the distinctiveness of the Brontë temperament, and therefore of the Brontë novels, results, in Ward's view, from the combination of their 'Celtic' dimension with two other influences. Since the Brontës' Irish heritage was Protestant rather than Catholic, as well as northern-Irish and thus much affected by English hegemony, 'the Bible and Puritanism have mingled with their Celtic blood', and in their conduct as it appears to the world, '[e]conomy, self-discipline, constancy, self-repression and order ... come easily to them' (xxix–xxx). Their life in Yorkshire, moreover, exposed them to the characteristic traits of 'the hard, frugal, persistent North' (xxviii), 'the heart of working England':

> all the English love of gain and the English thirst for success – watchful, jealous, thrifty, absorbed in this very tangible earth, and the struggle to subdue it, stained with many coarse and brutal things, scornful of the dreamer and the talker, and yet, by virtue of its very strength of striving life, its very excesses of rough force and will, holding in its deep breast powers of passion and of drama unsuspected even by itself. (xxviii–xxix).

In the Brontës' lives, the special combination of traits that Ward ascribes to them means that they learn and practise all household duties, and are 'docile, hard-working, hard-living ... poor, saving, industrious, keenly alive to the value of money and work, like the world about them'. But they 'take their revenge in dreams, – in the whims and passions of the imagination' (xxx). As a result, both Charlotte and Emily's novels possess 'value and originality' deriving from 'this mixture of Celtic dreaming with English realism and self-control' (xxx). So as to illustrate their distinctiveness, Ward makes the same kind of move as when she set a passage from *Persuasion* alongside one from Susan Ferrier's *Marriage*, to demonstrate the superiority of Austen's writing. Here she quotes from Lady Caroline Lamb's novel *Glenarvon*, and compares the passage with the scene from *Jane Eyre* when Jane and Rochester are reunited. Despite the 'vigour' of Lamb's sentences, they are but 'vague and mouthing falsity' when set against conversations in *Jane Eyre* such as that in the reunion scene: 'notice how clear and true – with the clearness and truth of poetry – are all the stages of recognition and of rapture' (xxxi).

Charlotte's literary influences, according to Ward, were just as hybrid as those of her heredity and environment. The Brontës became very well-read in the British classics, in contemporary British poetry and biography, and in periodical writing (xxxiii–xxxiv). But Charlotte was also steeped in French Romanticism – notably the works of Hugo, Musset, and especially George Sand (xxivff). What was 'English, Protestant, law-respecting' in her made her very different from Sand

– she claimed to find French fiction 'immoral'. But it 'quickened and fertilized her genius' (xxxvii). Sand's fiction, Ward argues, provided Charlotte Brontë with a model for combining 'restless imagination' with 'a fine and chosen realism' (xxxv). Although she does not imitate Sand directly, parts of *Shirley* bear traces of passages from Sand's *Lélia*, and Rochester's unearthly cry to Jane is foreshadowed by a passage in her *Jacques* (xxxvi–xxxvii). In the Introduction to *Villette*, Ward points out that Charlotte Brontë's response to the French actor Rachel, expressed in the chapter on 'Vashti', 'bears testimony once again to the close affinity between her genius and those more passionate and stormy influences let loose in French culture by the romantic movement' (xv). Ward's analysis thus accounts for the qualities registered by Mozley and Oliphant – the narrow but intense focus on the world Charlotte Brontë knew, transfigured by passion and a potent imagination – by going beyond a purely biographical explanation.

If Charlotte Brontë's temperament and fiction were passionate, and manifested Celtic imagination contained by Protestant self-control and a northern-English sense of quotidian reality, the same was true of her sister Emily. In her Introduction to *Wuthering Heights*, Ward quotes the lines paying tribute to Emily in Matthew Arnold's elegy, 'Haworth Churchyard', lines which emphasise her passionate nature. He describes her as one

> whose soul
> Knew no fellow for might,
> Passion, vehemence, grief,
> Daring, since Byron died …

before she 'sank / Baffled, unknown, self-consumed' (xl).

But Arnold's tribute was to Emily Brontë's poetry, rather than to her novel, and although Ward praises the poetry (xxxviii–xl), she is much more interested in *Wuthering Heights*. Arnold's lines also imply that if Emily Brontë's passions were held in check, then the self-restraint finally killed her. Ward, on the other hand, finds impressive Emily's combination in life of strong will and imagination, though it seems 'inhuman or terrible' (xxiii). More importantly, it contributed to making Emily Brontë a much less confessional artist than Charlotte: *Wuthering Heights* uses first-person narrators, but they are not the novel's protagonists – projections of the author, as Ward interpreted those of *Jane Eyre* and *Villette*. Unlike in Charlotte's novels, the artist in *Wuthering Heights* 'remains hidden and self-contained', and this gives the characters 'an independence behind which the maker is forgotten' (xxiv). Emily's impersonality also makes her male characters more consistently convincing than her sister's: while Charlotte can be 'parochial, womanish, and morbid in her imagination of men in relation to women', Emily 'is the true creator, using the most limited material in the puissant, detached, impersonal way that belongs only to the highest gifts – the way of Shakespeare' (Introduction to *Shirley*, xix–xxi). In her Introduction to *Wuthering Heights*, Ward notes as well the 'timidity' of both Charlotte Brontë and Elizabeth Gaskell in their accounts of the novel (xvi).

Ward presents Emily Brontë's work as influenced by European Romanticism, but in her case, it was German rather than French writers. She notes Emily's exposure, in the 1830s and 1840s, including during her stay in Brussels, to translations from German and periodical articles on German writing (xix–xxi), with E.T.A. Hoffmann being particularly important. Emily was hence familiar with Romantic monsters, hideous characters, abnormal situations, violent speech, and Romantic self-exaltation. These influences might have contributed to what Ward saw as Heathcliff's exaggerated cruelty to Edgar and the two Catherines in *Wuthering Heights* (xxvff). Nonetheless, 'all that is best in Romantic literature' contributes to the power of the second half of the novel – 'that fusion of terror and beauty, of ugliness and a flying magic – "settling unawares" – which is the characteristic note of the Brontës' (xxxvi). The tendency to exaggeration, moreover, was contained by 'a mind richly stored with English and local reality' (xxvi). Ward makes more than does Mozley of Emily Brontë here: Mozley could only see *Wuthering Heights* as the product of an idiosyncratic personality and isolation from normal human contact.

Ward conveys the impression that she considers Emily superior to Charlotte as a writer – but I concur with Beth Sutton-Ramspeck that, overall, her Introductions to the novels suggest that she 'responded far more intensely to Charlotte's work than to Emily's'.[97] It was the apparent direct contact with Charlotte's personality in her fiction that Ward relished, rather than the more subtle and impersonal art of her sister. The contrast perhaps recalls Oliphant's differing responses to Jane Austen and Mary Russell Mitford: Austen had to be acknowledged as the greater artist, but the broader scope and the cheerfulness of Mitford's writing made her appeal more directly to Oliphant.

And what of the third Brontë sister, Anne? In the twentieth century, she received little serious attention before the 1980s, and in the nineteenth century, she was, throughout, very much overshadowed by her sisters. Oliphant and Ward, no more than had Mozley, did nothing to counter the trend of neglecting her. In *The Victorian Age of English Literature*, Oliphant declares that Anne 'need never have been mentioned except for her relationship with the other two'.[98] Ward, meanwhile, in introducing a complete edition of the Brontë sisters' works, can hardly ignore Anne, but gives her short shrift, comparing her unfavourably with her sisters. Assuming, as had Mozley, that the sisters' experience of their brother Branwell was what gave them knowledge of the seamy side of male behaviour, she argued that for the older sisters, the ordeal 'troubled the waters of the soul, and brought them near to the more desperate realities of our "frail, fall'n humankind"' – but in Anne's case, 'her gift was not vigorous enough, to enable her thus to

---

[97]   'The Personal is Poetical', 72.
[98]   Vol. 1, p. 320.

transmute experience and grief'.[99] So, while *The Tenant of Wildfell Hall* possesses 'considerable narrative ability' and 'a sheer moral energy', it has only 'the truth of a tract or a report', rather than 'the truth of imagination', and was probably based largely on 'close transcripts from Branwell's conduct and language' (xv–xvi). The novel was for Ward factual autobiography, rather than imaginative and emotional autobiography – a view which recalls Mozley's. Even having a greater talent for friendship than her sisters works against Anne in Ward's view, in that it makes her less of the Romantic artist that Ward evidently considered Charlotte and Emily to be: 'she was not set apart, as they were, by the lonely and self-sufficing activities of great powers' (xix). Hence is it is only 'as the sister of Charlotte and Emily Brontë, that Anne Brontë escapes oblivion' (xix).

Mary Ward clearly respected Jane Austen's fiction as the work of a woman who had wrestled with experience and who, in her representation of it, had both exercised remarkable powers of discrimination and restraint, and produced a style of writing which was original and unrivalled. But the limits of Austen's interests and emotional power meant that she was not, for Ward, in the first rank of novelists. George Eliot, meanwhile, was a writer of apparently much greater fictional scope and intellectual range, yet Ward found her old-fashioned and overrated. Eliot was, however, hard to escape as a role model for women novelists of Ward's generation, and perhaps Ward did adapt to this situation and aspire to be Eliot's successor. It could be argued as well that when Ward started publishing literary criticism under her own name in *Macmillan's* in the early 1880s, this reflected not only the growing pervasiveness of signature in periodicals of the late nineteenth century, but also the growing acceptance of women's intellectual calibre – a development for which Eliot was partly responsible.

It was however Charlotte Brontë who most engaged Mary Ward. She responded strongly to the powerful feelings conveyed by the novels, and relished the way they apparently offered access to the novelist herself. Of British women novelists, in Ward's view, Charlotte and Emily Brontë had most successfully taken advantage of the opportunities afforded women by the genre – the chance to be 'poets', and to offer insights into the female experience of love. Unlike Anne Mozley, Ward valued the sisters as Romantic artists, with their 'lonely and self-sufficing activities of great powers'. Unusually for a critic of her period, she explained their achievement, not through a straightforward reading of their lives and their Yorkshire environment, but by analysing the varied hereditary and cultural influences affecting them. In particular, she identified the impact of various kinds of literature on their writing – mainly French for Charlotte, mainly German for Emily. It was exposure to literary Romanticism, more than to the Yorkshire moors, that, for Mary Ward, made Charlotte and Emily Brontë the writers they were.

---

[99]   Introduction to *The Tenant of Wildfell Hall*, vol. 6 of *The Life and Works of Charlotte Brontë and Her Sisters* (1903), p. xiii. Subsequent references to this Introduction will be included parenthetically in the text.

Chapter 6
Conclusion

When Mathilde Blind produced the first book on George Eliot in 1883, she situated the novelist at the outset in the context of her female predecessors, notably Jane Austen and the Brontës. She acknowledged Austen as foreshadowing Eliot in her 'microscopic fidelity of observation', with its 'well-nigh scientific accuracy', and quoted Scott's by-then-celebrated praise of Austen's 'exquisite touch, which renders ordinary commonplace things and characters interesting from the truth of the descriptions and sentiment'. She claimed as well that Scott's tribute to Austen showed that he 'recognised the eminently feminine inspiration of her writings' – and what Blind went on to say about the Brontës also focused on their femaleness. '[D]oes not one feel', she asks, 'the very heartbeats of womanhood in those powerful utterances that seem to spring from some central emotional energy?'. On the other hand, George Eliot combines masculine and feminine qualities, and this is one reason that she 'takes precedence of all writers of this or any other country'. Eliot adds to literature 'something which is specifically feminine', which Blind locates in her 'unparalleled vision for the homely details of life' (the quality she shares with Austen) – while at the same time 'her intellect excels precisely in those qualities habitually believed to be masculine', especially 'the grasp of abstract philosophical ideas'.[1]

Blind's summary here, like the 1860 quotation with which this study began, is an instance of canon-forming based on the achievements of nineteenth-century women novelists. It also demonstrates the widespread contemporary tendency to discuss their work in terms of 'masculine' and 'feminine' qualities. The writings of the women critics focused on here reflect both these trends. They also worked with a strong sense of their own implication in gender-related assumptions about women's writing, and this awareness informed both their choices about disseminating their ideas and their textual self-representations. With all this in mind, then, how did they contribute to the nineteenth-century critical discourse on Jane Austen, Charlotte Brontë and George Eliot?

Jane Austen's life and works drew from women critics much insightful commentary in the nineteenth century. Some of the most valuable arose from a perception seldom shared by the men – that there was an inconsistency between the figure represented by Austen's male relatives and the kind of personality that seemed to be behind the writing in the novels. Maria Jane Jewsbury explained the discrepancy by suggesting that Austen concealed in her social behaviour the

---

[1]   Mathilde Blind, *George Eliot* [1883] (new edn 1888, repr. New York: Haskell House, 1972), p. 5.

insights and satirical tendencies evident in her fiction, while Mary Ward, reviewing Austen's letters, claimed that in most of them Austen would have had to subdue the traits she could express in the novels. Margaret Oliphant, meanwhile, was convinced that the stance of the narrators in Austen's works was that of a writer highly perceptive about human behaviour but also fatalistic, as a woman, about her inability to influence it; Austen's 'feminine cynicism', for Oliphant, also derived from her family's lack of appreciation of the brilliant female in their midst.

There was a great deal of writing on Austen in the nineteenth century which characterised her as the miniaturist on 'little bit[s] of ivory', following her own apparent cue: what she achieved, she accomplished with perfection, but her aims, especially as regards the social and intellectual scope of her fiction, were limited. In addition, the representation of Austen and her environment in the 1869 *Memoir* encouraged a sentimental approach to the writer as the recorder of a simpler but irrevocably bygone era. Women critics were not guiltless of such an approach: what became one of the most widely quoted post-*Memoir* tributes to the novelist was penned by Anne Thackeray, who apostrophised the novels thus: 'Dear books! bright, sparkling with wit and animation, in which the homely heroines charm, the dull hours fly, and the very bores are enchanting.' Austen is one of those who can 'raise and ennoble all those who follow after, – true, gentle and strong and tender' because she teaches the lesson: 'Don't let us despise our nests – ... let us complete the daily duties; let us patiently gather the twigs and the little scraps of moss, of dried grass together; and see the result! – a whole, completed and coherent, beautiful even without the song.' Austen here is a kind of icon of true womanhood, her actual writing merely incidental.[2]

Other women critics, however, interpreted Austen's writing as feminine in less reductive ways. Sara Coleridge suggested that Austen's kind of novel was a female specialty, and could not be surpassed by men, but she was ambivalent about Austen's creative and intellectual powers. Julia Kavanagh was more forthright: like Sara Coleridge, she claimed 'delicacy' as a defining trait of Austen's writing, but extended the term's meaning to encompass Austen's sharp insights and careful, subtle discrimination in her portrayal of character. Several women critics, too – Kavanagh, Mozley, Oliphant and Ward – recognised that what was lacking from Austen's novels was often absent not because of Austen's limitations but because of her deliberate choices.

Charlotte Brontë's writing challenged nineteenth-century readers in quite different ways from Jane Austen's, not least because of the issue about her sex raised by her puzzling pseudonym, 'Currer Bell'. Sara Coleridge, for one, was initially convinced that the author was male, and judged *Jane Eyre*, with its plain and morally clear-sighted heroine, as a welcome change from what she considered some sentimental, and thus too-feminine, novels by women. She made the common

---

[2]   Review of *Memoir of Jane Austen, Cornhill Magazine*, 34 (1871): 158–78, repr. in Solveig C. Robinson (ed.), *A Serious Occupation: Literary Criticism by Victorian Women Writers* (Peterborough, Ontario and Orchard Park, NY: Broadview, 2003), pp. 234–53.

complaint about the 'coarseness' of Charlotte Brontë's fiction, too, but believed such strictures could be exaggerated.

One hostile contemporary treatment of Charlotte Brontë's fiction, the review of *Jane Eyre* in the *Quarterly Review*, was by a woman (Elizabeth Rigby); it was echoed in some respects by Anne Mozley's review of *Villette* in the *Christian Remembrancer*, which apparently targeted protagonist Lucy Snowe's unwomanly independence and her disclosure of the power of female desire. I have argued, however, that Mozley was probably accommodating here the *Remembrancer*'s conservative audience: most of the review praises the novel's originality, and elsewhere Mozley welcomed the advent in fiction by women of heroines who could think for themselves.

The more problematic aspect of the strength of Brontë's heroines – the power of their emotional and sexual desires – was a central theme of Margaret Oliphant's discussion of the novels. She recognised the assertion of this power as one kind of claim for women's rights, and insofar as she expressed reservations about it, this was mainly because of its legacy in the work of lesser writers: the emphasis on women's sexuality to the exclusion of all else represented for her just as reductive a view of women as the failure to acknowledge their sexuality at all. Moreover, the overall emotional force exerted by Brontë's novels on the reader – a power which was due partly but not entirely to their heroines' personalities – was focused on by Mozley, Oliphant and Ward. In their view, it was attributable to a sensibility which drew on a limited range of experience, but whose fine imagination worked with intensity and originality to produce compelling narratives from that restricted material. These critics were not unusual in pointing to these qualities in the fiction – they were after all central to the novels' popularity – but their emphasis on them shows a wish to welcome an exciting and innovative female presence in English fiction.

Important to the response to Charlotte Brontë's work after her death was the impact of Elizabeth Gaskell's biography. For the critics discussed here who reviewed the book, Hannah Lawrance and Anne Mozley, Charlotte Brontë's life as interpreted by Gaskell explained much that was puzzling, outré or offensive about the fiction. The two critics' emphases were nonetheless different. Hannah Lawrance read Brontë as a victim of men, both those in her family, and literary figures like Robert Southey who were fearful of female competition. Anne Mozley was more critical of Brontë's own choices, including her religious choices, but did acknowledge her suffering; to some extent, too, Charlotte Brontë remained for Mozley a mysterious figure.

Mary Ward's comprehensive treatment, especially in her prefaces to the new Haworth edition of the Brontë novels at the turn of the century, is especially significant in the history of responses to Charlotte Brontë and her works. Ward's reaction was clearly personal in part. She grappled as well with Brontë's handling of female passion, by stressing that insights into the female experience of love represented women's particular contribution to the novel as a genre, and a contribution that extended men's understanding of the inner life too. But Ward also went beyond the straightforwardly biographical readings of the Brontës' works that were common at the time, to trace more complex influences. We might now find problematic the explanation of life or literature by recourse to qualities associated with ethnicity. Yet Ward's account of the Brontës' Celtic heritage and its alleged impact on their works, did at least counter the domination of the 'purple heather' school of writing on the Brontës, with its obsession with their Yorkshire environment. Most importantly, she drew attention to some of the specifically literary influences on the Brontës' works: those of French Romanticism for Charlotte and those of German Romanticism for Emily. That is, the Brontë novels, according to Ward, engaged with other writing as much as with the writers' own life-experiences.

In reading the Gaskell biography, Margaret Oliphant was struck by the limited experience of its subject. She likewise found that George Eliot's life, as recounted in her widower's biography, suggested a very protected existence, and one where important personal choices were made with little emotional fallout for Eliot. But what has not been sufficiently recognised is how far Oliphant questioned J.W. Cross's version of his wife as a mystification, and also came to realise that she had been a hard-headed woman of business in her dealings with her publishers. She also registered that Eliot's achievement, especially her obvious intellectual attainments, had made it difficult for critics to treat her in the patronising way which was the lot of many women writers. The same awareness had lain behind Anne Mozley's welcoming, in her review of *Adam Bede* back in 1859, what she was unusual in identifying as a new female voice in fiction – there was little in either knowledge or powers of expression which was beyond a woman novelist's reach. And although Mozley could not accept Eliot's rejection of Christianity, she could not help being impressed by *The Spanish Gypsy* and engaging thoughtfully with the implications of its creed.

Margaret Oliphant and Mary Ward, however, were both influenced in their responses to George Eliot by their experiences as fellow novelists. Oliphant found her own *Chronicles of Carlingford* accused of being an imitation of Eliot in their treatment of small communities' religious life; she was as well acutely conscious of how the intense financial pressure she was always under affected the quality of her work, whereas Eliot was apparently free of such constraints. Ward, whose fiction-writing career followed hard upon Eliot's death in 1880, was in a paradoxical situation: she found Eliot's fiction dated, but her own salient success, *Robert Elsmere*, was in some measure attributable to Eliot's example. Public taste for and acceptance of novels by women that treated serious philosophical issues had been created partly by Eliot.

Oliphant, as both critic and novelist, also responded negatively to Eliot's novels from *Romola* onwards, because she considered them out of touch with the concerns of ordinary mortals. Oliphant was warm in her praise for *Adam Bede*, but the later novels conveyed to her an uncritical admiration on Eliot's part for figures supposedly superior to the normal run of humanity, such as Romola and *Middlemarch*'s Dorothea Brooke – figures she found lacking in humanity. It is possible that the protagonist and her career in Oliphant's own *Miss Marjoribanks* constituted in part a parody of *Romola*.

Oliphant and Ward's responses to George Eliot show something of the flipside of the pre-eminence the novelist had attained in the latter part of her career: her reputation, especially after Dickens's death in 1870, was unrivalled, and for other women novelists, she was the standard of comparison. This situation also suggests the negative side of canon-formation when women writers are concerned – the risk of relating them too much simply to one another. This was less likely to occur with male writers, since critics had no great concern to define what men were capable of: it was women who were 'the sex'. Oliphant had herself ridiculed a review's yoking of Austen and Eliot, as if it was incumbent on a critic discussing a new woman writer to analyse her achievement in relation to a very different one.

So when Eliot's work fell from favour in the latter years of the nineteenth century, the voices of prominent women critics like Oliphant and Ward were not there to counter the trend. The differences between the earlier novels and those from *Romola* onwards came to be constantly commented on – usually not in Oliphant's terms of their focus moving from ordinary to extraordinary characters, but rather, targeting a regrettable predominance of analytical reflectiveness and moral sententiousness over creativity and vitality. So A.V. Dicey, reviewing *Daniel Deronda* in 1876, comments that in the later works '[r]eflection prevails over description, and the moral purpose always discernible in George Eliot's works threatens to throw into the shade the author's creative power',[3] and his point was made repeatedly in later years. The overall popularity of the earlier works was sustained, too, partly by the nostalgia for the rural and provincial past which had also inflected the reception of Jane Austen and her fiction. Ward did not in any case value Eliot's earlier fiction, finding the often-lauded *Adam Bede* both shallow and dated. Meanwhile the impressionistic approach to literature taken by influential critics like Edmund Gosse and George Saintsbury tended to devalue the moral focus of Eliot's fiction.[4]

Eliot's novels had attracted serious and valuable commentary from male critics such as E.S. Dallas, R.H. Hutton, Richard Simpson, Sidney Colvin, Lord Acton and Henry James. But the decline in her reputation, which extended well into the twentieth century, had a misogynist side to it as well, unfortunately aggravated in some male commentary by distaste for both her physical appearance and the aura of moral solemnity with which she was invested in the last years of her life, with her Sunday afternoon gatherings of admirers. The work of W.E. Henley, as well as that of Gosse and Saintsbury, conveys almost a pleasure in belittling both the woman and her achievement. To some extent, too, the version of Eliot offered by

---

[3]   *Nation*, 19 October 1876: 245–6, repr. in Stuart Hutchinson (ed.), *George Eliot: Critical Assessments* (4 vols, Mountfield: Helm Information, 1996), vol. 1, pp. 392–7, at p. 392.

[4]   J. Russell Perkin, *A Reception-History of George Eliot's Fiction* (Rochester: University of Rochester Press, 1990), 93ff.

Cross fostered the view that her intellectual ideas were derived from a series of male figures in her life – so that the reviewer in the *Saturday Review* even argued that she passively adopted the beliefs of whichever male loomed largest in her life at the time, and concluded smugly that '[t]he person whom superficial critics took to be the most masculine of her sex was a very woman'.[5] The patronising treatment of women's writing which had been so recurrent earlier in the century resurfaces as this would-be intellectual female is cut down to size.

As this last quotation suggests, the discussion of women writers in terms of 'masculine' and 'feminine' qualities continued through the nineteenth century, and the critics treated here grappled with the issue of what these qualities meant, plus the extent to which they were determined by the writer's sex. For Maria Jane Jewsbury, women writers capable of 'masculine' intellectual rigour and cogency were admirable – the female and feminine 'sketchers' come across as lesser figures. On the other hand, masculine 'power' in men's writing could be taken to an extreme, while Felicia Hemans's womanliness was an asset to her poetry, especially as her work manifested masculine intellect as well. Sara Coleridge's take on the issue seems less consistent – but consistency is less likely to be characteristic of letter-writing over a number of years than of publications, and it could be argued that her various treatments of the question express the potential difficulties it raised for a woman of her time. Women can write a certain kind of novel better than men can – but isn't this a more limited form of achievement? Does a writer like Jane Austen really possess a creative imagination? How 'masculine' can the writing of a woman like Charlotte Brontë be without her own femininity being at stake? Can women's fiction actually be too 'feminine'? Is there really a fit between the character conveyed by a woman's writing and the personality that emerges in social intercourse with her? All these issues are at stake in Sara Coleridge's discussions of women writers.

All three historians of women and women's writing treated here make demarcations between masculine and feminine qualities in women's lives and works. Hannah Lawrance highlights their household management, their charitable endeavours, and, in both life and literature, their roles as mothers. Jane Williams focuses on women's domestic virtues, and, in their writing, draws attention to female intuition, 'tenderness' and 'delicacy'. Julia Kavanagh fixes too on 'tenderness' and 'delicacy' as distinctive traits of women's writing, adding to them 'purity' and 'sympathy' – all qualities of course associated with women themselves. But all three writers champion women's intellectual capacities, and register the prejudices and barriers that had, over the centuries, hampered the development of these. Lawrance points to Elizabeth Barrett Browning as an example of how a woman writer could expand the boundaries of female awareness without endangering female 'delicacy', while also contributing to poetry distinctively maternal

---

    5   *Saturday Review*, 7 February 1885: 181–2, repr. in David R. Carroll (ed.), *George Eliot: The Critical Heritage* (London: Routledge & Kegan Paul; New York: Barnes & Noble, 1971), pp. 483–9, at p. 487.

emotion. Considering the novel, Julia Kavanagh claims it as the most influential contemporary form of creative literature, and as a genre to which women had made groundbreaking contributions, notably to its habitual focus on the inner life.

Lawrance, Williams and Kavanagh, writing often under their own names, are to some extent accommodating traditional assumptions about women in their readers. This is also the case with Anne Mozley, who writes anonymously, but generally for conservative periodicals. So she sometimes endorses notions such as women's necessary subordination to men, their incapacity for public office and male professions, and the advisability of their sticking to feminine intuition rather than essaying 'masculine' modes of ratiocination. But she works into her articles strong claims for women's mental and literary abilities being on a par with those of men, and welcomes the opening up of writing as a possible career path for them.

Oliphant gives some attention to the capacities of novelists of each sex to create characters of the opposite sex: although she criticises what she sees as the reductive views of women implied by the novels of Thackeray, Dickens and Hardy, she also pays tribute to Trollope and Richardson for their perceptive representations of female figures. Yet she was concerned as well with how women writers could be treated condescendingly, like the female purveyors of three-deckers whom she saw as maligned by contrast with the prolix and tedious George Meredith. In Austen's case, Oliphant argued that the narrative viewpoints of the novels were inflected by the writer's sense of social and intellectual powerlessness as a female. Ward's gender-related commentary, however, like Kavanagh's, was more focused on women's distinctive contribution to the novel. She echoed Kavanagh's identification of fiction as the genre where women's input had been most significant; she argued too that the restrictions of the material at their disposal yielded particularly valuable insights into the very field where they could claim most knowledge – the female experience of love. In this sense, women's powerlessness in other areas, paradoxically, had its benefits.

The women critics discussed here made strategic choices as to the ways they disseminated their ideas. For Maria Jane Jewsbury, anonymous periodical criticism enabled her to eschew the quest for fame which both her own religious convictions and the ideological forces of her culture discouraged in women; but it also meant that she could express her views more forcibly and openly than if her sex and identity had been known. She was very aware of the possibility afforded by anonymous criticism for adopting an array of voices and attitudes. Anne Mozley and Margaret Oliphant, meanwhile, in some of their periodical writing, adopted overtly male personae. In Mozley's case, where conservative periodicals were concerned, she was able to assure her readers of her traditional attitudes while working into her articles claims for women's intellectual and literary potential. As regards Oliphant, male ventriloquism was relatively rare in the criticism considered here – her voice is usually not overtly gendered – although her initial commentary on Charlotte Brontë aped in parts an archly masculine condescension. When writing under her own name, she could adapt to the circumstances. So in defending women, as in the reviews of *Jude the Obscure* and of Froude's publications on the Carlyles, she wrote as an outspoken representative of her sex – but in publishing on Charlotte Brontë at the end of her life, she was circumspect about the novelist's passion, possibly because she was writing in a book to mark Victoria's Jubilee.

Sara Coleridge found letter-writing a less constrained way of conveying her thoughts than periodical publication – albeit she needed to take account of the sensibilities of her correspondents, as is shown by her revising of her letter about Elizabeth Barrett's poetry that was directed to Barrett's cousin John Kenyon. Letter-writing was an accepted mode of female self-expression, and it enabled Sara Coleridge to write extensively beyond her literary roles of dutiful daughter and helpful wife, if only for private consumption.

In the publications that came out under their own names, Lawrance, Williams and Kavanagh accommodated in various ways conservative ideas about women: all of them highlighted 'feminine' qualities in life and/or writing, and Williams asserted both the subordinate role of women in the poetic tradition and the primacy of domestic duty in women writers' lives. But the actual content of their books foregrounds women's important contributions to literature (Williams and Kavanagh) and history (Lawrance). Lawrance also disclaims any foray into discussing public events in the mode of a male historian – but incorporates such discussion into her treatment of women and especially of queens of the past. Mary Ward, however, publishing in her own name on the Brontës at the turn of the century, could be more direct in her claims; she also both capitalised on her fame as a novelist and hinted that she was herself Charlotte's successor.

Women critics understood gender as at least partly performance, adumbrating the perceptions of recent theorists like Judith Butler, who have explored gender as socially constructed and habitually performed, rather than as expressing any kind of ontological essence.[6] While sometimes performing masculinity herself, Jewsbury showed in her discussions of books by Elizabeth Sandford and Anna Jameson how women writers might be constrained to perform a kind of femininity which pandered to traditional cultural notions of womanhood. Her published celebration of the 'womanly' qualities of Hemans's poetry, meanwhile, reflected in part her private knowledge of the circumstances of her life that belied the accepted wifely and maternal image of the poet. Jane Williams and Hannah Lawrance, also dealing with Hemans (and in Williams's case with Letitia Landon as well), pointed to how they tailored both their public personae and the poetry which expressed these to early nineteenth-century models of the 'poetess'.

Yet when women critics grappled with the lives and works of female writers, they still generally sought some access to the personality of the women themselves, some understanding of the novelists as fellow women. So Jewsbury, Oliphant and Ward may have discounted the version of Jane Austen offered by her male relatives, but they found her character expressed in her novels. Likewise, although

---

6   Judith Butler, *Gender Trouble: Feminism and the Subversion of Identity* (London: Routledge, 1990), *Bodies That Matter: On the Discursive Limits of Sex* (London: Routledge, 1993).

Oliphant distrusted Cross's representation of George Eliot, she found the woman, with all her deficiencies (as Oliphant saw them), in her fiction and unpublished letters. Mozley, meanwhile, was perplexed by the apparent gap between the narrative presence apparently behind *Adam Bede* and the woman Marian Evans. For Lawrance, Mozley, Oliphant and Ward, Charlotte Brontë's personality, which they saw variously as compelling, forceful, pitiable, limited and puzzling, emerged in both her novels and Gaskell's biography.

The popularity of Gaskell's biography, as well as of Austen-Leigh's *Memoir* and Cross's *Life and Letters of George Eliot*, shows that seeking the woman behind the fiction was habitual in the nineteenth century. In the cases of Austen-Leigh's text and the *Life of Charlotte Brontë*, too, the biographical accounts established images of modest and self-effacing femininity which were to inflect interpretations of the Austen and Brontë novels for years to come. This was despite the insights of some of the women critics treated here. Ironically, two of them, Sara Coleridge and Anne Mozley, were themselves to suffer from a kind of memorialisation which owed something to Austen's relatives and to Gaskell.

When Edith Coleridge issued her *Memoir and Letters* of her mother in 1873, the 'Memoir' section assembled substantial commentary on Sara from those who had known her. But its emphasis recalls that of S.T. Coleridge's encomium on his daughter, when presenting her with a translation of Virgil at her marriage back in 1829: her erudition is impressive, but less important than – and perhaps excused by – her 'feminine' qualities. So Sara's old friend the poet Sir Henry Taylor told Edith, 'I only know that the admirable strength and subtlety of her reasoning faculty shown in her writings and conversation, were less to me than the beauty and simplicity and feminine tenderness of her face'.[7] Another male poet, Aubrey de Vere, commented that Sara Coleridge's 'intellectual fervour' was 'ever modulated by a womanly instinct of reserve and dignity', such that '[s]he was more a woman than those who had not a tenth part of her intellectual energy', possessing 'domestic affections so tender, so dutiful, and so self-sacrificing'.[8] Sara had performed her femininity well, and Edith continues the performance, emphasising that her mother's aim as a widow was to devote 'the whole of her intellectual existence to the great object of carrying out a husband's wishes, of doing justice to a father's name'. But this harping on what Edith calls 'my mother's truly feminine authorship',[9] before she presents the actual letters, becomes insistent and repetitive, as if there is behind it all the awareness that what Sara's extensive literary and intellectual correspondence really shows is a relish for discussion of subjects that were not directly related to either her husband's wishes or her father's name.

---

[7]   Edith Coleridge (ed.), *Memoir and Letters of Sara Coleridge* (2 vols, London: Henry S. King, 1873), vol. 1, p. 29.

[8]   Ibid., vol. 1, pp. 51–2.

[9]   Ibid., vol. 1, p. 46.

In 1892, the year after Anne Mozley's death, her sister Fanny and nephew Frank disclosed her long and prolific career as a contributor to leading periodicals and republished some of her articles. They did outline her literary activities and comment that her writing represented 'a world of her own, which for the great part of the day was indeed the world that interested her'.[10] But like Gaskell and Austen-Leigh, they pointed out that for a long time no one outside the woman writer's family circle had any knowledge of the resident female author's literary activity. They stressed, too, that '[i]n more directly feminine occupations Anne bore her full share', including 'delicate and tasteful embroidery'.[11] Moreover, Anne Mozley's 'feminine' aspect extended to her writing, since this manifests 'instinctive habit of observation' and 'the power of drawing conclusions from slight traits'.[12]

So in the latter part of the nineteenth century, accounts of women writers of considerable intellect and erudition were still haunted by the images of Charlotte Brontë living for her father and siblings, of Jane Austen's 'little bit of ivory'. Both Sara Coleridge and Anne Mozley came from families whose male members were some of them published writers and intellectuals – from what Sara Coleridge's father would have called the 'clerisy'. Yet, although family members in both cases considered the women's literary criticism worth publishing and identifying as theirs, the publications were posthumous. To recall Maria Jane Jewsbury's comment on Jane Austen – 'being dead', they could be 'quoted without impropriety'.

---

[10] 'Memoir', in *Essays from 'Blackwood'. By the late Anne Mozley* (Edinburgh and London: William Blackwood and Sons, 1892), p. vii.

[11] Ibid., p. xi.

[12] Ibid., p. viii.

Bibliography

Manuscript Sources

Letters from Maria Jane Jewsbury to Geraldine Jewsbury, John Rylands University Library of Manchester.

Letters from Maria Jane Jewsbury to Dora Wordsworth, Wordsworth Trust, Dove Cottage, Cumbria.

Letters from Sara Coleridge to Dora Wordsworth, Wordsworth Trust, Dove Cottage, Cumbria.

Letters from Sara Coleridge to various correspondents, Harry Ransom Center, University of Texas at Austin.

Unpublished MSS by Sara Coleridge, 'The Princess, A Medley' (two versions), 'Fielding', Harry Ransom Center, University of Texas at Austin.

Correspondence between Anne Mozley and members of the Blackwood publishing firm, Blackwood Papers, National Library of Scotland, Edinburgh.

Correspondence between Margaret Oliphant and members of the Blackwood publishing firm, Blackwood Papers, National Library of Scotland, Edinburgh.

Printed Primary Sources

Allott, Miriam (ed.), *The Brontës: The Critical Heritage* (London: Routledge & Kegan Paul; New York: Barnes & Noble, 1974).

Armstrong, Isobel and Joseph Bristow with Cath Sharrock (eds), *Nineteenth-Century Women Poets: An Oxford Anthology* (Oxford: Clarendon Press, 1996).

Austen, Henry, 'Biographical Notice of the Author' [1817], repr. in B.C. Southam (ed.), *Jane Austen: The Critical Heritage* (London: Routledge & Kegan Paul; New York: Barnes & Noble, 1968), pp. 73–8.

Austen, Jane, *Emma* [1815], ed. James Kinsley, intro. David Lodge (London and Oxford: World's Classics, 1990).

Austen, Jane, *Northanger Abbey* [1817], ed. Claire Grogan (Peterborough, Ontario and Orchard Park, NY: Broadview, 1996).

Austen-Leigh, James Edward, *A Memoir of Jane Austen and Other Family Recollections*, ed. Kathryn Sutherland (London and Oxford: Oxford University Press, 2002).

Barnett Smith, G., 'More Views of Jane Austen', *Gentleman's Magazine*, 258 (January 1885): 26–45.

Blind, Mathilde, *George Eliot* [1883] (new edn, 1888, repr. New York: Haskell House, 1972).

Brabourne, Edward, Lord (ed.), *Letters of Jane Austen* (2 vols, London: Richard Bentley and Son, 1884).

'The British Press: Its Growth, Liberty, and Power', *North British Review*, 30 (May 1859): 367–402.

Carroll, David R. (ed.), *George Eliot: The Critical Heritage* (London: Routledge & Kegan Paul; New York: Barnes & Noble, 1971).

[Chorley, Henry Fothergill], '*French Women of Letters*', *Athenaeum*, 30 November 1861: 717–18.

Chorley, Henry Fothergill, *Memorials of Mrs. Hemans* (2 vols, London: Saunders & Otley, 1836).

[Chorley, Henry Fothergill], '*Woman in France During the Eighteenth Century*', *Athenaeum*, 2 March 1850: 226–7.

Coleridge, Edith (ed.), *Memoir and Letters of Sara Coleridge* (2 vols, London: Henry S. King, 1873).

[Coleridge, Sara], 'Dyce's Edition of Beaumont and Fletcher', *Quarterly Review*, 83 (September 1848): 377–418.

[Coleridge, Sara], 'Tennyson's *Princess: A Medley*', *Quarterly Review*, 82 (March 1848): 427–53.

Costello, Louisa Stuart, *Memoirs of Eminent Englishwomen* (4 vols, London: Richard Bentley, 1844).

[Croker, J.W.], 'Poems by Alfred Tennyson', *Quarterly Review*, 49 (April 1833): 81–96.

[Dallas, Eneas Sweetland], '*Felix Holt, the Radical*', *Times*, 26 June 1866, repr. David R. Carroll (ed.), *George Eliot: The Critical Heritage* (London: Routledge & Kegan Paul; New York: Barnes & Noble, 1971), pp. 263–70.

[Dallas, Eneas Sweetland], 'Popular Literature: The Periodical Press', *Blackwood's Edinburgh Magazine*, 85 (February 1859): 180–95.

[Dicey, A.V.], '*Daniel Deronda*', *Nation*, 19 October 1876: 245–6, repr. in Stuart Hutchinson (ed.), *George Eliot: Critical Assessments* (4 vols, Mountfield: Helm Information, 1996), vol. 1, pp. 392–7.

Easson, Angus (ed.), *Elizabeth Gaskell: The Critical Heritage* (London and New York: Routledge & Kegan Paul, 1991).

[Eliot, George], 'Belles Lettres', *Westminster Review*, 67 (January 1857): 306–10.

[Eliot, George], 'Silly Novels by Lady Novelists', *Westminster Review*, 66 (1856): 442–61, repr. in Solveig C. Robinson (ed.), *A Serious Occupation: Literary Criticism by Victorian Women Writers* (Peterborough, Ontario and Orchard Park, NY: Broadview, 2003), pp. 88–115.

Elwood, Anne, *Memoirs of the Literary Ladies of England from the Commencement of the Last Century* (2 vols, London: Henry Colburn, 1843).

Espinasse, Francis, *Lancashire Worthies* (2nd series; London: Simpkin, Marshall, & Co., 1877).

'French Women of Letters', *Saturday Review*, 18 January 1862: 75–7.

Gaskell, Elizabeth, *The Life of Charlotte Brontë* [1857], ed. Linda H. Peterson, vol. 8 of *The Works of Elizabeth Gaskell* (London: Pickering & Chatto, 2005).

[Greg, W.R.], 'The Newspaper Press', *Edinburgh Review*, 102 (October 1855): 470–98.

Griggs, Grace Evelyn and Earl Leslie Griggs, *The Letters of Hartley Coleridge* (London: Oxford University Press, 1936).

Haight, Gordon S. (ed.), *The George Eliot Letters* (6 vols, New Haven and London: Yale University Press, 1954), vols 2 and 3.

Hardy, Thomas, Postscript (1912) to the Preface to *Jude the Obscure* [1895], ed. Cedric Watts (Peterborough, Ontario and Orchard Park, NY: Broadview, 2004), pp. 40–42.

Hill, Alan G. (ed.), *The Letters of William and Dorothy Wordsworth*, 2nd edn, III, *The Later Years, Pt I, 1821–28* (Oxford: Clarendon Press, 1978).

[Howitt, William], '*Shirley*', *Standard of Freedom*, 10 November 1849: 11, repr. in Miriam Allott (ed.), *The Brontës: The Critical Heritage* (London: Routledge & Kegan Paul; New York: Barnes & Noble, 1974), pp. 133–5.

Hughes, C. Harriett, *Works of Mrs. Hemans, With a Memoir of Her Life* (2 vols, Edinburgh: William Blackwood and Sons, 1839).

Hutchinson, Stuart (ed.), *George Eliot: Critical Assessments* (4 vols, Mountfield: Helm Information, 1996), vol. 1, *Biography, Nineteenth-Century Reviews and Responses.*

[Hutton, Richard Holt], 'George Eliot's Moral Anatomy', *Spectator*, 5 October 1872: 1262–4, repr. in Stuart Hutchinson (ed.), *George Eliot: Critical Assessments* (4 vols, Mountfield: Helm Information, 1996), vol. 1, pp. 285–8.

[Jeffrey, Francis], 'Felicia Hemans', *Edinburgh Review*, 50 (October 1829): 32–47.

[Jewsbury, Maria Jane], *Letters to the Young* (London: J. Hatchard & Son, 1828).

[Jewsbury, Maria Jane], 'Literary Sketches – No. 1 Mrs Hemans', *Athenaeum*, 12 February 1831: 104– 5.

[Jewsbury, Maria Jane], 'Literary Women – No. 2 Jane Austen', *Athenaeum*, 27 August 1831: 553–4.

[Jewsbury, Maria Jane], '*Memoirs of Celebrated Female Sovereigns*', *Athenaeum*, 12 November 1831: 730–31.

[Jewsbury, Maria Jane], '*The Nature and Dignity of Christ*', *Athenaeum*, 28 May 1831: 337.

Jewsbury, Maria Jane, *Occasional Papers*, ed. Eric Gillett (London: Oxford University Press, 1932).

[Jewsbury, Maria Jane], *Phantasmagoria; or, Sketches of Life and Literature* (2 vols, London: Hurst, Robinson and Co., 1825).

[Jewsbury, Maria Jane], 'Shelley's "Wandering Jew"', *Athenaeum*, 16 July 1831: 456–7.

Jewsbury, Maria Jane, *The Three Histories* (London: Frederick Westley and A.H. Davis, 1830).

[Jewsbury, Maria Jane], '*Woman, in her Social and Domestic Character*', *Athenaeum*, 5 May 1832: 282–3.

Kavanagh, Julia, *English Women of Letters*: *Biographical Sketches* (2 vols, London: Hurst and Blackett, 1862).

Kavanagh, Julia, *French Women of Letters: Biographical Sketches* (2 vols, London: Hurst and Blackett, 1861).

Kavanagh, Julia, *Woman in France During the Eighteenth Century* (2 vols, 1850, repr. London: G.P. Putnam's Sons, 1893).

Kavanagh, Julia, *Women of Christianity, Exemplary for Acts of Piety and Charity* (London: Smith, Elder, 1852).

Kebbel, T.E., 'Jane Austen at Home', *Fortnightly Review* ns 37 (February 1885): 262–70.

Kelley, Philip and Ronald Hudson (eds), *The Brownings' Correspondence* (Winfield, KS: Wedgestone Press, 1984–), vols 4–10 (1986–92).

[Lawrance, Hannah], 'The Anglo-Norman Poets of the Twelfth Century', *British Quarterly Review*, 5 (March 1847): 159–86.

[Lawrance, Hannah], 'George Herbert and Contemporary Religious Poets', *British Quarterly Review*, 19 (April 1854): 377–407.

Lawrance, Hannah, *Historical Memoirs of the Queens of England from the Commencement of the Twelfth Century* (2 vols, London: Edward Moxon, 1838).

Lawrance, Hannah, *The History of Woman in England and Her Influence on Society and Literature, From the Earliest Period.* Vol. 1 *To the Year 1200* [no further vols published] (London: Henry Colburn, 1843).

[Lawrance, Hannah], 'The Life of Charlotte Brontë', *British Quarterly Review*, 26 (July 1857): 218–31.

[Lawrance, Hannah], *The Mabinogion*, reviews in the *Athenaeum*: pt 1, 24 November 1838: 833–5; pt 2, 14 September 1839: 694; pt 3, 23 April 1842: 360–61; pt 4, 30 April 1842: 378–9; pt 6, 17 May 1845: 479–81; pt 7, 17 November 1849: 1149–51.

[Lawrance, Hannah], 'Mistress Hannah Woolley', *Household Words*, 4 August 1855: 18–22.

[Lawrance, Hannah], 'Mrs. Browning's Poetry', *British Quarterly Review*, 42 (October 1865): 359–84.

[Lawrance, Hannah], 'Tennyson's Idylls of the King', *British Quarterly Review*, 30 (October 1859): 481–510.

Le Faye, Deirdre (ed.), *Jane Austen's Letters*, 3rd edn (London and New York: Oxford University Press, 1995).

'*Letters of Jane Austen*', *Athenaeum*, 8 November 1884: 585–6.

'*Letters of Jane Austen*', *Times*, 6 February 1885: 3.

[Lewes, George Henry], 'The Novels of Jane Austen', *Blackwood's Edinburgh Magazine*, 86 (July 1859): 99–113, repr. in B.C. Southam (ed.), *Jane Austen: The Critical Heritage* (London: Routledge & Kegan Paul; New York: Barnes & Noble, 1968), pp. 148–66.

[Lewes, George Henry], '*Shirley*', *Edinburgh Review*, 91 (January 1850): 153–73, partly repr. in Miriam Allott (ed.), *The Brontës: The Critical Heritage* (London: Routledge & Kegan Paul; New York: Barnes & Noble, 1974), pp. 160–70.

Littlewood, Ian (ed.), *Jane Austen: Critical Assessments* (4 vols, Mountfield: Helm Information, 1998).

Lyster, Thomas William, '*Letters of Jane Austen*', *Academy*, 22 November 1884: 333–4.

McCarthy, William and Elizabeth Kraft (eds), *Anna Letitia Barbauld: Selected Poetry and Prose* (Peterborough, Ontario and Orchard Park, NY: Broadview, 2002).

McNees, Eleanor (ed.), *The Brontë Sisters: Critical Assessments* (4 vols, Mountfield: Helm Information, 1996).

'*The Mill on the Floss*', *Saturday Review*, 14 April 1860: 470–71, repr. in Stuart Hutchinson (ed.), *George Eliot: Critical Assessments* (4 vols, Mountfield: Helm Information, 1996), vol. 1, pp. 118–22.

Morley, John, 'Anonymous Journalism', *Fortnightly Review*, ns 2 (September 1867): 287–92.

[Mozley, Anne], '*Adam Bede* and Recent Novels', *Bentley's Quarterly Review*, no. 2 (July 1859): 433–72.

[Mozley, Anne], 'Clever Women', *Blackwood's Edinburgh Magazine*, 104 (October 1868): 410–27.

Mozley, Anne, *Essays from 'Blackwood'. By the Late Anne Mozley* (Edinburgh and London: William Blackwood and Sons, 1892). (Memoir by Fanny and Frank Mozley, and John Wordsworth, Bishop of Salisbury, [vii]–xx).

[Mozley, Anne], *Essays on Social Subjects from the Saturday Review* (2 vols, Edinburgh and London: William Blackwood and Sons, vol. 1, 1864; vol. 2, 1865).

[Mozley, Anne], 'Female Occupation and Influence', *Christian Remembrancer*, 35 (June 1858): 436–87.

[Mozley, Anne], 'Illustration', *Blackwood's Edinburgh Magazine*, 110 (December 1871): 754–70.

Mozley, Anne (ed.), *Letters and Correspondence of John Henry Newman During His Life in the English Church, With a Brief Autobiography* (2 vols, Longmans, Green and Co., 1891).

Mozley, Anne (ed.), *Letters of the Rev. J.B. Mozley, D.D.* (London: Rivingtons, 1885).

[Mozley, Anne], '*The Life of Charlotte Brontë*', *Christian Remembrancer*, 34 (July 1857): 87–145.

[Mozley, Anne], 'Mr Mill on *The Subjection of Women*', *Blackwood's Edinburgh Magazine*, 106 (September 1869): 309–21.

[Mozley, Anne], 'New Novels by Lady G. Fullerton and Currer Bell', *Christian Remembrancer*, 25 (April 1853): 401–43.

[Mozley, Anne], 'Novels by Sir Edward Bulwer-Lytton', *Bentley's Quarterly Review*, no. 1 (March 1859): 73–105.

[Mozley, Anne], 'On Fiction as an Educator', *Blackwood's Edinburgh Magazine*, 108 (October 1870): 449–59.

[Mozley, Anne], 'Our Female Novelists', *Christian Remembrancer*, 38 (October 1859): 305–39.

[Mozley, Anne], 'Prolixity', *Blackwood's Edinburgh Magazine*, 109 (May 1871): 610–26.

[Mozley, Anne], *Tales of Female Heroism* (London: James Burns, 1846).

[Mozley, Anne], 'Vapours, Fears and Tremors', *Blackwood's Edinburgh Magazine*, 104 (February 1869): 228–37.

[Mozley, Anne], 'Youth as Depicted in Modern Fiction', *Christian Remembrancer*, 52 (July 1866): 184–211.

Mozley, Dorothea (ed.), *Newman Family Letters* (London: SPCK, 1962).

Mozley, Rev. Tom, *Reminiscences Chiefly of Towns, Villages and Schools* (2 vols, London: Longmans, Green & Co., 1885).

Oliphant, Margaret, *Annals of a Publishing House: William Blackwood and His Sons, Their Magazine and Friends* (2 vols, Edinburgh and London: William Blackwood and Sons, 1897).

Oliphant, Margaret, 'The Anti-Marriage League', *Blackwood's Edinburgh Magazine*, 159 (January 1896): 135–49.

Oliphant, Margaret, *Autobiography and Letters of Mrs Margaret Oliphant* (1899), ed. Mrs Harry Coghill, intro. Q.D. Leavis (Leicester: Leicester University Press, 1974).

Oliphant, Margaret, *Autobiography of Margaret Oliphant: The Complete Text*, ed. Elisabeth Jay (Oxford and New York: Oxford University Press, 2002).

[Oliphant, Margaret], 'Charles Dickens', *Blackwood's Edinburgh Magazine*, 77 (April 1855): 451–66.

[Oliphant, Margaret], 'Charles Dickens', *Blackwood's Edinburgh Magazine*, 109 (June 1871): 673–95.

[Oliphant, Margaret], 'The Correspondence of M. de Balzac', *Edinburgh Review*, 148 (October 1878): 528–58.

[Oliphant, Margaret], 'Historical Sketches of the Reign of George II. No. X The Novelist', *Blackwood's Edinburgh Magazine*, 105 (March 1869): 253–76.

[Oliphant, Margaret], '*The Life and Letters of George Eliot*', *Edinburgh Review*, 161 (April 1885): 514–53.

Oliphant, Margaret, *Literary History of England in the End of the Eighteenth and Beginning of the Nineteenth Century* (3 vols, London: Macmillan, 1882), vol. 3.

[Oliphant, Margaret], 'The Lives of Two Ladies', *Blackwood's Edinburgh Magazine*, 91 (April 1862): 401–23.

[Oliphant, Margaret], 'Miss Austen and Miss Mitford', *Blackwood's Edinburgh Magazine*, 107 (March 1870): 290–313.

[Oliphant, Margaret], 'Modern Novelists – Great and Small', *Blackwood's Edinburgh Magazine*, 77 (May 1855): 554–68.

[Oliphant, Margaret], 'Mr Thackeray and His Novels', *Blackwood's Edinburgh Magazine*, 77 (January 1855): 86–96.

Oliphant, Margaret, 'Mrs Carlyle', *Contemporary Review*, 44 (May 1883): 609–28.

[Oliphant, Margaret], 'New Books (No. XIII)', *Blackwood's Edinburgh Magazine*, 114 (September 1873): 368–90.

[Oliphant, Margaret], 'New Novels', *Blackwood's Edinburgh Magazine*, 128 (September 1880): 378–404.

[Oliphant, Margaret], 'Novels', *Blackwood's Edinburgh Magazine*, 102 (September 1867): 257–80, partly repr. in Solveig C. Robinson (ed.), *A Serious Occupation: Literary Criticism by Victorian Women Writers* (Peterborough, Ontario and Orchard Park, NY: Broadview, 2003), pp. 144–74.

[Oliphant, Margaret], 'The Old Saloon (No. XIII)', *Blackwood's Edinburgh Magazine*, 144 (September 1888): 419–42.

[Oliphant, Margaret], 'The Rev. W. Lucas Collins', *Blackwood's Edinburgh Magazine*, 141 (June 1887): 734–6.

Oliphant, Margaret, 'The Sisters Brontë', in Margaret Oliphant and others, *Women Novelists of Queen Victoria's Reign: A Book of Appreciations* (London: Hurst and Blackett, 1897), pp. 3–61.

Oliphant, Margaret, 'Thomas Carlyle', *Macmillan's Magazine*, 43 (April 1881): 482–96.

[Oliphant, Margaret], 'Two Cities – Two Books', *Blackwood's Edinburgh Magazine*, 116 (July 1874): 72–91.

Oliphant, Margaret with F.R. Oliphant, *The Victorian Age of English Literature* (2 vols, London: Percival & Co., 1892).

Porter, Mrs Gerald, *Annals of a Publishing House: William Blackwood and His Sons, Their Magazine and Friends*, vol. 3 *John Blackwood* (Edinburgh and London: William Blackwood and Sons, 1898).

Raymond, Meredith B. and Mary Rose Sullivan (eds), *The Letters of Elizabeth Barrett Browning to Mary Russell Mitford* (3 vols, Waco, TX: Wedgestone Press, 1983), vol. 3.

[Rigby, Elizabeth], '*Vanity Fair* and *Jane Eyre*', *Quarterly Review*, 84 (December 1848): 153–85, repr. in Solveig C. Robinson (ed.), *A Serious Occupation: Literary Criticism by Victorian Women Writers* (Peterborough, Ontario and Orchard Park, NY: Broadview, 2003), pp. 46–73.

Robinson, Solveig C. (ed.), *A Serious Occupation: Literary Criticism by Victorian Women Writers* (Peterborough, Ontario and Orchard Park, NY: Broadview, 2003).

[Simpson, Richard], 'George Eliot's Novels', *Home and Foreign Review*, 3 (October 1863): 522–49, repr. in Stuart Hutchinson (ed.), *George Eliot: Critical Assessments* (Mountfield: Helm Information, 1996), vol. 1, pp. 576–600.

[Simpson, Richard], '*Memoir of Jane Austen*', *North British Review*, 52 (April 1870): 129–52, repr. in B.C. Southam (ed.), *Jane Austen: The Critical Heritage* (London: Routledge & Kegan Paul; New York: Barnes & Noble, 1968), pp. 241–65.

Southam, B.C. (ed.), *Jane Austen: the Critical Heritage* (London: Routledge & Kegan Paul; New York: Barnes & Noble, vol. 1, 1968, vol. 2 *(1870–1940)*, 1987).

[Sweat, Margaret], '*The Life of Charlotte Brontë*', *North American Review*, 85 (October 1857): 293–329, partly repr. in Miriam Allott (ed.), *The Brontës: The Critical Heritage* (London: Routledge & Kegan Paul; New York: Barnes & Noble, 1974), pp. 379–85.

Thackeray, Anne, '*Memoir of Jane Austen*', *Cornhill Magazine*, 34 (1871): 158–74, repr. in Solveig C. Robinson (ed.), *A Serious Occupation: Literary Criticism by Victorian Women Writers* (Peterborough, Ontario and Orchard Park, NY: Broadview, 2003), pp. 234–53.

Vincent, Howard P. (ed.), *Letters of Dora Wordsworth* (Chicago: Packard, 1944).

[Ward, Mary A.], 'Anthony Trollope', *Times*, 7 December 1882: 9.

[Ward, Mary A.], '*Charlotte Brontë and Her Circle*', *Times*, 23 October 1896: 10.

Ward, Mary A., 'Elizabeth Barrett Browning', *Atalanta*, 1 (September 1888): 708–12.

Ward, Mary A., Introductions to *The Life and Works of Charlotte Brontë and Her Sisters* (7 vols, London: Smith, Elder & Co., 1899–1903).

Ward, Mary A., 'The Literature of Introspection', *Macmillan's Magazine*, 49 (January 1884): 190–201; (February 1884): 264–78.

Ward, Mary A., '*Marius the Epicurean*', *Macmillan's Magazine*, 52 (June 1885): 132–9.

Ward, Mary A., 'Recent Fiction in England and France', *Macmillan's Magazine*, 50 (August 1884): 250–60.

Ward, Mary A., 'Some Thoughts on Charlotte Brontë', in Butler Wood (ed.), *Charlotte Brontë 1816–1916: A Centenary Memorial* (London: T. Fisher Unwin, 1917): 13–38.

Ward, Mary A., 'Style and Miss Austen', *Macmillan's Magazine*, 51 (December 1884): 84–91, repr. in Solveig C. Robinson (ed.), *A Serious Occupation: Literary Criticism by Victorian Women Writers* (Peterborough, Ontario and Orchard Park, NY: Broadview, 2003), pp. 254–68.

Watts, Alaric Alfred, *Alaric Watts: A Narrative of His Life* (2 vols, London: Richard Bentley, 1884; repr. New York: AMS Press, 1974).

[Whately, Richard], '*Northanger Abbey* and *Persuasion*', *Quarterly Review*, 24 (January 1821): 352–76, repr. in B.C. Southam (ed.), *Jane Austen: the Critical Heritage* (London: Routledge & Kegan Paul; New York: Barnes & Noble, 1968), pp. 87–105.

Williams (Ysgafell), Jane (ed.), *The Autobiography of Elizabeth Davis A Balaclava Nurse. Daughter of Dafydd Cadwaladyr* (2 vols, London: Hurst and Blackett, 1857).

Williams, Jane (ed.), *The Autobiography of Elizabeth Davis Betsy Cadwaladyr: a Balaclava Nurse* [1857], ed. with a new intro. by Deirdre Beddoe (Cardiff: Honno, 1987).

Williams, Jane, *The Literary Women of England: Including a Biographical Epitome of all the Most Eminent to the Year 1700; and Sketches of the Poetesses to the Year 1850; with Extracts from Their Works, and Critical Remarks* (London: Saunders, Otley and Co., 1861).

Williams, Jane, *The Origin, Rise, and Progress of the Paper People, For My Little Friends* (London: Grant and Griffith, 1856).

[Yonge, Charlotte M.], 'In Memoriam. Anne Mozley', *Monthly Packet* (September 1891): 341.

Secondary Sources

Anderson, Nancy Fix, *Woman Against Women in Victorian England: A Life of Eliza Lynn Linton* (Bloomington and Indianapolis: Indiana University Press, 1987).

Auerbach, Emily, *Searching for Jane Austen* (Madison, WI: University of Wisconsin Press, 2004).

Barker, Juliet, *The Brontës* (London: Weidenfeld, 1994).

Beetham, Margaret, *A Magazine of Her Own? Domesticity and Desire in the Woman's Magazine 1800–1914* (London: Routledge, 1996).

Bellamy, Joan, 'A Lifetime of Reviewing: Margaret Oliphant on Charlotte Brontë', *Brontë Studies*, 29 (2004): 37–42.

Bellamy, Joan, 'Margaret Oliphant: "mightier than the mightiest of her sex"', in Joan Bellamy, Anne Laurence and Gill Perry (eds), *Women, Scholarship and Criticism: Gender and Knowledge c.1790–1900* (Manchester: Manchester University Press, 2000), pp. 143–58.

Bevington, Merle Mowbray, *The Saturday Review 1855–1868: Representative Educated Opinion in Victorian England* (New York: Columbia University Press, 1941; repr. New York: AMS Press, 1966).

Booth, Alison, *How to Make it as a Woman: Collective Biographical History from Victoria to the Present* (Chicago and London: University of Chicago Press, 2004).

Brake, Laurel, *Subjugated Knowledges: Journalism, Gender and Literature in the Nineteenth Century* (Houndmills, Basingstoke: Macmillan, 1994).

Brake, Laurel, Bill Bell and David Finkelstein (eds), *Nineteenth-Century Media and the Construction of Identities* (Houndmills, Basingstoke: Palgrave, 2000).

Broughton, Trev Lynn, 'Impotence, Biography, and the Froude–Carlyle Controversy: "Revelations on Ticklish Topics"', *Journal of the History of Sexuality*, 7 (1997): 502–36.

Butler, Judith, *Bodies That Matter: On the Discursive Limits of Sex* (London: Routledge, 1993).

Butler, Judith, *Gender Trouble: Feminism and the Subversion of Identity* (New York and London: Routledge, 1990).

Clarke, John Stock (comp.), *Margaret Oliphant (1828–1897): Non-Fictional Writings: A Bibliography* (St. Lucia, Queensland: Department of English, University of Queensland, 1997).

Clarke, Norma, *Ambitious Heights: Writing, Friendship, Love – the Jewsbury Sisters, Felicia Hemans, and Jane Carlyle* (London and New York: Routledge, 1990).

Clarke, Norma, *The Rise and Fall of the Woman of Letters* (London: Pimlico Random House, 2004).

Collins, Amanda J., 'Grave Duties of the Caretaker in the Lives of Charlotte Brontë' (PhD thesis, Sydney: University of Sydney, 2004).

Curran, Elaine, '"Holding on by a Pen": The Story of a Lady Reviewer, Mary Margaret Busk (1779–1863)', *Victorian Periodicals Review*, 31/1 (1998): 9–30.

Easley, Alexis, *First-Person Anonymous: Women Writers and Victorian Print Media, 1830–1870* (Aldershot and Burlington, VT: Ashgate, 2004).

Ezell, Margaret J.M., *Writing Women's Literary History* (Baltimore: Johns Hopkins University Press, 1993).

Fraser, Hilary, Stephanie Green and Judith Johnston, *Gender and the Victorian Periodical* (Cambridge: Cambridge University Press, 2003).

Fryckstedt, Monica Correa, 'The Hidden Rill: The Life and Career of Maria Jane Jewsbury', *Bulletin of the John Rylands University Library of Manchester*, 66/2 (1983–4): 177–203, 67/1 (1984–5): 450–73.

Gilbert, Elliot L., 'Rescuing Reality: Carlyle, Froude, and Biographical Truth-Telling', *Victorian Studies*, 34/3 (1991): 295–314.

Gilson, David, *A Bibliography of Jane Austen* (Oxford: Clarendon Press, 1982).

Gilson, David, 'Henry Austen's "Memoir of Jane Austen"', *Persuasions*, 19 (1997): 12–19.

Gordon, Lyndall, *Charlotte Brontë: A Passionate Life* (London: Chatto & Windus, 1994).

Grantz, Carl L., 'Letters of Sara Coleridge: A Calendar and Index to the Manuscript Correspondence in the University of Texas Library' (PhD thesis, Austin: University of Texas at Austin, 1968).

Griggs, Earl Leslie, *Coleridge Fille* (London, New York, Toronto: Oxford University Press, 1940).

Haythornthwaite, J., 'Friendly Encounters: A Study of the Relationship Between the House of Blackwood and Margaret Oliphant in her Role as Literary Critic', *Publishing History*, 28 (1990): 79–88.

Haythornthwaite, J., 'A Victorian Novelist and Her Publisher: Margaret Oliphant and the House of Blackwood', *The Bibliothek*, 15/2 (1988): 37–50.

Heilmann, Ann, 'Mrs Grundy's Rebellion: Margaret Oliphant Between Orthodoxy and the New Woman', *Women's Writing*, 6/2 (1999): 25–37.

Helsinger, Elizabeth K., Robin Lauterbach Sheets and William Veeder (eds), *The Woman Question: Society and Literature in Britain and America 1837–1883* (3 vols, Chicago and London: University of Chicago Press, 1983), vol. 3, *Literary Issues*.

Hickey, Alison, '"The Body of My Father's Writings": Sara Coleridge's Genial Labor', in Marjorie Stone and Judith Thompson (eds), *Literary Couplings: Writing Couples, Collaborators, and the Construction of Authorship* (Madison, WI: University of Wisconsin Press, 2006), pp. 124–47.

Houghton, Walter and others (eds), *The Wellesley Index to Victorian Periodicals* (5 vols, Toronto: University of Toronto Press, 1966–89).

Jay, Elisabeth, *Mrs Oliphant: 'A Fiction to Herself' A Literary Life* (Oxford: Clarendon Press, 1995).

Jones, Kathleen, *Passionate Sisterhood: The Sisters, Wives and Daughters of the Lake Poets* (London: Constable, 1997).

Jordan, Ellen, 'Sister as Journalist: The Almost Anonymous Career of Anne Mozley', *Victorian Periodicals Review*, 37/3 (2004): 315–41.

Jordan, Ellen, Hugh Craig and Alexis Antonia, 'The Brontë Sisters and the *Christian Remembrancer*', *Victorian Periodicals Review*, 39/1 (2006): 21–45.

Korn, Frederick, 'An Unpublished Letter by Thomas Hood: Hannah Lawrance and *Hood's Magazine*', *English Language Notes*, 18 (1981): 192–4.

Le Faye, Deirdre, 'Lord Brabourne's Edition of Jane Austen's Letters', *Review of English Studies*, ns 52 (2001): 91–102.

Liddle, Dallas, 'Salesmen, Sportsmen, Mentors: Anonymity in Mid-Victorian Theories of Journalism', *Victorian Studies*, 41/1 (1997): 31–58.

Lohrli, Anne (ed.), *Household Words: A Weekly Journal Conducted by Charles Dickens: Table of Contents, List of Contributors and Their Contributions* (Toronto: University of Toronto Press, 1973).

Low, Dennis, *The Literary Protégées of the Lake Poets* (Aldershot and Burlington, VT: Ashgate, 2006).

Maitzen, Rohan A., *Gender, Genre, and Victorian Historical Writing* (New York and London: Garland, 1998).

Marchand, Leslie A., *The Athenaeum: A Mirror of Victorian Culture* (1941; repr. New York: Octagon Books, 1971).

Miller, Lucasta, *The Brontë Myth* (London: Jonathan Cape, 2001).

Mitchell, Rosemary, 'Hannah Lawrance (1795–1875)', *Dictionary of National Biography* (Oxford: Oxford University Press, 2004).

Mitchell, Rosemary, *Picturing the Past: English History in Text and Image. 1830–1870* (Oxford: Clarendon Press, 2000).

Morris, Pam, *Imagining Inclusive Society in Nineteenth-Century Novels: The Code of Sincerity in the Public Sphere* (Baltimore and London: Johns Hopkins University Press, 2004).

Mudge, Bradford Keyes, 'On Tennyson's *The Princess*: Sara Coleridge in the *Quarterly Review*', *The Wordsworth Circle* 15/1 (1984): 51–4.

Mudge, Bradford Keyes, *Sara Coleridge, A Victorian Daughter: Her Life and Essays* (New Haven: Yale University Press, 1989).

Nicoll, W. Robertson, 'Charlotte Brontë and Anne Mozley', *Brontë Society Transactions*, 29 (1919): 255–64.

Onslow, Barbara, *Women of the Press in Nineteenth-Century Britain* (Houndmills, Basingstoke: Macmillan; New York: St Martin's, 2000).

Perkin, J. Russell, *A Reception-History of George Eliot's Fiction* (Rochester: University of Rochester Press, 1990).

Peterson, William S., *Victorian Heretic: Mrs Humphry Ward's 'Robert Elsmere'* (Leicester: Leicester University Press, 1976).

Robinson, Solveig C., 'Expanding a "Limited Orbit": Margaret Oliphant, Blackwood's Edinburgh Magazine, and the Development of a Critical Voice', *Victorian Periodicals Review*, 38/2 (2005): 199–220.

Ross, Marlon B., *The Contours of Masculine Desire: Romanticism and the Rise of Women's Poetry* (New York and Oxford: Oxford University Press, 1989).

Sanders, Valerie, *Eve's Renegades: Victorian Anti-Feminist Women Novelists* (Houndmills, Basingstoke and London: Macmillan; New York: St Martin's, 1996).

Sanders, Valerie, '"I'm your Man": Harriet Martineau and the *Edinburgh Review*', *Australasian Victorian Studies Journal*, 6 (2000): 36–47.

Scriven, Anne M., 'Margaret Oliphant's "Marriage" to *Maga*', *Scottish Studies Review*, 8/1 (2007): 27–36.

Shattock, Joanne, 'The Construction of the Woman Writer', in Joanne Shattock (ed.), *Women and Literature in Britain 1800–1900* (Cambridge: Cambridge University Press, 2001), pp. 8–34.

Shattock, Joanne, 'Reviewing Generations: Professionalism and the Mid-Victorian Reviewer', *Victorian Periodicals Review*, 35/4 (2002): 384–400.

Shattock, Joanne, 'Work for Women: Margaret Oliphant's Journalism', in Laurel Brake, Bill Bell and David Finkelstein (eds), *Nineteenth-Century Media and the Construction of Identities* (Houndmills, Basingstoke: Palgrave, 2000), pp. 165–77.

Showalter, Elaine, *A Literature of Their Own: British Women Novelists from Brontë to Lessing* (Princeton, NJ: Princeton University Press, 1977).

Small, Ian, *Conditions for Criticism: Authority, Knowledge, and Literature in the Late Nineteenth Century* (Oxford: Clarendon Press, 1991).

Spencer, Sandra, 'Words, Terms, and Other "Unchancy" Things: Rhetorical Strategies and Self-Definition in "The Laws Concerning Women"', *Women's Writing*, 6/2 (1999): 251–9.

Spongberg, Mary, *Writing Women's History Since the Renaissance* (Houndmills, Basingstoke and London: Macmillan; New York: St Martin's, 2002).

Stang, Richard, *The Theory of the Novel in England 1850–1870* (London: Routledge & Kegan Paul, 1959).

Stephenson, Glennis, 'Letitia Landon and the Victorian Improvisatrice: the Construction of L.E.L.', *Victorian Poetry*, 30/1 (1992): 1–17.

Sutherland, John, *Mrs Humphry Ward: Eminent Victorian, Pre-Eminent Edwardian* (Oxford and New York: Oxford University Press, 1991).

Sutherland, Kathryn, *Jane Austen's Textual Lives: From Aeschylus to Bollywood* (Oxford: Clarendon Press, 2005).

Sutton-Ramspeck, Beth, 'The Personal is Poetical: Feminist Criticism and Mary Ward's Reading of the Brontës', *Victorian Studies*, 34/1 (1990): 55–75.

Sutton-Ramspeck, Beth, *Raising the Dust: The Literary Housekeeping of Mary Ward, Sarah Grand, and Charlotte Perkins Gilman* (Athens, OH: Ohio University Press, 2004).

Thompson, Nicola Diane, *Reviewing Sex: Gender and the Reception of Victorian Novels* (New York: New York University Press, 1996).

Todd, Janet, *The Critical Fortunes of Aphra Behn* (Columbia, SC: Camden House, 1998).

Tredrey, F., *The House of Blackwood 1804–1954 The History of a Publishing Firm* (Edinburgh and London: William Blackwood and Sons, 1954).

Trela, D.J., 'Margaret Oliphant, James Anthony Froude and the Carlyles' Reputations: Defending the Dead', *Victorian Periodicals Review*, 29/3 (1996): 199–215.

Waters, Mary A., *British Women Writers and the Profession of Literary Criticism, 1789–1832* (Houndmills, Basingstoke: Palgrave Macmillan, 2004).

Wilkes, Joanne, 'Remaking the Canon', in Joanne Shattock (ed.), *Women and Literature in Britain 1800–1900* (Cambridge: Cambridge University Press, 2001), pp. 35–54.

Wilkes, Joanne, 'Snuffing Out an Article: Sara Coleridge and the Early Victorian Reception of Keats', in Joel Faflak and Julia M. Wright (eds), *Nervous Reactions: Victorian Recollections of Romanticism* (New York: State University of New York Press, 2004), pp. 189–206.

Winston, Elizabeth, '"Taking off" the Neighbours: Margaret Oliphant's Parody of *Romola*', in William Baker and Ira Bruce Nadel (eds), *Redefining the Modern: Essays on Literature and Society in Honor of Joseph Wiesenfarth* (Madison and Teaneck: Fairleigh Dickinson University Press; London: Associated University Presses, 2004), pp. 115–29.

Wolfson, Susan J., *Borderlines: The Shiftings of Gender in British Romanticism* (Stanford: Stanford University Press, 2006).

Worth, George, 'Margaret Oliphant and Macmillan's Magazine', in Elizabeth James (ed.), *Macmillan: A Publishing Tradition* (Houndmills, Basingstoke: Palgrave, 2002), pp. 83–101.

Index